CW01643394

EAST INDIA
Publishing Company

AYESHA

H. Rider Haggard

Published by the
EAST INDIA PUBLISHING COMPANY
Ottawa, Canada

9781774269442

www.eastindiapublishing.com

Contents

INTRODUCTION

Verily and indeed it is the unexpected that happens! Probably if there was one person upon the earth from whom the Editor of this, and of a certain previous history, did not expect to hear again, that person was Ludwig Horace Holly. This, too, for a good reason; he believed him to have taken his departure from the earth.

When Mr. Holly last wrote, many, many years ago, it was to transmit the manuscript of She, and to announce that he and his ward, Leo Vincey, the beloved of the divine Ayesha, were about to travel to Central Asia in the hope, I suppose, that there she would fulfil her promise and appear to them again.

Often I have wondered, idly enough, what happened to them there; whether they were dead, or perhaps droning their lives away as monks in some Thibetan Lamasery, or studying magic and practising asceticism under the tuition of the Eastern Masters trusting that thus they would build a bridge by which they might pass to the side of their adored Immortal.

Now at length, when I had not thought of them for months, without a single warning sign, out of the blue as it were, comes the answer to these wonderings!

To think—only to think—that I, the Editor aforesaid, from its appearance suspecting something quite familiar and without interest, pushed aside that dingy, unregistered, brown-paper parcel directed in an unknown hand, and for two whole days let it lie forgotten. Indeed there it might be lying now, had not another person been moved to curiosity, and opening it, found within a bundle of manuscript badly burned upon the back, and with this two letters addressed to myself.

Although so great a time had passed since I saw it, and it was shaky now because of the author's age or sickness, I knew the writing at once—nobody ever made an "H" with that peculiar twirl under it except Mr. Holly. I tore open the sealed envelope, and sure enough the first thing my eye fell upon was the signature, L. H. Holly. It is long since I read anything so eagerly as I did that letter. Here it is:—

"My dear Sir,—I have ascertained that you still live, and strange to say I still live also—for a little while.

"As soon as I came into touch with civilization again I found a copy of your book She, or rather of my book, and read it—first of all in a Hindostani translation. My host—he was a minister of some religious body, a man of worthy but prosaic mind—expressed surprise that a 'wild romance' should absorb me so much. I answered that those who have wide experience of the hard facts of life often find interest in romance. Had he known what were the hard facts to which I alluded, I wonder what that excellent person would have said?

"I see that you carried out your part of the business well and faithfully. Every instruction has been obeyed, nothing has been added or taken away. Therefore, to you, to whom some twenty years ago I entrusted the beginning of the history, I wish to entrust its end also. You were the first to learn of She-Who-Must-Be-Obeyed, who from century to century sat alone, clothed with unchanging loveliness in the sepulchres of Kor, waiting till her lost love was born again, and Destiny brought him back to her.

"It is right, therefore, that you should be the first to learn also of Ayesha, Hesea and Spirit of the Mountain, the priestess of that Oracle which since the time of Alexander the Great has reigned between the flaming pillars in the Sanctuary, the last holder of the sceptre of Hes or Isis upon the earth. It is right also that to you first among men I should reveal the mystic consummation of the wondrous tragedy which began at Kor, or perchance far earlier in Egypt and elsewhere.

"I am very ill; I have struggled back to this old house of mine to die, and my end is at hand. I have asked the doctor here, after all is over, to send you the Record, that is unless I change my mind and burn it first. You will also receive, if you receive anything at all, a case containing several rough sketches which may be of use to you, and a sistrum, the instrument that has been always used in the worship of the Nature goddesses of the old Egyptians, Isis and Hathor, which you will see is as beautiful as it is ancient. I give it to you for two reasons; as a token of my gratitude and regard, and as the only piece of evidence that is left to me of the literal truth of what I have written in the accompanying manuscript, where you will find it often mentioned. Perhaps also you will value it as a souvenir of, I suppose, the strangest and loveliest being who ever was, or rather, is. It was her sceptre, the rod of her power, with which I saw her salute the Shadows in the Sanctuary, and her gift to me.

"It has virtues also; some part of Ayesha's might yet haunts the symbol to which even spirits bowed, but if you should discover them, beware how they are used.

"I have neither the strength nor the will to write more. The Record must speak for itself. Do with it what you like, and believe it or not as you like. I care nothing who know that it is true.

"Who and what was Ayesha, nay, what is Ayesha? An incarnate essence, a materialised spirit of Nature the unforeseeing, the lovely, the cruel and the immortal; ensouled alone, redeemable only by Humanity and its piteous sacrifice? Say you! I have done with speculations who depart to solve these mysteries.

"I wish you happiness and good fortune. Farewell to you and to all.

"L. Horace Holly."

I laid the letter down, and, filled with sensations that it is useless to attempt to analyse or describe, opened the second envelope, of which I also print the contents, omitting only certain irrelevant portions, and the name of the writer as, it will be noted, he requests me to do.

This epistle, that was dated from a remote place upon the shores of Cumberland, ran as follows:—

"Dear Sir,—As the doctor who attended Mr. Holly in his last illness I am obliged, in obedience to a promise that I made to him, to become an intermediary in a some what strange business, although in truth it is one of which I know very little, however much it may have interested me. Still I do so only on the strict understanding that no mention is to be made of my name in connexion with the matter, or of the locality in which I practise.

"About ten days ago I was called in to see Mr. Holly at an old house upon the Cliff that for many years remained untenanted except by the caretakers, which house was his property, and had been in his family for generations. The housekeeper who summoned me told me that her master had but just returned from abroad, somewhere in Asia, she said, and that he was very ill with his heart—dying, she believed; both of which suppositions proved to be accurate.

"I found the patient sitting up in bed (to ease his heart), and a strange-looking old man he was. He had dark eyes, small but full of fire and intelligence, a magnificent and snowy-white beard that covered a chest of extraordinary breadth, and hair also white, which encroached upon his forehead and face so much that it met the whiskers upon his cheeks.

His arms were remarkable for their length and strength, though one of them seemed to have been much torn by some animal. He told me that a dog had done this, but if so it must have been a dog of unusual power. He was a very ugly man, and yet, forgive the bull, beautiful. I cannot describe what I mean better than by saying that his face was not like the face of any ordinary mortal whom I have met in my limited experience. Were I an artist who wished to portray a wise and benevolent, but rather grotesque spirit, I should take that countenance as a model.

"Mr. Holly was somewhat vexed at my being called in, which had been done without his knowledge. Soon we became friendly enough, however, and he expressed gratitude for the relief that I was able to give him, though I could not hope to do more. At different times he talked a good deal of the various countries in which he had travelled, apparently for very many years, upon some strange quest that he never clearly defined to me. Twice also he became light-headed, and spoke, for the most part in languages that I identified as Greek and Arabic; occasionally in English also, when he appeared to be addressing himself to a being who was the object of his veneration, I might almost say of his worship. What he said then, however, I prefer not to repeat, for I heard it in my professional capacity.

"One day he pointed to a rough box made of some foreign wood (the same that I have now duly despatched to you by train), and, giving me your name and address, said that without fail it was to be forwarded to you after his death. Also he asked me to do up a manuscript, which, like the box, was to be sent to you.

"He saw me looking at the last sheets, which had been burned away, and said (I repeat his exact words)—

"'Yes, yes, that can't be helped now, it must go as it is. You see I made up my mind to destroy it after all, and it was already on the fire when the command came—the clear, unmistakable command—and I snatched it off again.'

"What Mr. Holly meant by this 'command' I do not know, for he would speak no more of the matter.

"I pass on to the last scene. One night about eleven o'clock, knowing that my patient's end was near, I went up to see him, proposing to inject some strychnine to keep the heart going a little longer. Before I reached the house I met the caretaker coming to seek me in a great fright, and asked her if her master was dead. She answered No; but he was gone—had got out of bed and, just as he was, barefooted, left the house, and was last seen by her grandson among the very Scotch firs where we were talking. The lad, who was terrified out of his wits, for he thought that he beheld a ghost, had told her so.

"The moonlight was very brilliant that night, especially as fresh snow had fallen, which reflected its rays. I was on foot, and began to search among the firs, till presently just outside of them I found the track of naked feet in the snow. Of course I followed, calling to the housekeeper to go and wake her husband, for no one else lives near by. The spoor proved very easy to trace across the clean sheet of snow. It ran up the slope of a hill behind the house.

"Now, on the crest of this hill is an ancient monument of upright monoliths set there by some primeval people, known locally as the Devil's Ring—a sort of miniature Stonehenge in fact. I had seen it several times, and happened to have been present not long ago at a meeting of an archaeological society when its origin and purpose were discussed. I remember that one learned but somewhat eccentric gentleman read a short paper upon a rude, hooded bust and head that are cut within the chamber of a tall, flat-topped cromlech, or dolmen, which stands alone in the centre of the ring.

"He said that it was a representation of the Egyptian goddess, Isis, and that this place had once been sacred to some form of her worship, or at any rate to that of a Nature goddess with like attributes, a suggestion which the other learned gentlemen treated as absurd. They declared that Isis had never travelled into Britain, though for my part I do not see why the Phoenicians, or even the Romans, who adopted her cult, more or less, should not have brought it here. But I know nothing of such matters and will not discuss them.

"I remembered also that Mr. Holly was acquainted with this place, for he had mentioned it to me on the previous day, asking if the stones were still uninjured as they used to be when he was young. He added also, and the remark struck me, that yonder was where he would wish to die. When I answered that I feared he would never take so long a walk again, I noted that he smiled a little.

"Well, this conversation gave me a clue, and without troubling more about the footprints I went on as fast as I could to the Ring, half a mile or so away. Presently I reached it, and there—yes, there—standing by the cromlech, bareheaded, and clothed in his night-things only, stood Mr. Holly in the snow, the strangest figure, I think, that ever I beheld.

"Indeed never shall I forget that wild scene. The circle of rough, single stones pointing upwards to the star-strewn sky, intensely lonely and intensely solemn: the tall trilithon towering above them in the centre, its shadow, thrown by the bright moon behind it, lying long and black upon the dazzling sheet of snow, and, standing clear of this shadow so that I could distinguish his every motion, and even the rapt look upon his dying face, the white-draped figure of Mr. Holly. He appeared to be uttering some invocation—in Arabic, I think—for long before I reached him I could catch the tones of his full, sonorous voice, and see his waving, outstretched arms. In his right hand he held the looped sceptre which, by his express wish I send to you with the drawings. I could see the flash of the jewels strung upon the wires, and in the great stillness, hear the tinkling of its golden bells.

"Presently, too, I seemed to become aware of another presence, and now you will understand why I desire and must ask that my identity should be suppressed. Naturally enough I do not wish to be mixed up with a superstitious tale which is, on the face of it, impossible and absurd. Yet under all the circumstances I think it right to tell you that I saw, or thought I saw, something gather in the shadow of the central dolmen, or emerge from its rude chamber—I know not which for certain—something bright and glorious which gradually took the form of a woman upon whose forehead burned a star-like fire.

"At any rate the vision or reflection, or whatever it was, startled me so much that I came to a halt under the lee of one of the monoliths, and found myself unable even to call to the distraught man whom I pursued.

"Whilst I stood thus it became clear to me that Mr. Holly also saw something. At least he turned towards the Radiance in the shadow, uttered one cry; a wild, glad cry, and stepped forward; then seemed to fall through it on to his face.

"When I reached the spot the light had vanished, and all I found was Mr. Holly, his arms still outstretched, and the sceptre gripped tightly in his hand, lying quite dead in the shadow of the trilithon."

The rest of the doctor's letter need not be quoted as it deals only with certain very improbable explanations of the origin of this figure of light, the details of the removal of Holly's body, and of how he managed to satisfy the coroner that no inquest was necessary.

The box of which he speaks arrived safely. Of the drawings in it I need say nothing, and of the sistrum or sceptre only a few words. It was fashioned of crystal to the well-known shape of the Crux-ansata, or the emblem of life of the Egyptians; the rod, the cross and the loop combined in one. From side to side of this loop ran golden wires, and on these were strung gems of three colours, glittering diamonds, sea-blue sapphires, and blood-red rubies, while to the fourth wire, that at the top, hung four little golden bells.

When I took hold of it first my arm shook slightly with excitement, and those bells began to sound; a sweet, faint music like to that of chimes heard far away at night in the silence of the sea. I thought too, but perhaps this was fancy, that a thrill passed from the hallowed and beautiful thing into my body.

On the mystery itself, as it is recorded in the manuscript, I make no comment. Of it and its inner significations every reader must form his or her own judgment. One thing alone is clear to me—on the hypothesis that Mr. Holly tells the truth as to what he and Leo Vincey saw and experienced, which I at least believe—that though sundry interpretations of this mystery were advanced by Ayesha and others, none of them are quite satisfactory.

Indeed, like Mr. Holly, I incline to the theory that She, if I may still call her by that name although it is seldom given to her in these pages, put forward some of them, such as the vague Isis-myth, and the wondrous picture-story of the Mountain-fire, as mere veils to hide the truth which it was her purpose to reveal at last in that song she never sang.

The Editor

I. THE DOUBLE SIGN

Hard on twenty years have gone by since that night of Leo's vision—the most awful years, perhaps, which were ever endured by men—twenty years of search and hardship ending in soul-shaking wonder and amazement.

My death is very near to me, and of this I am glad, for I desire to pursue the quest in other realms, as it has been promised to me that I shall do. I desire to learn the beginning and the end of the spiritual drama of which it has been my strange lot to read some pages upon earth.

I, Ludwig Horace Holly, have been very ill; they carried me, more dead than alive, down those mountains whose lowest slopes I can see from my window, for I write this on the northern frontiers of India. Indeed any other man had long since perished, but Destiny kept my breath in me, perhaps that a record might remain. I must bide here a month or two till I am strong enough to travel homewards, for I have a fancy to die in the place where I was born. So while I have strength I will put the story down, or at least those parts of it that are most essential, for much can, or at any rate must, be omitted. I shrink from attempting too long a book, though my notes and memory would furnish me with sufficient material for volumes.

I will begin with the Vision.

After Leo Vincey and I came back from Africa in 1885, desiring solitude, which indeed we needed sorely to recover from the fearful shock we had experienced, and to give us time and opportunity to think, we went to an old house upon the shores of Cumberland that has belonged to my family for many generations. This house, unless somebody has taken it believing me to be dead, is still my property and thither I travel to die.

Those whose eyes read the words I write, if any should ever read them, may ask—What shock?

Well, I am Horace Holly, and my companion, my beloved friend, my son in the spirit whom I reared from infancy was—nay, is—Leo Vincey.

We are those men who, following an ancient clue, travelled to the Caves of Kor in Central Africa, and there discovered her whom we sought, the immortal She-who-must-be-obeyed. In Leo she found her love, that re-born Kallikrates, the Grecian priest of Isis whom some two thousand years before she had slain in her jealous rage, thus executing on him the judgment of the angry goddess. In her also I found the divinity whom I was doomed to worship from afar, not with the flesh, for that is all lost and gone from me, but, what is sorer still, because its burden is undying, with the will and soul which animate a man throughout the countless eons of his being. The flesh dies, or at least it changes, and its passions pass, but that other passion of the spirit—that longing for oneness—is undying as itself.

What crime have I committed that this sore punishment should be laid upon me? Yet, in truth, is it a punishment? May it not prove to be but that black and terrible Gate which leads to the joyous palace of Rewards? She swore that I should ever be her friend and his and dwell with them eternally, and I believe her.

For how many winters did we wander among the icy hills and deserts! Still, at length, the Messenger came and led us to the Mountain, and on the Mountain we found the Shrine, and in the Shrine the Spirit. May not these things be an allegory prepared for our instruction? I will take comfort. I will hope that it is so. Nay, I am sure that it is so.

It will be remembered that in Kor we found the immortal woman. There before the flashing rays and vapours of the Pillar of Life she declared her mystic love, and then in our very sight was swept to a doom so horrible that even now, after all which has been and gone, I shiver at its recollection. Yet what were Ayesha's last words? "Forget me not . . . have pity on my shame. I die not. I shall come again and shall once more be beautiful. I swear it—it is true."

Well, I cannot set out that history afresh. Moreover it is written; the man whom I trusted in the matter did not fail me, and the book he made of it seems to be known throughout the world, for I have found it here in English, yes, and read it first translated into Hindostani. To it then I refer the curious.

In that house upon the desolate sea-shore of Cumberland, we dwelt a year, mourning the lost, seeking an avenue by which it might be found again and discovering none. Here our strength came back to us, and Leo's hair, that had been whitened in the horror of the Caves, grew again from grey to golden. His beauty returned to him also, so that his face was as it had been, only purified and saddened.

Well I remember that night—and the hour of illumination. We were heart-broken, we were in despair. We sought signs and could find none. The dead remained dead to us and no answer came to all our crying.

It was a sullen August evening, and after we had dined we walked upon the shore, listening to the slow surge of the waves and watching the lightning flicker from the bosom of a distant cloud. In silence we walked, till at last Leo groaned—it was more of a sob than a groan—and clasped my arm.

"I can bear it no longer, Horace," he said—for so he called me now—"I am in torment. The desire to see Ayesha once more saps my brain. Without hope I shall go quite mad. And I am strong, I may live another fifty years."

"What then can you do?" I asked.

"I can take a short road to knowledge—or to peace," he answered solemnly, "I can die, and die I will—yes, tonight."

I turned upon him angrily, for his words filled me with fear.

"Leo, you are a coward!" I said. "Cannot you bear your part of pain as—others do?"

"You mean as you do, Horace," he answered with a dreary laugh, "for on you also the curse lies—with less cause. Well, you are stronger than I am, and more tough; perhaps because you have lived longer. No, I cannot bear it. I will die."

"It is a crime," I said, "the greatest insult you can offer to the Power that made you, to cast back its gift of life as a thing outworn, contemptible and despised. A crime, I say, which will bring with it worse punishment than any you can dream; perhaps even the punishment of everlasting separation."

"Does a man stretched in some torture-den commit a crime if he snatches a knife and kills himself, Horace? Perhaps; but surely that sin should find forgiveness—if torn flesh and quivering nerves may plead for mercy. I am such a man, and I will use that knife and take my chance. She is dead, and in death at least I shall be nearer her."

"Why so, Leo? For aught you know Ayesha may be living."

"No; for then she would have given me some sign. My mind is made up, so talk no more, or, if talk we must, let it be of other things."

Then I pleaded with him, though with little hope, for I saw that what I had feared for long was come to pass. Leo was mad: shock and sorrow had destroyed his reason. Were it not so, he, in his own way a very religious man, one who held, as I knew, strict opinions on such matters, would never have purposed to commit the wickedness of suicide.

"Leo," I said, "are you so heartless that you would leave me here alone? Do you pay me thus for all my love and care, and wish to drive me to my death? Do so if you will, and my blood be on your head."

"Your blood! Why your blood, Horace?"

"Because that road is broad and two can travel it. We have lived long years together and together endured much; I am sure that we shall not be long parted."

Then the tables were turned and he grew afraid for me. But I only answered, "If you die I tell you that I shall die also. It will certainly kill me."

So Leo gave way. "Well," he exclaimed suddenly, "I promise you it shall not be to-night. Let us give life another chance."

"Good," I answered; but I went to my bed full of fear. For I was certain that this desire of death, having once taken hold of him, would grow and grow, until at length it became too strong, and then—then I should wither and die who could not live on alone. In my despair I threw out my soul towards that of her who was departed.

"Ayesha!" I cried, "if you have any power, if in any way it is permitted, show that you still live, and save your lover from this sin and me from a broken heart. Have pity on his sorrow and breathe hope into his spirit, for without hope Leo cannot live, and without him I shall not live."

Then, worn out, I slept.

I was aroused by the voice of Leo speaking to me in low, excited tones through the darkness.

"Horace," he said, "Horace, my friend, my father, listen!"

In an instant I was wide awake, every nerve and fibre of me, for the tones of his voice told me that something had happened which bore upon our destinies.

"Let me light a candle first," I said.

"Never mind the candle, Horace; I would rather speak in the dark. I went to sleep, and I dreamed the most vivid dream that ever came to me. I seemed to stand under the vault of heaven, it was black, black, not a star shone in it, and a great loneliness possessed me. Then suddenly high up in the vault, miles and miles away, I saw a little light and thought that a planet had appeared to keep me company. The light began to descend slowly, like a floating flake of fire. Down it sank, and down and down, till it was but just above me, and I perceived that it was shaped like a tongue or fan of flame. At the height of my head from the ground it stopped and stood steady, and by its ghostly radiance I saw that beneath was the shape of a woman and that the flame burned upon her forehead. The radiance gathered strength and now I saw the woman.

"Horace, it was Ayesha herself, her eyes, her lovely face, her cloudy hair, and she looked at me sadly, reproachfully, I thought, as one might who says, 'Why did you doubt?'

"I tried to speak to her but my lips were dumb. I tried to advance and to embrace her, my arms would not move. There was a barrier between us. She lifted her hand and beckoned as though bidding me to follow her.

"Then she glided away, and, Horace, my spirit seemed to loose itself from the body and to be given the power to follow. We passed swiftly eastward, over lands and seas, and—I knew the road. At one point she paused and I looked downwards. Beneath, shining in the moonlight, appeared the ruined palaces of Kor, and there not far away was the gulf we trod together.

"Onward above the marshes, and now we stood upon the Ethiopian's Head, and gathered round, watching us earnestly, were the faces of the Arabs, our companions who drowned in the sea beneath. Job was among them also, and he smiled at me sadly and shook his head, as though he wished to accompany us and could not.

"Across the sea again, across the sandy deserts, across more sea, and the shores of India lay beneath us. Then northward, ever northward, above the plains, till we reached a place of mountains capped with eternal snow. We passed them and stayed for an instant above a building set upon the brow of a plateau. It was a monastery, for old monks droned prayers upon its terrace. I shall know it again, for it is built in the shape of a half-moon and in front of it sits the gigantic, ruined statue of a god who gazes everlastingly across the desert. I knew, how I cannot say, that now we were far past the furthest borders of Thibet and that in front of us lay untrodden lands. More mountains stretched beyond that desert, a sea of snowy peaks, hundreds and hundreds of them.

"Near to the monastery, jutting out into the plain like some rocky headland, rose a solitary hill, higher than all behind. We stood upon its snowy crest and waited, till presently, above the mountains and the desert at our feet shot a sudden beam of light that beat upon us like some signal flashed across the sea. On we went, floating down the beam—on over the desert and the mountains, across a great flat land beyond, in which were many villages and a city on a mound, till we lit upon a towering peak. Then I saw that this peak was loop-shaped like the symbol of Life of the Egyptians—the crux-ansata—and supported by a lava stem hundreds of feet in height. Also I saw that the fire which shone through it rose from the crater of a volcano beyond. Upon the very crest of this loop we rested a while, till the Shadow of Ayesha pointed downward with its hand, smiled and vanished. Then I awoke.

"Horace, I tell you that the sign has come to us."

His voice died away in the darkness, but I sat still, brooding over what I had heard. Leo groped his way to me and, seizing my arm, shook it.

"Are you asleep?" he asked angrily. "Speak, man, speak!"

"No," I answered, "never was I more awake. Give me time."

Then I rose, and going to the open window, drew up the blind and stood there staring at the sky, which grew pearl-hued with the first faint tinge of dawn. Leo came also and leant upon the window-sill, and I could feel that his body was trembling as though with cold. Clearly he was much moved.

"You talk of a sign," I said to him, "but in your sign I see nothing but a wild dream."

"It was no dream," he broke in fiercely; "it was a vision."

"A vision then if you will, but there are visions true and false, and how can we know that this is true? Listen, Leo. What is there in all that wonderful tale which could not have been fashioned in your own brain, distraught as it is almost to madness with your sorrow and your longings? You dreamed that you were alone in the vast universe. Well, is not every living creature thus alone? You dreamed that the shadowy shape of Ayesha came to you. Has it ever left your side? You dreamed that she led you over sea and land, past places haunted by your memory, above the mysterious mountains of the Unknown to an undiscovered peak. Does she not thus lead you through life to that peak which lies beyond the Gates of Death? You dreamed——"

"Oh! no more of it," he exclaimed. "What I saw, I saw, and that I shall follow. Think as you will, Horace, and do what you will. To-morrow I start for India, with you if you choose to come; if not, without you."

"You speak roughly, Leo," I said. "You forget that I have had no sign, and that the nightmare of a man so near to insanity that but a few hours ago he was determined upon suicide, will be a poor staff to lean on when we are perishing in the snows of Central Asia. A mixed vision, this of yours, Leo, with its mountain peak shaped like a crux-ansata and the rest. Do you suggest that Ayesha is re-incarnated in Central Asia—as a female Grand Lama or something of that sort?"

"I never thought of it, but why not?" asked Leo quietly. "Do you remember a certain scene in the Caves of Kor yonder, when the living looked upon the dead, and dead and living were the same? And do you remember what Ayesha swore, that she would come again—yes, to this world; and how could that be except by re-birth, or, what is the same thing, by the transmigration of the spirit?"

I did not answer this argument. I was struggling with myself.

"No sign has come to me," I said, "and yet I have had a part in the play, humble enough, I admit, and I believe that I have still a part."

"No," he said, "no sign has come to you. I wish that it had. Oh! how I wish you could be convinced as I am, Horace!"

Then we were silent for a long while, silent, with our eyes fixed upon the sky.

It was a stormy dawn. Clouds in fantastic masses hung upon the ocean. One of them was like a great mountain, and we watched it idly. It changed its shape, the crest of it grew hollow like a crater. From this crater sprang a projecting cloud, a rough pillar with a knob or lump resting on its top. Suddenly the rays of the risen sun struck upon this mountain and the column and they turned white like snow. Then as though melted by those fiery arrows, the centre of the excrescence above the pillar thinned out and vanished, leaving an enormous loop of inky cloud.

"Look," said Leo in a low, frightened voice, "that is the shape of the mountain which I saw in my vision. There upon it is the black loop, and there through it shines the fire. It would seem that the sign is for both of us, Horace."

I looked and looked again till presently the vast loop vanished into the blue of heaven. Then I turned and said—"I will come with you to Central Asia, Leo."

II. THE LAMASERY

Sixteen years had passed since that night vigil in the old Cumberland house, and, behold! we two, Leo and I, were still travelling, still searching for that mountain peak shaped like the Symbol of Life which never, never could be found.

Our adventures would fill volumes, but of what use is it to record them. Many of a similar nature are already written of in books; those that we endured were more prolonged, that is all. Five years we spent in Thibet, for the most part as guests of various monasteries, where we studied the law and traditions of the Lamas. Here we were once sentenced to death in punishment for having visited a forbidden city, but escaped through the kindness of a Chinese official.

Leaving Thibet, we wandered east and west and north, thousands and thousands of miles, sojourning amongst many tribes in Chinese territory and elsewhere, learning many tongues, enduring much hardship. Thus we would hear a legend of a place, say nine hundred miles away, and spend two years in reaching it, to find when we came there, nothing.

And so the time went on. Yet never once did we think of giving up the quest and returning, since, before we started, we had sworn an oath that we would achieve or die. Indeed we ought to have died a score of times, yet always were preserved, most mysteriously preserved.

Now we were in country where, so far as I could learn, no European had ever set a foot. In a part of the vast land called Turkestan there is a great lake named Balhkash, of which we visited the shores. Two hundred miles or so to the westward is a range of mighty mountains marked on the maps as Arkarty-Tau, on which we spent a year, and five hundred or so miles to the eastward are other mountains called Cherga, whither we journeyed at last, having explored the triple ranges of the Tau.

Here it was that at last our true adventures began. On one of the spurs of these awful Cherga mountains—it is unmarked on any map—we well-nigh perished of starvation. The winter was coming on and we could find no game. The last traveller we had met, hundreds of miles south, told us that on that range was a monastery inhabited by Lamas of surpassing holiness. He said that they dwelt in this wild land, over which no power claimed dominion and where no tribes lived, to acquire "merit," with no other company than that of their own pious contemplations. We did not believe in its existence, still we were searching for that monastery, driven onward by the blind fatalism which was our only guide through all these endless wanderings. As we were starving and could find no "argals," that is fuel with which to make a fire, we walked all night by the light of the moon, driving between us a single yak—for now we had no attendant, the last having died a year before.

He was a noble beast, that yak, and had the best constitution of any animal I ever knew, though now, like his masters, he was near his end. Not that he was over-laden, for a few rifle cartridges, about a hundred and fifty, the remnant of a store which we had fortunately been able to buy from a caravan two years before, some money in gold and silver, a little tea and a bundle of skin rugs and sheepskin garments were his burden. On, on we trudged across a plateau of snow, having the great mountains on our right, till at length the yak gave a sigh and stopped. So we stopped also, because we must, and wrapping ourselves in the skin rugs, sat down in the snow to wait for daylight.

"We shall have to kill him and eat his flesh raw," I said, patting the poor yak that lay patiently at our side.

"Perhaps we may find game in the morning," answered Leo, still hopeful.

"And perhaps we may not, in which case we must die."

"Very good," he replied, "then let us die. It is the last resource of failure. We shall have done our best."

"Certainly, Leo, we shall have done our best, if sixteen years of tramping over mountains and through eternal snows in pursuit of a dream of the night can be called best."

"You know what I believe," he answered stubbornly, and there was silence between us, for here arguments did not avail. Also even then I could not think that all our toils and sufferings would be in vain.

The dawn came, and by its light we looked at one another anxiously, each of us desiring to see what strength was left to his companion. Wild creatures we should have seemed to the eyes of any civilized person. Leo was now over forty years of age, and certainly his maturity had fulfilled the promise of his youth, for a more magnificent man I never knew. Very tall, although he seemed spare to the eye, his girth matched his height, and those many years of desert life had turned his muscles to steel. His hair had grown long, like my own, for it was a protection from sun and cold, and hung upon his neck, a curling, golden mane, as his great beard hung upon his breast, spreading outwards almost to the massive shoulders. The face, too—what could be seen of it—was beautiful though burnt brown with weather; refined and full of thought, sombre almost, and in it, clear as crystal, steady as stars, shone his large grey eyes.

And I—I was what I have always been—ugly and hirsute, iron-grey now also, but in spite of my sixty odd years, still wonderfully strong, for my strength seemed to increase with time, and my health was perfect. In fact, during all this period of rough travels, although now and again we had met with accidents which laid us up for awhile, neither of us had known a day of sickness. Hardship seemed to have turned our constitutions to iron and made them impervious to every human ailment. Or was this because we alone amongst living men had once inhaled the breath of the Essence of Life?

Our fears relieved—for notwithstanding our foodless night, as yet neither of us showed any signs of exhaustion—we turned to contemplate the landscape. At our feet beyond a little belt of fertile soil, began a great desert of the sort with which we were familiar—sandy, salt-encrusted, treeless, waterless, and here and there streaked with the first snows of winter. Beyond it, eighty or a hundred miles away—in that lucent atmosphere it was impossible to say how far exactly—rose more mountains, a veritable sea of them, of which the white peaks soared upwards by scores.

As the golden rays of the rising sun touched their snows to splendour, I saw Leo's eyes become troubled. Swiftly he turned and looked along the edge of the desert.

"See there!" he said, pointing to something dim and enormous. Presently the light reached it also. It was a mighty mountain not more than ten miles away, that stood out by itself among the sands. Then he turned once more, and with his back to the desert stared at the slope of the hills, along the base of which we had been travelling. As yet they were in gloom, for the sun was behind them, but presently light began to flow over their crests like a flood. Down it crept, lower, and yet lower, till it reached a little plateau not three hundred yards above us. There, on the edge of the plateau, looking out solemnly across the waste, sat a great ruined idol, a colossal Buddha, while to the rear of the idol, built of yellow stone, appeared the low crescent-shaped mass of a monastery.

"At last!" cried Leo, "oh, Heaven! at last!" and, flinging himself down, he buried his face in the snow as though to hide it there, lest I should read something written on it which he did not desire that even I should see.

I let him lie a space, understanding what was passing in his heart, and indeed in mine also. Then going to the yak that, poor brute, had no share in these joyous emotions but only lowed and looked round with hungry eyes, I piled the sheepskin rugs on to its back. This done, I laid my hand on Leo's shoulder, saying, in the most matter-of-fact voice I could command—"Come. If that place is not deserted, we may find food and shelter there, and it is beginning to storm again."

He rose without a word, brushed the snow from his beard and garments and came to help me to lift the yak to its feet, for the worn-out beast was too stiff and weak to rise of itself. Glancing at him covertly, I saw on Leo's face a very strange and happy look; a great peace appeared to possess him.

We plunged upwards through the snow slope, dragging the yak with us, to the terrace whereon the monastery was built. Nobody seemed to be about there, nor could I discern any footprints. Was the place but a ruin? We had found many such; indeed this ancient land is full of buildings that had once served as the homes of men, learned and pious enough after their own fashion, who lived and died hundreds, or even thousands, of years ago, long before our Western civilization came into being.

My heart, also my stomach, which was starving, sank at the thought, but while I gazed doubtfully, a little coil of blue smoke sprang from a chimney, and never, I think, did I see a more joyful sight. In the centre of the edifice was a large building, evidently the temple, but nearer to us I saw a small door, almost above which the smoke appeared. To this door I went and knocked, calling aloud—"Open! open, holy Lamas. Strangers seek your charity." After awhile there was a sound of shuffling feet and the door creaked upon its hinges, revealing an old, old man, clad in tattered, yellow garments.

"Who is it? Who is it?" he exclaimed, blinking at me through a pair of horn spectacles. "Who comes to disturb our solitude, the solitude of the holy Lamas of the Mountains?"

"Travellers, Sacred One, who have had enough of solitude," I answered in his own dialect, with which I was well acquainted. "Travellers who are starving and who ask your charity, which," I added, "by the Rule you cannot refuse."

He stared at us through his horn spectacles, and, able to make nothing of our faces, let his glance fall to our garments which were as ragged as his own, and of much the same pattern. Indeed, they were those of Thibetan monks, including a kind of quilted petticoat and an outer vestment not unlike an Eastern burnous. We had adopted them because we had no others. Also they protected us from the rigours of the climate and from remark, had there been any to remark upon them.

"Are you Lamas?" he asked doubtfully, "and if so, of what monastery?"

"Lamas sure enough," I answered, "who belong to a monastery called the World, where, alas! one grows hungry."

The reply seemed to please him, for he chuckled a little, then shook his head, saying—"It is against our custom to admit strangers unless they be of our own faith, which I am sure you are not."

"And much more is it against your Rule, holy Khubilghan," for so these abbots are entitled, "to suffer strangers to starve"; and I quoted a well-known passage from the sayings of Buddha which fitted the point precisely.

"I perceive that you are instructed in the Books," he exclaimed with wonder on his yellow, wrinkled face, "and to such we cannot refuse shelter. Come in, brethren of the monastery called the World. But stay, there is the yak, who also has claims upon our charity," and, turning, he struck upon a gong or bell which hung within the door.

At the sound another man appeared, more wrinkled and to all appearance older than the first, who stared at us open-mouthed.

"Brother," said the abbot, "shut that great mouth of yours lest an evil spirit should fly down it; take this poor yak and give it fodder with the other cattle."

So we unstrapped our belongings from the back of the beast, and the old fellow whose grandiloquent title was "Master of the Herds," led it away.

When it had gone, not too willingly—for our faithful friend disliked parting from us and distrusted this new guide—the abbot, who was named Kou-en, led us into the living room or rather the kitchen of the monastery, for it served both purposes. Here we found the rest of the monks, about twelve in all, gathered round the fire of which we had seen the smoke, and engaged, one of them in preparing the morning meal, and the rest in warming themselves.

They were all old men; the youngest could not have been less than sixty-five. To these we were solemnly introduced as "Brethren of the Monastery called the World, where folk grow hungry," for the abbot Kou-en could not make up his mind to part from this little joke.

They stared at us, they rubbed their thin hands, they bowed and wished us well and evidently were delighted at our arrival. This was not strange, however, seeing that ours were the first new faces which they had seen for four long years.

Nor did they stop at words, for while they made water hot for us to wash in, two of them went to prepare a room—and others drew off our rough hide boots and thick outer garments and brought us slippers for our feet. Then they led us to the guest chamber, which they informed us was a "propitious place," for once it had been slept in by a noted saint. Here a fire was lit, and, wonder of wonders! clean garments, including linen, all of them ancient and faded, but of good quality, were brought for us to put on.

So we washed—yes, actually washed all over—and having arrayed ourselves in the robes, which were somewhat small for Leo, struck the bell that hung in the room and were conducted by a monk who answered it, back to the kitchen, where the meal was now served. It consisted of a kind of porridge, to which was added new milk brought in by the "Master of the Herds," dried fish from a lake, and buttered tea, the last two luxuries produced in our special honour. Never had food tasted more delicious to us, and, I may add, never did we eat more. Indeed, at last I was obliged to request Leo to stop, for I saw the monks staring at him and heard the old abbot chuckling to himself.

"Oho! The Monastery of the World, where folk grow hungry," to which another monk, who was called the "Master of the Provisions," replied uneasily, that if we went on like this, their store of food would scarcely last the winter. So we finished at length, feeling, as some book of maxims which I can remember in my youth said all polite people should do—that we could eat more, and much impressed our hosts by chanting a long Buddhist grace.

"Their feet are in the Path! Their feet are in the Path!" they said, astonished.

"Yes," replied Leo, "they have been in it for sixteen years of our present incarnation. But we are only beginners, for you, holy Ones, know how star-high, how ocean-wide and how desert-long is that path. Indeed it is to be instructed as to the right way of walking therein that we have been miraculously directed by a dream to seek you out, as the most pious, the most saintly and the most learned of all the Lamas in these parts."

"Yes, certainly we are that," answered the abbot Kou-en, "seeing that there is no other monastery within five months' journey," and again he chuckled, "though, alas!" he added with a pathetic little sigh, "our numbers grow few."

After this we asked leave to retire to our chamber in order to rest, and there, upon very good imitations of beds, we slept solidly for four and twenty hours, rising at last perfectly refreshed and well.

Such was our introduction to the Monastery of the Mountains—for it had no other name—where we were destined to spend the next six months of our lives. Within a few days—for they were not long in giving us their complete confidence—those good-hearted and simple old monks told us all their history.

It seemed that of old time there was a Lamasery here, in which dwelt several hundred brethren. This, indeed, was obviously true, for the place was enormous, although for the most part ruined, and, as the weather-worn statue of Buddha showed, very ancient. The story ran, according to the old abbot, that two centuries or so before, the monks had been killed out by some fierce tribe who lived beyond the desert and across the distant mountains, which tribe were heretics and worshippers of fire. Only a few of them escaped to bring the sad news to other communities, and for five generations no attempt was made to re-occupy the place.

At length it was revealed to him, our friend Kou-en, when a young man, that he was a re-incarnation of one of the old monks of this monastery, who also was named Kou-en, and that it was his duty during his present life to return thither, as by so doing he would win much merit and receive many wonderful revelations. So he gathered a band of zealots and, with the blessing and consent of his superiors, they started out, and after many hardships and losses found and took possession of the place, repairing it sufficiently for their needs.

This happened about fifty years before, and here they had dwelt ever since, only communicating occasionally with the outside world. At first their numbers were recruited from time to time by new brethren, but at length these ceased to come, with the result that the community was dying out.

"And what then?" I asked.

"And then," the abbot answered, "nothing. We have acquired much merit; we have been blest with many revelations, and, after the repose we have earned in Devachan, our lots in future existences will be easier. What more can we ask or desire, removed as we are from all the temptations of the world?"

For the rest, in the intervals of their endless prayers, and still more endless contemplations, they were husbandmen, cultivating the soil, which was fertile at the foot of the mountain, and tending their herd of yaks. Thus they wore away their blameless lives until at last they died of old age, and, as they believed—and who shall say that they were wrong—the eternal round repeated itself elsewhere.

Immediately after, indeed on the very day of our arrival at the monastery the winter began in earnest with bitter cold and snowstorms so heavy and frequent that all the desert was covered deep. Very soon it became obvious to us that here we must stay until the spring, since to attempt to move in any direction would be to perish. With some misgivings we explained this to the abbot Kou-en, offering to remove to one of the empty rooms in the ruined part of the building, supporting ourselves with fish that we could catch by cutting a hole in the ice of the lake above the monastery, and if we were able to find any, on game, which we might trap or shoot in the scrub-like forest of stunted pines and junipers that grew around its border. But he would listen to no such thing. We had been sent to be their guests, he said, and their guests we should remain for so long as might be convenient to us. Would we lay upon them the burden of the sin of inhospitality? Besides, he remarked with his chuckle—"We who dwell alone like to hear about that other great monastery called the World, where the monks are not so favoured as we who are set in this blessed situation, and where folk even go hungry in body, and," he added, "in soul."

Indeed, as we soon found out, the dear old man's object was to keep our feet in the Path until we reached the goal of Truth, or, in other words, became excellent Lamas like himself and his flock.

So we walked in the Path, as we had done in many another Lamasery, and assisted at the long prayers in the ruined temple and studied the Kandjur, or "Translation of the Words" of Buddha, which is their bible and a very long one, and generally showed that our "minds were open." Also we expounded to them the doctrines of our own faith, and greatly delighted were they to find so many points of similarity between it and theirs. Indeed, I am not certain but that if we could have stopped there long enough, say ten years, we might have persuaded some of them to accept a new revelation of which we were the prophets. Further, in spare hours we told them many tales of "the Monastery called the World," and it was really delightful, and in a sense piteous, to see the joy with which they listened to these stories of wondrous countries and new races of men; they who knew only of Russia and China and some semi-savage tribes, inhabitants of the mountains and the deserts.

"It is right for us to learn all this," they declared, "for, who knows, perhaps in future incarnations we may become inhabitants of these places."

But though the time passed thus in comfort and indeed, compared to many of our experiences, in luxury, oh! our hearts were hungry, for in them burned the consuming fire of our quest. We felt that we were on the threshold—yes, we knew it, we knew it, and yet our wretched physical limitations made it impossible for us to advance by a single step. On the desert beneath fell the snow, moreover great winds arose suddenly that drove those snows like dust, piling them in heaps as high as trees, beneath which any unfortunate traveller would be buried. Here we must wait, there was nothing else to be done.

One alleviation we found, and only one. In a ruined room of the monastery was a library of many volumes, placed there, doubtless, by the monks who were massacred in times bygone. These had been more or less cared for and re-arranged by their successors, who gave us liberty to examine them as often as we pleased. Truly it was a strange collection, and I should imagine of priceless value, for among them were to be found Buddhistic, Sivaistic and Shamanistic writings that we had never before seen or heard of, together with the lives of a multitude of Bodhisatvas, or distinguished saints, written in various tongues, some of which we did not understand.

What proved more interesting to us, however, was a diary in many tomes that for generations had been kept by the Khubilghans or abbots of the old Lamasery, in which every event of importance was recorded in great detail. Turning over the pages of one of the last volumes of this diary, written apparently about two hundred and fifty years earlier, and shortly before the destruction of the monastery, we came upon an entry of which the following—for I can only quote from memory—is the substance—

"In the summer of this year, after a very great sandstorm, a brother (the name was given, but I forget it) found in the desert a man of the people who dwell beyond the Far Mountains, of whom rumours have reached this Lamasery from time to time. He was living, but beside him were the bodies of two of his companions who had been overwhelmed by sand and thirst. He was very fierce looking. He refused to say how he came into the desert, telling us only that he had followed the road known to the ancients before communication between his people and the outer world ceased. We gathered, however, that his brethren with whom he fled had committed some crime for which they had been condemned to die, and that he had accompanied them in their flight. He told us that there was a fine country beyond the mountains, fertile, but plagued with droughts and earthquakes, which latter, indeed, we often feel here.

"The people of that country were, he said, warlike and very numerous but followed agriculture. They had always lived there, though ruled by Khans who were descendants of the Greek king called Alexander, who conquered much country to the south-west of us. This may be true, as our records tell us that about two thousand years ago an army sent by that invader penetrated to these parts, though of his being with them nothing is said.

"The stranger-man told us also that his people worship a priestess called Hes or the Hesea, who is said to reign from generation to generation. She lives in a great mountain, apart, and is feared and adored by all, but is not the queen of the country, in the government of which she seldom interferes. To her, however, sacrifices are offered, and he who incurs her vengeance dies, so that even the chiefs of that land are afraid of her. Still their subjects often fight, for they hate each other.

"We answered that he lied when he said that this woman was immortal—for that was what we supposed he meant—since nothing is immortal; also we laughed at his tale of her power. This made the man very angry. Indeed he declared that our Buddha was not so strong as this priestess, and that she would show it by being avenged upon us.

"After this we gave him food and turned him out of the Lamasery, and he went, saying that when he returned we should learn who spoke the truth. We do not know what became of him, and he refused to reveal to us the road to his country, which lies beyond the desert and the Far Mountains. We think that perhaps he was an evil spirit sent to frighten us, in which he did not succeed."

Such is a precis of this strange entry, the discovery of which, vague as it was, thrilled us with hope and excitement. Nothing more appeared about the man or his country, but within a little over a year from that date the diary of the abbot came to a sudden end without any indication that unusual events had occured or were expected.

Indeed, the last item written in the parchment book mentioned the preparation of certain new lands to be used for the sowing of grain in future seasons, which suggested that the brethren neither feared nor expected disturbance. We wondered whether the man from beyond the mountains was as good as his word and had brought down the vengeance of that priestess called the Hesea upon the community which sheltered him. Also we wondered—ah! how we wondered—who and what this Hesea might be.

On the day following this discovery we prayed the abbot, Kou-en, to accompany us to the library, and having read him the passage, asked if he knew anything of the matter. He swayed his wise old head, which always reminded me of that of a tortoise, and answered—"A little. Very little, and that mostly about the army of the Greek king who is mentioned in the writing."

We inquired what he could possibly know of this matter, whereon Kou-en replied calmly—"In those days when the faith of the Holy One was still young, I dwelt as a humble brother in this very monastery, which was one of the first built, and I saw the army pass, that is all. That," he added meditatively, "was in my fiftieth incarnation of this present Round—no, I am thinking of another army—in my seventy-third."*

Here Leo began a great laugh, but I managed to kick him beneath the table and he turned it into a sneeze. This was fortunate, as such ribald merriment would have hurt the old man's feelings terribly. After all, also, as Leo himself had once said, surely we were not the people to mock at the theory of re-incarnation, which, by the way, is the first article of faith among nearly one quarter of the human race, and this not the most foolish quarter.

"How can that be—I ask for instruction, learned One—seeing that memory perishes with death?"

"Ah!" he answered, "Brother Holly, it may seem to do so, but oftentimes it comes back again, especially to those who are far advanced upon the

* As students of their lives and literature will be aware, it is common for Buddhist priests to state positively that they remember events which occurred during their previous incarnations.—ed.

Path. For instance, until you read this passage I had forgotten all about that army, but now I see it passing, passing, and myself with other monks standing by the statue of the big Buddha in front yonder, and watching it go by. It was not a very large army, for most of the soldiers had died, or been killed, and it was being pursued by the wild people who lived south of us in those days, so that it was in a great hurry to put the desert between it and them. The general of the army was a swarthy man—I wish that I could remember his name, but I cannot.

"Well," he went on, "that general came up to the Lamasery and demanded a sleeping place for his wife and children, also provisions and medicines, and guides across the desert. The abbot of that day told him it was against our law to admit a woman under our roof, to which he answered that if we did not, we should have no roof left, for he would burn the place and kill every one of us with the sword. Now, as you know, to be killed by violence means that we must pass sundry incarnations in the forms of animals, a horrible thing, so we chose the lesser evil and gave way, and afterwards obtained absolution for our sins from the Great Lama. Myself I did not see this queen, but I saw the priestess of their worship—alas! alas!" and Kou-en beat his breast.

"Why alas?" I asked, as unconcernedly as I could, for this story interested me strangely.

"Why? Oh! because I may have forgotten the army, but I have never forgotten that priestess, and she has been a great hindrance to me through many ages, delaying me upon my journey to the Other Side, to the Shore of Salvation. I, as a humble Lama, was engaged in preparing her apartment when she entered and threw aside her veil; yes, and perceiving a young man, spoke to me, asking many questions, and even if I was not glad to look again upon a woman."

"What—what was she like?" said Leo, anxiously.

"What was she like? Oh! She was all loveliness in one shape; she was like the dawn upon the snows; she was like the evening star above the mountains; she was like the first flower of the spring. Brother, ask me not what she was like, nay, I will say no more. Oh! my sin, my sin. I am slipping backward and you draw my black shame out into the light of day. Nay, I will confess it that you may know how vile a thing I am—I whom perhaps you have thought holy—like yourselves. That woman, if woman she were, lit a fire in my heart which will not burn out, oh! and more, more," and Kou-en rocked himself to and fro upon his stool while tears of contrition trickled from beneath his horn spectacles, "she made me worship her! For first she asked me of my faith and listened eagerly as I expounded it, hoping that the light would come into her heart; then, after I had finished she said—"'So your Path is Renunciation and your Nirvana a most excellent Nothingness which some would think it scarce worth while to strive so hard to reach. Now I will show you a more joyous way and a goddess more worthy of your worship.'

"'What way, and what goddess?' I asked of her.

"'The way of Love and Life!" she answered, 'that makes all the world to be, that made you, O seeker of Nirvana, and the goddess called Nature!'

"Again I asked where is that goddess, and behold! she drew herself up, looking most royal, and touching her ivory breast, she said, 'I am She. Now kneel you down and do me homage!'

"My brethren, I knelt, yes, I kissed her foot, and then I fled away shamed and broken-hearted, and as I went she laughed, and cried: 'Remember me when you reach Devachan, O servant of the Budda-saint, for though I change, I do not die, and even there I shall be with you who once gave me worship!'

"And it is so, my brethren, it is so; for though I obtained absolution for my sin and have suffered much for it through this, my next incarnation, yet I cannot be rid of her, and for me the Utter Peace is far, far away," and Kou-en placed his withered hands before his face and sobbed outright.

A ridiculous sight, truly, to see a holy Khublighan well on the wrong side of eighty, weeping like a child over a dream of a beautiful woman which he imagined he had once dreamt in his last life more than two thousand years ago. So the reader will say. But I, Holly, for reasons of my own, felt deep sympathy with that poor old man, and Leo was also sympathetic. We patted him on the back; we assured him that he was the victim of some evil hallucination which could never be brought up against him in this or any future existence, since, if sin there were, it must have been forgiven long ago, and so forth. When his calm was somewhat restored we tried also to extract further information from him, but with poor results, so far as the priestess was concerned.

He said that he did not know to what religion she belonged, and did not care, but thought that it must be an evil one. She went away the next morning with the army, and he never saw or heard of her any more, though it came into his mind that he was obliged to be locked in his cell for eight days to prevent himself from following her. Yes, he had heard one thing, for the abbot of that day had told the brethren. This priestess was the real general of the army, not the king or the queen, the latter of whom hated her. It was by her will that they pushed on northwards across the desert to some country beyond the mountains, where she desired to establish herself and her worship.

We asked if there really was any country beyond the mountains, and Kou-en answered wearily that he believed so. Either in this or in a previous life he had heard that people lived there who worshipped fire. Certainly also it was true that about thirty years ago a brother who had climbed the great peak yonder to spend some days in solitary meditation, returned and reported that he had seen a marvellous thing, namely, a shaft of fire burning in the heavens beyond those same mountains, though whether this were a vision, or what, he could not say. He recalled, however, that about that time they had felt a great earthquake.

Then the memory of that fancied transgression again began to afflict Kou-en's innocent old heart, and he crept away lamenting and was seen no more for a week. Nor would he ever speak again to us of this matter.

But we spoke of it much with hope and wonder, and made up our minds that we would at once ascend this mountain.

III. THE BEACON LIGHT

A week later came our opportunity of making this ascent of the mountain, for now in mid-winter it ceased storming, and hard frost set in, which made it possible to walk upon the surface of the snow. Learning from the monks that at this season ovis poli and other kinds of big-horned sheep and game descended from the hills to take refuge in certain valleys, where they scraped away the snow to find food, we announced that we were going out to hunt. The excuse we gave was that we were suffering from confinement and needed exercise, having by the teaching of our religion no scruples about killing game.

Our hosts replied that the adventure was dangerous, as the weather might change at any moment. They told us, however, that on the slopes of this very mountain which we desired to climb, there was a large natural cave where, if need be, we could take shelter, and to this cave one of them, somewhat younger and more active than the rest, offered to guide us. So, having manufactured a rougri tent from skins, and laden our old yak, now in the best of condition, with food and garments, on one still morning we started as soon as it was light. Under the guidance of the monk, who, notwithstanding his years, walked very well, we reached the northern slope of the peak before mid-day. Here, as he had said, we found a great cave of which the opening was protected by an over-hanging ledge of rock. Evidently this cave was the favourite place of shelter for game at certain seasons of the year, since in it were heaped vast accumulations of their droppings, which removed any fear of a lack of fuel.

The rest of that short day we spent in setting up our tent in the cave, in front of which we lit a large fire, and in a survey of the slopes of the mountain, for we told the monk that we were searching for the tracks of wild sheep. Indeed, as it happened, on our way back to the cave we came across a small herd of ewes feeding upon the mosses in a sheltered spot where in summer a streamlet ran. Of these we were so fortunate as to kill two, for no sportsman had ever come here, and they were tame enough, poor things. As meat would keep for ever in that temperature, we had now sufficient food to last us for a fortnight, and dragging the animals down the snow slopes to the cave, we skinned them by the dying light.

That evening we supped upon fresh mutton, a great luxury, which the monk enjoyed as much as we did, since, whatever might be his views as to taking life, he liked mutton. Then we turned into the tent and huddled ourselves together for warmth, as the temperature must have been some degrees below zero. The old monk rested well enough, but neither Leo nor I slept over much, for wonder as to what we might see from the top of that mountain banished sleep.

Next morning at the dawn, the weather being still favourable, our companion returned to the monastery, whither we said we would follow him in a day or two.

Now at last we were alone, and without wasting an instant began our ascent of the peak. It was many thousand feet high and in certain places steep enough, but the deep, frozen snow made climbing easy, so that by midday we reached the top. Hence the view was magnificent. Beneath us stretched the desert, and beyond it a broad belt of fantastically shaped, snow-clad mountains, hundreds and hundreds of them; in front, to the right, to the left, as far as the eye could reach.

"They are just as I saw them in my dream so many years ago," muttered Leo; "the same, the very same."

"And where was the fiery light?" I asked.

"Yonder, I think;" and he pointed north by east.

"Well, it is not there now," I answered, "and this place is cold."

So, since it was dangerous to linger, lest the darkness should overtake us on our return journey, we descended the peak again, reaching the cave about sunset. The next four days we spent in the same way. Every morning we crawled up those wearisome banks of snow, and every afternoon we slid and tobogganed down them again, till I grew heartily tired of the exercise.

On the fourth night, instead of coming to sleep in the tent Leo sat himself down at the entrance to the cave. I asked him why he did this, but he answered impatiently, because he wished it, so I left him alone. I could see, indeed, that he was in a strange and irritable mood, for the failure of our search oppressed him. Moreover, we knew, both of us, that it could not be much prolonged, since the weather might break at any moment, when ascents of the mountain would become impossible.

In the middle of the night I was awakened by Leo shaking me and saying—"Come here, Horace, I have something to show you."

Reluctantly enough I crept from between the rugs and out of the tent. To dress there was no need, for we slept in all our garments. He led me to the mouth of the cave and pointed northward. I looked. The night was very dark; but far, far away appeared a faint patch of light upon the sky, such as might be caused by the reflection of a distant fire.

"What do you make of it?" he asked anxiously.

"Nothing in particular," I answered, "it may be anything. The moon—no, there is none, dawn—no, it is too northerly, and it does not break for three hours. Something burning, a house, or a funeral pyre, but how can there be such things here? I give it up."

"I think it is a reflection, and that if we were on the peak we should see the light which throws it," said Leo slowly.

"Yes, but we are not, and cannot get there in the dark."

"Then, Horace, we must spend a night there."

"It will be our last in this incarnation," I answered with a laugh, "that is if it comes on to snow."

"We must risk it, or I will risk it. Look, the light has faded;" and there at least he was right, for undoubtedly it had. The night was as black as pitch.

"Let's talk it over to-morrow," I said, and went back to the tent, for I was sleepy and incredulous, but Leo sat on by the mouth of the cave.

At dawn I awoke and found breakfast already cooked.

"I must start early," Leo explained.

"Are you mad?" I asked. "How can we camp on that place?"

"I don't know, but I am going. I must go, Horace."

"Which means that we both must go. But how about the yak?"

"Where we can climb, it can follow," he answered.

So we strapped the tent and other baggage, including a good supply of cooked meat, upon the beast's back, and started. The tramp was long since we were obliged to make some detours to avoid slopes of frozen snow in which, on our previous ascents, we had cut footholds with an axe, for up these the laden animal could not clamber. Reaching the summit at length, we dug a hole, and there pitched the tent, piling the excavated snow about its sides. By this time it began to grow dark, and having descended into the tent, yak and all, we ate our food and waited.

Oh! what cold was that. The frost was fearful, and at this height a wind blew whose icy breath passed through all our wrappings, and seemed to burn our flesh beneath as though with hot irons. It was fortunate that we had brought the yak, for without the warmth from its shaggy body I believe that we should have perished, even in our tent. For some hours we watched, as indeed we must, since to sleep might mean to die, yet saw nothing save the lonely stars, and heard nothing in that awful silence, for here even the wind made no noise as it slid across the snows. Accustomed as I was to such exposure, my faculties began to grow numb and my eyes to shut, when suddenly Leo said—"Look, below the red star!"

I looked, and there high in the sky was the same curious glow which we had seen upon the previous night. There was more than this indeed, for beneath it, almost on a line with us and just above the crests of the intervening peaks, appeared a faint sheet of fire and revealed against it, something black. Whilst we watched, the fire widened, spread upwards and grew in power and intensity. Now against its flaming background the black object became clearly visible, and lo! it was the top of a soaring pillar surmounted by a loop. Yes, we could see its every outline. It was the crux ansata, the Symbol of Life itself.

The symbol vanished, the fire sank. Again it blazed up more fiercely than before and the loop appeared afresh, then once more disappeared. A third time the fire shone, and with such intensity, that no lightning could surpass its brilliance. All around the heavens were lit up, and, through the black needle-shaped eye of the symbol, as from the flare of a beacon, or the search-light of a ship, one fierce ray shot across the sea of mountain tops and the spaces of the desert, straight as an arrow to the lofty peak on which we lay. Yes, it lit upon the snow, staining it red, and upon the wild, white faces of us who watched, though to the right and left of us spread thick darkness. My compass lay before me on the snow, and I could even see its needle; and beyond us the shape of a white fox that had crept near, scenting food. Then it was gone as swiftly as it came. Gone too were the symbol and the veil of flame behind it, only the glow lingered a little on the distant sky.

For awhile there was silence between us, then Leo said—"Do you remember, Horace, when we lay upon the Rocking Stone where her cloak fell upon me—" as he said the words the breath caught in his throat—"how the ray of light was sent to us in farewell, and to show us a path of escape from the Place of Death? Now I think that it has been sent again in greeting to point out the path to the Place of Life where Ayesha dwells, whom we have lost awhile."

"It may be so," I answered shortly, for the matter was beyond speech or argument, beyond wonder even. But I knew then, as I know now that we were players in some mighty, predestined drama; that our parts were written and we must speak them, as our path was prepared and we must tread it to the end unknown. Fear and doubt were left behind, hope was sunk in certainty; the fore-shadowing visions of the night had found an actual fulfilment and the pitiful seed of the promise of her who died, growing unseen through all the cruel, empty years, had come to harvest.

No, we feared no more, not even when with the dawn rose the roaring wind, through which we struggled down the mountain slopes, as it would seem in peril of our lives at every step; not even as hour by hour we fought our way onwards through the whirling snow-storm, that made us deaf and blind. For we knew that those lives were charmed. We could not see or hear, yet we were led. Clinging to the yak, we struggled downward and homewards, till at length out of the turmoil and the gloom its instinct brought us unharmed to the door of the monastery, where the old abbot embraced us in his joy, and the monks put up prayers of thanks. For they were sure that we must be dead. Through such a storm, they said, no man had ever lived before.

It was still mid-winter, and oh! the awful weariness of those months of waiting. In our hands was the key, yonder amongst those mountains lay the door, but not yet might we set that key within its lock. For between us and these stretched the great desert, where the snow rolled like billows, and until that snow melted we dared not attempt its passage. So we sat in the monastery, and schooled our hearts to patience.

Still even to these frozen wilds of Central Asia spring comes at last. One evening the air felt warm, and that night there were only a few degrees of frost. The next the clouds banked up, and in the morning not snow was falling from them, but rain, and we found the old monks preparing their instruments of husbandry, as they said that the season of sowing was at hand. For three days it rained, while the snows melted before our eyes. On the fourth torrents of water were rushing down the mountain and the desert was once more brown and bare, though not for long, for within another week it was carpeted with flowers. Then we knew that the time had come to start.

"But whither go you? Whither go you?" asked the old abbot in dismay. "Are you not happy here? Do you not make great strides along the Path, as may be known by your pious conversation? Is not everything that we have your own? Oh! why would you leave us?"

"We are wanderers," we answered, "and when we see mountains in front of us we must cross them."

Kou-en looked at us shrewdly, then asked—"What do you seek beyond the mountains? And, my brethren, what merit is gathered by hiding the truth from an old man, for such concealments are separated from falsehoods but by the length of a single barleycorn. Tell me, that at least my prayers may accompany you."

"Holy abbot," I said, "awhile ago yonder in the library you made a certain confession to us."

"Oh! remind me not of it," he said, holding up his hands. "Why do you wish to torment me?"

"Far be the thought from us, most kind friend and virtuous man," I answered. "But, as it chances, your story is very much our own, and we think that we have experience of this same priestess."

"Speak on," he said, much interested.

So I told him the outlines of our tale; for an hour or more I told it while he sat opposite to us swaying his head like a tortoise and saying nothing. At length it was done.

"Now," I added, "let the lamp of your wisdom shine upon our darkness. Do you not find this story wondrous, or do you perchance think that we are liars?"

"Brethren of the great monastery called the World," Kou-en answered with his customary chuckle, "why should I think you liars who, from the moment my eyes fell upon you, knew you to be true men? Moreover, why should I hold this tale so very wondrous? You have but stumbled upon the fringe of a truth with which we have been acquainted for many, many ages.

"Because in a vision she showed you this monastery, and led you to a spot beyond the mountains where she vanished, you hope that this woman whom you saw die is re-incarnated yonder. Why not? In this there is nothing impossible to those who are instructed in the truth, though the lengthening of her last life was strange and contrary to experience. Doubtless you will find her there as you expect, and doubtless her khama, or identity, is the same as that which in some earlier life of hers once brought me to sin.

"Only be not mistaken, she is no immortal; nothing is immortal. She is but a being held back by her own pride, her own greatness if you will, upon the path towards Nirvana. That pride will be humbled, as already it has been humbled; that brow of majesty shall be sprinkled with the dust of change and death, that sinful spirit must be purified by sorrows and by separations. Brother Leo, if you win her, it will be but to lose, and then the ladder must be reclimbed. Brother Holly, for you as for me loss is our only gain, since thereby we are spared much woe. Oh! bide here and pray with me. Why dash yourselves against a rock? Why labour to pour water into a broken jar whence it must sink into the sands of profitless experience, and there be wasted, whilst you remain athirst?"

"Water makes the sand fertile," I answered. "Where water falls, life comes, and sorrow is the seed of joy."

"Love is the law of life," broke in Leo; "without love there is no life. I seek love that I may live. I believe that all these things are ordained to an end which we do not know. Fate draws me on—I fulfil my fate——"

"And do but delay your freedom. Yet I will not argue with you, brother, who must follow your own road. See now, what has this woman, this priestess of a false faith if she be so still, brought you in the past? Once in another life, or so I understand your story, you were sworn to a certain nature-goddess, who was named Isis, were you not, and to her alone? Then a woman tempted you, and you fled with her afar. And there what found you? The betrayed and avenging goddess who slew you, or if not the goddess, one who had drunk of her wisdom and was the minister of her vengeance. Having that wisdom this minister—woman or evil spirit—refused to die because she had learned to love you, but waited knowing that in your next life she would find you again, as indeed she would have done more swiftly in Devachan had she died without living on alone in so much misery. And she found you, and she died, or seemed to die, and now she is re-born, as she must be, and doubtless you will meet once more, and again there must come misery. Oh! my friends, go not across the mountains; bide here with me and lament your sins."

"Nay," answered Leo, "we are sworn to a tryst, and we do not break our word."

"Then, brethren, go keep your tryst, and when you have reaped its harvest think upon my sayings, for I am sure that the wine you crush from the vintage of your desire will run red like blood, and that in its drinking you shall find neither forgetfulness nor peace. Made blind by a passion of which well I know the sting and power, you seek to add a fair-faced evil to your lives, thinking that from this unity there shall be born all knowledge and great joy.

"Rather should you desire to live alone in holiness until at length your separate lives are merged and lost in the Good Unspeakable, the eternal bliss that lies in the last Nothingness. Ah! you do not believe me now; you shake your heads and smile; yet a day will dawn, it may be after many incarnations, when you shall bow them in the dust and weep, saying to me, 'Brother Kou-en, yours were the words of wisdom, ours the deeds of foolishness;'" and with a deep sigh the old man turned and left us.

"A cheerful faith, truly," said Leo, looking after him, "to dwell through aeons in monotonous misery in order that consciousness may be swallowed up at last in some void and formless abstraction called the 'Utter Peace.' I would rather take my share of a bad world and keep my hope of a better. Also I do not think that he knows anything of Ayesha and her destiny."

"So would I," I answered, "though perhaps he is right after all. Who can tell? Moreover, what is the use of reasoning? Leo, we have no choice; we follow our fate. To what that fate may lead us we shall learn in due season."

Then we went to rest, for it was late, though I found little sleep that night. The warnings of the ancient abbot, good and learned man as he was, full also of ripe experience and of the foresighted wisdom that is given to such as he, oppressed me deeply. He promised us sorrow and bloodshed beyond the mountains, ending in death and rebirths full of misery. Well, it might be so, but no approaching sufferings could stay our feet. And even if they could, they should not, since to see her face again I was ready to brave them all. And if this was my case what must be that of Leo!

A strange theory that of Kou-en's, that Ayesha was the goddess in old Egypt to whom Kallikrates was priest, or at the least her representative. That the royal Amenartas, with whom he fled, seduced him from the goddess to whom he was sworn. That this goddess incarnate in Ayesha—or using the woman Ayesha and her passions as her instruments—was avenged upon them both at Kor, and that there in an after age the bolt she shot fell back upon her own head.

Well, I had often thought as much myself. Only I was sure that She herself could be no actual divinity, though she might be a manifestation of one, a priestess, a messenger, charged to work its will, to avenge or to reward, and yet herself a human soul, with hopes and passions to be satisfied, and a destiny to fulfil. In truth, writing now, when all is past and done with, I find much to confirm me in, and little to turn me from that theory, since life and powers of a quality which are more than human do not alone suffice to make a soul divine. On the other hand, however, it must be borne in mind that on one occasion at any rate, Ayesha did undoubtedly suggest that in the beginning she was "a daughter of Heaven," and that there were others, notably the old Shaman Simbri, who seemed to take it for granted that her origin was supernatural. But of all these things I hope to speak in their season.

Meanwhile what lay beyond the mountains? Should we find her there who held the sceptre and upon earth wielded the power of the outraged Isis, and with her, that other woman who wrought the wrong? And if so, would the dread, inhuman struggle reach its climax around the person of the sinful priest? In a few months, a few days even, we might begin to know.

Thrilled by this thought at length I fell asleep.

IV. THE AVALANCHE

On the morning of the second day from that night the sunrise found us already on our path across the desert. There, nearly a mile behind us, we could see the ruined statue of Buddha seated in front of the ancient monastery, and in that clear atmosphere could even distinguish the bent form of our friend, the old abbot, Kou-en, leaning against it until we were quite lost to sight. All the monks had wept when we parted from them, and Kou-en even more bitterly than the rest, for he had learned to love us.

"I am grieved," he said, "much grieved, which indeed I should not be, for such emotion partakes of sin. Yet I find comfort, for I know well that although I must soon leave this present life, yet we shall meet again in many future incarnations, and after you have put away these follies, together tread the path to perfect peace. Now take with you my blessings and my prayers and begone, forgetting not that should you live to return"—and he shook his head, doubtfully—"here you will be ever welcome."

So we embraced him and went sorrowfully.

It will be remembered that when the mysterious light fell upon us on the peak I had my compass with me and was able roughly to take its bearings. For lack of any better guide we now followed these bearings, travelling almost due north-east, for in that direction had shone the fire. All day in the most beautiful weather we marched across the flower-strewn desert, seeing nothing except bunches of game and one or two herds of wild asses which had come down from the mountains to feed upon the new grass. As evening approached we shot an antelope and made our camp—for we had brought the yak and a tent with us—among some tamarisk scrub, of which the dry stems furnished us with fuel. Nor did we lack for water, since by scraping in the sand soaked with melted snow, we found plenty of fair quality. So that night we supped in luxury upon tea and antelope meat, which indeed we were glad to have, as it spared our little store of dried provisions.

The next morning we ascertained our position as well as we could, and estimated that we had crossed about a quarter of the desert, a guess which proved very accurate, for on the evening of the fourth day of our journey we reached the bottom slopes of the opposing mountains, without having experienced either accident or fatigue. As Leo said, things were "going like clockwork," but I reminded him that a good start often meant a bad finish. Nor was I wrong, for now came our hardships. To begin with, the mountains proved to be exceeding high; it took us two days to climb their lower slopes. Also the heat of the sun had softened the snow, which made walking through it laborious, whilst, accustomed though we were to such conditions through long years of travelling, its continual glitter affected our eyes.

The morning of the seventh day found us in the mouth of a defile which wound away into the heart of the mountains. As it seemed the only possible path, we followed it, and were much cheered to discover that here must once have run a road. Not that we could see any road, indeed, for everything was buried in snow. But that one lay beneath our feet we were certain, since, although we marched along the edge of precipices, our path, however steep, was always flat; moreover, the rock upon one side of it had often been scarped by the hand of man. Of this there could be no doubt, for as the snow did not cling here, we saw the tool marks upon its bare surface.

Also we came to several places where galleries had been built out from the mountain side, by means of beams let into it, as is still a common practice in Thibet. These beams of course had long since rotted away, leaving a gulf between us and the continuation of the path. When we met with such gaps we were forced to go back and make a detour round or over some mountain; but although much delayed thereby, as it happened, we always managed to regain the road, if not without difficulty and danger.

What tried us more—for here our skill and experience as mountaineers could not help us—was the cold at night, obliged as we were to camp in the severe frost at a great altitude, and to endure through the long hours of darkness penetrating and icy winds, which soughed ceaselessly down the pass.

At length on the tenth day we reached the end of the defile, and as night was falling, camped there in the most bitter cold. Those were miserable hours, for now we had no fuel with which to boil water, and must satisfy our thirst by eating frozen snow, while our eyes smarted so sorely that we could not sleep, and notwithstanding all our wraps and the warmth that we gathered from the yak in the little tent, the cold caused our teeth to chatter like castanets.

The dawn came, and, after it, the sunrise. We crept from the tent, and leaving it standing awhile, dragged our stiffened limbs a hundred yards or so to a spot where the defile took a turn, in order that we might thaw in the rays of the sun, which at that hour could not reach us where we had camped.

Leo was round it first, and I heard him utter an exclamation. In a few seconds I reached his side, and lo! before us lay our Promised Land.

Far beneath us, ten thousand feet at least—for it must be remembered that we viewed it from the top of a mountain—it stretched away and away till its distances met the horizon. In character it was quite flat, an alluvial plain that probably, in some primeval age, had been the bottom of one of the vast lakes of which a number exist in Central Asia, most of them now in process of desiccation. One object only relieved this dreary flatness, a single, snow-clad, and gigantic mountain, of which even at that distance—for it was very far from us—we could clearly see the outline. Indeed we could see more, for from its rounded crest rose a great plume of smoke, showing that it was an active volcano, and on the hither lip of the crater an enormous pillar of rock, whereof the top was formed to the shape of a loop.

Yes, there it stood before us, that symbol of our vision which we had sought these many years, and at the sight of it our hearts beat fast and our breath came quickly. We noted at once that although we had not seen it during our passage of the mountains, since the peaks ahead and the rocky sides of the defile hid it from view, so great was its height that it overtopped the tallest of them. This made it clear to us how it came to be possible that the ray of light passing through the loop could fall upon the highest snows of that towering pinnacle which we had climbed upon the further side of the desert.

Also now we were certain of the cause of that ray, for the smoke behind the loop explained this mystery. Doubtless, at times when the volcano was awake, that smoke must be replaced by flame, emitting light of fearful intensity, and this light it was that reached us, concentrated and directed by the loop.

For the rest we thought that about thirty miles away we could make out a white-roofed town set upon a mound, situated among trees upon the banks of a wide river, which flowed across the plain. Also it was evident that this country had a large population who cultivated the soil, for by the aid of a pair of field glasses, one of our few remaining and most cherished possessions, we could see the green of springing crops pierced by irrigation canals and the lines of trees that marked the limits of the fields.

Yes, there before us stretched the Promised Land, and there rose the mystic Mount, so that all we had to do was to march down the snow slopes and enter it where we would.

Thus we thought in our folly, little guessing what lay before us, what terrors and weary suffering we must endure before we stood at length beneath the shadow of the Symbol of Life.

Our fatigues forgotten, we returned to the tent, hastily swallowed some of our dried food, which we washed down with lumps of snow that gave us toothache and chilled us inside, but which thirst compelled us to eat, dragged the poor yak to its feet, loaded it up, and started.

All this while, so great was our haste and so occupied were each of us with our own thoughts that, if my memory serves me, we scarcely interchanged a word. Down the snow slopes we marched swiftly and without hesitation, for here the road was marked for us by means of pillars of rock set opposite to one another at intervals. These pillars we observed with satisfaction, for they told us that we were still upon a highway which led to the Promised Land.

Yet, as we could not help noting, it was one which seemed to have gone out of use, since with the exception of a few wild-sheep tracks and the spoor of some bears and mountain foxes, not a single sign of beast or man could we discover. This, however, was to be explained, we reflected, by the fact that doubtless the road was only used in the summer season. Or perhaps the inhabitants of the country were now stay-at-home people who never travelled it at all.

Those slopes were longer than we thought; indeed, when darkness closed in we had not reached the foot of them. So we were obliged to spend another night in the snow, pitching our tent in the shelter of an overhanging rock. As we had descended many thousand feet, the temperature proved, fortunately, a little milder; indeed, I do not think that there were more than eighteen or twenty degrees of frost that night. Also here and there the heat of the sun had melted the snow in secluded places, so that we were able to find water to drink, while the yak could fill its poor old stomach with dead-looking mountain mosses, which it seemed to think better than nothing.

Again, the still dawn came, throwing its red garment over the lonesome, endless mountains, and we dragged ourselves to our numbed feet, ate some of our remaining food, and started onwards. Now we could no longer see the country beneath, for it and even the towering volcano were hidden from us by an intervening ridge that seemed to be pierced by a single narrow gulley, towards which we headed. Indeed, as the pillars showed us, thither ran the buried road. By mid-day it appeared quite close to us, and we tramped on in feverish haste. As it chanced, however, there was no need to hurry, for an hour later we learned the truth.

Between us and the mouth of the gulley rose, or rather sank, a sheer precipice that was apparently three or four hundred feet in depth, and at its foot we could hear the sound of water.

Right to the edge of this precipice ran the path, for one of the stone pillars stood upon its extreme brink, and yet how could a road descend such a place as that? We stared aghast; then a possible solution occurred to us.

"Don't you see," said Leo, with a hollow laugh, "the gulf has opened since this track was used: volcanic action probably."

"Perhaps, or perhaps there was a wooden bridge or stairway which has rotted. It does not matter. We must find another path, that is all," I answered as cheerfully as I could.

"Yes, and soon," he said, "if we do not wish to stop here for ever."

So we turned to the right and marched along the edge of the precipice till, a mile or so away, we came to a small glacier, of which the surface was sprinkled with large stones frozen into its substance. This glacier hung down the face of the cliff like a petrified waterfall, but whether or no it reached the foot we could not discover. At any rate, to think of attempting its descent seemed out of the question. From this point onwards we could see that the precipice increased in depth and far as the eye could reach was absolutely sheer.

So we went back again and searched to the left of our road. Here the mountains receded, so that above us rose a mighty, dazzling slope of snow and below us lay that same pitiless, unclimbable gulf. As the light began to fade we perceived, half a mile or more in front a bare-topped hillock of rock, which stood on the verge of the precipice, and hurried to it, thinking that from its crest we might be able to discover a way of descent.

When at length we had struggled to the top, it was about a hundred and fifty feet high; what we did discover was that, here also, as beyond the glacier, the gulf was infinitely deeper than at the spot where the road ended, so deep indeed that we could not see its bottom, although from it came the sound of roaring water. Moreover, it was quite half a mile in width.

Whilst we stared round us the sinking sun vanished behind a mountain and, the sky being heavy, the light went out like that of a candle. Now the ascent of this hillock had proved so steep, especially at one place, where we were obliged to climb a sort of rock ladder, that we scarcely cared to attempt to struggle down it again in that gloom. Therefore, remembering that there was little to choose between the top of this knoll and the snow plain at its foot in the matter of temperature or other conveniences, and being quite exhausted, we determined to spend the night upon it, thereby, as we were to learn, saving our lives.

Unloading the yak, we pitched our tent under the lee of the topmost knob of rock and ate a couple of handfuls of dried fish and corn-cake. This was the last of the food that we had brought with us from the Lamasery, and we reflected with dismay that unless we could shoot something, our commissariat was now represented by the carcass of our old friend the yak. Then we wrapped ourselves up in our thick rugs and fur garments and forgot our miseries in sleep.

It cannot have been long before daylight when we were awakened by a sudden and terrific sound like the boom of a great cannon, followed by thousands of other sounds, which might be compared to the fusillade of musketry.

"Great Heaven! What is that?" I said.

We crawled from the tent, but as yet could see nothing, whilst the yak began to low in a terrified manner. But if we could not see we could hear and feel. The booming and cracking had ceased, and was followed by a soft, grinding noise, the most sickening sound, I think, to which I ever listened. This was accompanied by a strange, steady, unnatural wind, which seemed to press upon us as water presses. Then the dawn broke and we saw.

The mountain-side was moving down upon us in a vast avalanche of snow.

Oh! what a sight was that. On from the crest of the precipitous slopes above, two miles and more away, it came, a living thing, rolling, sliding, gliding; piling itself in long, leaping waves, hollowing itself into cavernous valleys, like a tempest-driven sea, whilst above its surface hung a powdery cloud of frozen spray.

As we watched, clinging to each other terrified, the first of these waves struck our hill, causing the mighty mass of solid rock to quiver like a yacht beneath the impact of an ocean roller, or an aspen in a sudden rush of wind. It struck and slowly separated, then with a majestic motion flowed like water over the edge of the precipice on either side, and fell with a thudding sound into the unmeasured depths beneath. And this was but a little thing, a mere forerunner, for after it, with a slow, serpentine movement, rolled the body of the avalanche.

It came in combers, it came in level floods. It piled itself against our hill, yes, to within fifty feet of the head of it, till we thought that even that rooted rock must be torn from its foundations and hurled like a pebble to the deeps beneath. And the turmoil of it all! The screaming of the blast caused by the compression of the air, the dull, continuous thudding of the fall of millions of tons of snow as they rushed through space and ended their journey in the gulf.

Nor was this the worst of it, for as the deep snows above thinned, great boulders that had been buried beneath them, perhaps for centuries, were loosened from their resting-places and began to thunder down the hill. At first they moved slowly, throwing up the hard snow around them as the prow of a ship throws foam. Then gathering momentum, they sprang into the air with leaps such as those of shells ricocheting upon water, till in the end, singing and hurtling, many of them rushed past and even over us to vanish far beyond. Some indeed struck our little mountain with the force of shot fired from the great guns of a battleship, and shattered there, or if they fell upon its side, tore away tons of rock and passed with them into the chasm like a meteor surrounded by its satellites. Indeed, no bombardment devised and directed by man could have been half so terrible or, had there been anything to destroy, half so destructive.

The scene was appalling in its unchained and resistless might evolved suddenly from the completest calm. There in the lap of the quiet mountains, looked down upon by the peaceful, tender sky, the powers hidden in the breast of Nature were suddenly set free, and, companioned by whirlwinds and all the terrifying majesty of sound, loosed upon the heads of us two human atoms.

At the first rush of snow we had leapt back behind our protecting peak and, lying at full length upon the ground, gripped it and clung there, fearing lest the wind should whirl us to the abyss. Long ago our tent had gone like a dead leaf in an autumn gale, and at times it seemed as if we must follow.

The boulders hurtled over and past us; one of them, fell full upon the little peak, shattering its crest and bursting into fragments, which fled away, each singing its own wild song. We were not touched, but when we looked behind us it was to see the yak, which had risen in its terror, lying dead and headless. Then in our fear we lay still, waiting for the end, and wondering dimly whether we should be buried in the surging snow or swept away with the hill, or crushed by the flying rocks, or lifted and lost in the hurricane.

How long did it last? We never knew. It may have been ten minutes or two hours, for in such a scene time loses its proportion. Only we became aware that the wind had fallen, while the noise of grinding snow and hurtling boulders ceased. Very cautiously we gained our feet and looked.

In front of us was sheer mountain side, for a depth of over two miles, the width of about a thousand yards, which had been covered with many feet of snow, was now bare rock. Piled up against the face of our hill, almost to its summit, lay a tongue of snow, pressed to the consistency of ice and spotted with boulders that had lodged there. The peak itself was torn and shattered, so that it revealed great gleaming surfaces and pits, in which glittered mica, or some other mineral. The vast gulf behind was half filled with the avalanche and its debris. But for the rest, it seemed as though nothing had happened, for the sun shone sweetly overhead and the solemn snows reflected its rays from the sides of a hundred hills. And we had endured it all and were still alive; yes, and unhurt.

But what a position was ours! We dared not attempt to descend the mount, lest we should sink into the loose snow and be buried there. Moreover, all along the breadth of the path of the avalanche boulders from time to time still thundered down the rocky slope, and with them came patches of snow that had been left behind by the big slide, small in themselves, it is true, but each of them large enough to kill a hundred men. It was obvious, therefore, that until these conditions changed, or death released us, we must abide where we were upon the crest of the hillock.

So there we sat, foodless and frightened, wondering what our old friend Kou-en would say if he could see us now. By degrees hunger mastered all our other sensations and we began to turn longing eyes upon the headless body of the yak.

"Let's skin him," said Leo, "it will be something to do, and we shall want his hide to-night."

So with affection, and even reverence, we performed this office for the dead companion of our journeyings, rejoicing the while that it was not we who had brought him to his end. Indeed, long residence among peoples who believed fully that the souls of men could pass into, or were risen from, the bodies of animals, had made us a little superstitious on this matter. It would be scarcely pleasant, we reflected, in some future incarnation, to find our faithful friend clad in human form and to hear him bitterly reproach us for his murder.

Being dead, however, these arguments did not apply to eating him, as we were sure he would himself acknowledge. So we cut off little bits of his flesh and, rolling them in snow till they looked as though they were nicely floured, hunger compelling us, swallowed them at a gulp. It was a disgusting meal and we felt like cannibals: but what could we do?

V. THE GLACIER

Even that day came to an end at last, and after a few more lumps of yak, our tent being gone, we drew his hide over us and rested as best we could, knowing that at least we had no more avalanches to fear. That night it froze sharply, so that had it not been for the yak's hide and the other rugs and garments, which fortunately we were wearing when the snow-slide began, it would, I think, have gone hard with us. As it was, we suffered a great deal.

"Horace," said Leo at the dawn, "I am going to leave this. If we have to die, I would rather do so moving; but I don't believe that we shall die."

"Very well," I said, "let us start. If the snow won't bear us now, it never will."

So we tied up our rugs and the yak's hide in two bundles and, having cut off some more of the frozen meat, began our descent. Now, although the mount was under two hundred feet high, its base, fortunately for us—for otherwise it must have been swept away by the mighty pressure of the avalanche—was broad, so that there was a long expanse of piled-up snow between us and the level ground.

Since, owing to the overhanging conformation of the place, it was quite impossible for us to descend in front where pressure had made the snow hard as stone, we were obliged to risk a march over the looser material upon its flank. As there was nothing to be gained by waiting, off we went, Leo leading and step by step trying the snow. To our joy we discovered that the sharp night frost had so hardened its surface that it would support us. About half way down, however, where the pressure had been less, it became much softer, so that we were forced to lie upon our faces, which enabled us to distribute our weight over a larger surface, and thus slither gently down the hill.

All went well until we were within twenty paces of the bottom, where we must cross a soft mound formed of the powdery dust thrown off by the avalanche in its rush. Leo slipped over safely, but I, following a yard or two to his right, of a sudden felt the hard crust yield beneath me. An ill-judged but quite natural flounder and wriggle, such as a newly-landed flat-fish gives upon the sand, completed the mischief, and with one piercing but swiftly stifled yell, I vanished.

Any one who has ever sunk in deep water will know that the sensation is not pleasant, but I can assure him that to go through the same experience in soft snow is infinitely worse; mud alone could surpass its terrors. Down I went, and down, till at length I seemed to reach a rock which alone saved me from disappearing for ever. Now I felt the snow closing above me and with it came darkness and a sense of suffocation. So soft was the drift, however, that before I was overcome I contrived with my arms to thrust away the powdery dust from about my head, thus forming a little hollow into which air filtered slowly. Getting my hands upon the stone, I strove to rise, but could not, the weight upon me was too great.

Then I abandoned hope and prepared to die. The process proved not altogether unpleasant. I did not see visions from my past life as drowning men are supposed to do, but—and this shows how strong was her empire over me—my mind flew back to Ayesha. I seemed to behold her and a man at her side, standing over me in some dark, rocky gulf. She was wrapped in a long travelling cloak, and her lovely eyes were wild with fear. I rose to salute her, and make report, but she cried in a fierce, concentrated voice—"What evil thing has happened here? Thou livest; then where is my lord Leo? Speak, man, and say where thou hast hid my lord—or die."

The vision was extraordinarily real and vivid, I remember, and, considered in connection with a certain subsequent event, in all ways most remarkable, but it passed as swiftly as it came.

Then my senses left me.

I saw a light again. I heard a voice, that of Leo. "Horace," he cried, "Horace, hold fast to the stock of the rifle." Something was thrust against my outstretched hand. I gripped it despairingly, and there came a strain. It was useless, I did not move. Then, bethinking me, I drew up my legs and by chance or the mercy of Heaven, I know not, got my feet against a ridge of the rock on which I was lying. Again I felt the strain, and thrust with all my might. Of a sudden the snow gave, and out of that hole I shot like a fox from its earth.

I struck something. It was Leo straining at the gun, and I knocked him backwards. Then down the steep slope we rolled, landing at length upon the very edge of the precipice. I sat up, drawing in the air with great gasps, and oh! how sweet it was. My eyes fell upon my hand, and I saw that the veins stood out on the back of it, black as ink and large as cords. Clearly I must have been near my end.

"How long was I in there?" I gasped to Leo, who sat at my side, wiping off the sweat that ran from his face in streams.

"Don't know. Nearly twenty minutes, I should think."

"Twenty minutes! It seemed like twenty centuries. How did you get me out? You could not stand upon the drift dust."

"No; I lay upon the yak skin where the snow was harder and tunnelled towards you through the powdery stuff with my hands, for I knew where you had sunk and it was not far off. At last I saw your finger tips; they were so blue that for a few seconds I took them for rock, but thrust the butt of the rifle against them. Luckily you still had life enough to catch hold of it, and you know the rest. Were we not both very strong, it could never have been done."

"Thank you, old fellow," I said simply.

"Why should you thank me?" he asked with one of his quick smiles. "Do you suppose that I wished to continue this journey alone? Come, if you have got your breath, let us be getting on. You have been sleeping in a cold bed and want exercise. Look, my rifle is broken and yours is lost in the snow. Well, it will save us the trouble of carrying the cartridges," and he laughed drearily.

Then we began our march, heading for the spot where the road ended four miles or so away, for to go forward seemed useless. In due course we reached it safely. Once a mass of snow as large as a church swept down just in front of us, and once a great boulder loosened from the mountain rushed at us suddenly like an attacking lion, or the stones thrown by Polyphemus at the ship of Odysseus, and, leaping over our heads, vanished with an angry scream into the depths beneath. But we took little heed of these things: our nerves were deadened, and no danger seemed to affect them.

There was the end of the road, and there were our own footprints and the impress of the yak's hoofs in the snow. The sight of them affected me, for it seemed strange that we should have lived to look upon them again. We stared over the edge of the precipice. Yes, it was sheer and absolutely unclimbable.

"Come to the glacier," said Leo.

So we went on to it, and scrambling a little way down its root, made an examination. Here, so far as we could judge, the cliff was about four hundred feet deep. But whether or no the tongue of ice reached to the foot of it we were unable to tell, since about two thirds of the way down it arched inwards, like the end of a bent bow, and the conformation of the overhanging rocks on either side was such that we could not see where it terminated. We climbed back again and sat down, and despair took hold of us, bitter, black despair.

"What are we to do?" I asked. "In front of us death. Behind us death, for how can we recross those mountains without food or guns to shoot it with? Here death, for we must sit and starve. We have striven and failed. Leo, our end is at hand. Only a miracle can save us."

"A miracle," he answered. "Well, what was it that led us to the top of the mount so that we were able to escape the avalanche? And what was it which put that rock in your way as you sank into the bed of dust, and gave me wit and strength to dig you out of your grave of snow? And what is it that has preserved us through seventeen years of dangers such as few men have known and lived? Some directing Power. Some Destiny that will accomplish itself in us. Why should the Power cease to guide? Why should the Destiny be baulked at last?"

He paused, then added fiercely, "I tell you, Horace, that even if we had guns, food, and yaks, I would not turn back upon our spoor, since to do so would prove me a coward and unworthy of her. I will go on."

"How?" I asked.

"By that road," and he pointed to the glacier.

"It is a road to death!"

"Well, if so, Horace, it would seem that in this land men find life in death, or so they believe. If we die now, we shall die travelling our path, and in the country where we perish we may be born again. At least I am determined, so you must choose."

"I have chosen long ago. Leo, we began this journey together and we will end it together. Perhaps Ayesha knows and will help us," and I laughed drearily. "If not—come, we are wasting time."

Then we took counsel, and the end of it was that we cut a skin rug and the yak's tough hide into strips and knotted these together into two serviceable ropes, which we fastened about our middles, leaving one end loose, for we thought that they might help us in our descent.

Next we bound fragments of another skin rug about our legs and knees to protect them from the chafing of the ice and rocks, and for the same reason put on our thick leather gloves. This done, we took the remainder of our gear and heavy robes and, having placed stones in them, threw them over the brink of the precipice, trusting to find them again, should we ever reach its foot. Now our preparations were complete, and it was time for us to start upon perhaps one of the most desperate journeys ever undertaken by men of their own will.

Yet we stayed a little, looking at each other in piteous fashion, for we could not speak. Only we embraced, and I confess, I think I wept a little. It all seemed so sad and hopeless, these longings endured through many years, these perpetual, weary travellings, and now—the end. I could not bear to think of that splendid man, my ward, my most dear friend, the companion of my life, who stood before me so full of beauty and of vigour, but who must within a few short minutes be turned into a heap of quivering, mangled flesh. For myself it did not matter. I was old, it was time that I should die. I had lived innocently, if it were innocent to follow this lovely image, this Siren of the caves, who lured us on to doom.

No, I don't think that I thought of myself then, but I thought a great deal of Leo, and when I saw his determined face and flashing eyes as he nerved himself to the last endeavour, I was proud of him. So in broken accents I blessed him and wished him well through all the aeons, praying that I might be his companion to the end of time. In few words and short he thanked me and gave me back my blessing. Then he muttered—"Come."

So side by side we began the terrible descent. At first it was easy enough, although a slip would have hurled us to eternity. But we were strong and skilful, accustomed to such places moreover, and made none. About a quarter of the way down we paused, standing upon a great boulder that was embedded in the ice, and, turning round cautiously, leaned our backs against the glacier and looked about us. Truly it was a horrible place, almost sheer, nor did we learn much, for beneath us, a hundred and twenty feet or more, the projecting bend cut off our view of what lay below.

So, feeling that our nerves would not bear a prolonged contemplation of that dizzy gulf, once more we set our faces to the ice and proceeded on the downward climb. Now matters were more difficult, for the stones were fewer and once or twice we must slide to reach them, not knowing if we should ever stop again. But the ropes which we threw over the angles of the rocks, or salient points of ice, letting ourselves down by their help and drawing them after us when we reached the next foothold, saved us from disaster.

Thus at length we came to the bend, which was more than half way down the precipice, being, so far as I could judge, about two hundred and fifty feet from its lip, and say one hundred and fifty from the darksome bottom of the narrow gulf. Here were no stones, but only some rough ice, on which we sat to rest.

"We must look," said Leo presently.

But the question was, how to do this. Indeed, there was only one way, to hang over the bend and discover what lay below. We read each other's thought without the need of words, and I made a motion as though I would start.

"No," said Leo, "I am younger and stronger than you. Come, help me," and he began to fasten the end of his rope to a strong, projecting point of ice. "Now," he said, "hold my ankles."

It seemed an insanity, but there was nothing else to be done, so, fixing my heels in a niche, I grasped them and slowly he slid forward till his body vanished to the middle. What he saw does not matter, for I saw it all afterwards, but what happened was that suddenly all his great weight came upon my arms with such a jerk that his ankles were torn from my grip.

Or, who knows! perhaps in my terror I loosed them, obeying the natural impulse which prompts a man to save his own life. If so, may I be forgiven, but had I held on, I must have been jerked into the abyss. Then the rope ran out and remained taut.

"Leo!" I screamed, "Leo!" and I heard a muffled voice saying, as I thought, "Come." What it really said was—"Don't come." But indeed—and may it go to my credit—I did not pause to think, but face outwards, just as I was sitting, began to slide and scramble down the ice.

In two seconds I had reached the curve, in three I was over it. Beneath was what I can only describe as a great icicle broken off short, and separated from the cliff by about four yards of space. This icicle was not more than fifteen feet in length and sloped outwards, so that my descent was not sheer. Moreover, at the end of it the trickling of water, or some such accident, had worn away the ice, leaving a little ledge as broad, perhaps, as a man's hand. There were roughnesses on the surface below the curve, upon which my clothing caught, also I gripped them desperately with my fingers. Thus it came about that I slid down quite gently and, my heels landing upon the little ledge, remained almost upright, with outstretched arms—like a person crucified to a cross of ice.

Then I saw everything, and the sight curdled the blood within my veins.

Hanging to the rope, four or five feet below the broken point, was Leo, out of reach of it, and out of reach of the cliff; as he hung turning slowly round and round, much as—for in a dreadful, inconsequent fashion the absurd similarity struck me even then—a joint turns before the fire. Below yawned the black gulf, and at the bottom of it, far, far beneath, appeared a faint, white sheet of snow. That is what I saw.

Think of it! Think of it! I crucified upon the ice, my heels resting upon a little ledge; my fingers grasping excrescences on which a bird could scarcely have found a foothold; round and below me dizzy space. To climb back whence I came was impossible, to stir even was impossible, since one slip and I must be gone.

And below me, hung like a spider to its cord, Leo turning slowly round and round!

I could see that rope of green hide stretch beneath his weight and the double knots in it slip and tighten, and I remember wondering which would give first, the hide or the knots, or whether it would hold till he dropped from the noose limb by limb.

Oh! I have been in many a perilous place, I who sprang from the Swaying Stone to the point of the Trembling Spur, and missed my aim, but never, never in such a one as this. Agony took hold of me; a cold sweat burst from every pore. I could feel it running down my face like tears; my hair bristled upon my head. And below, in utter silence, Leo turned round and round, and each time he turned his up-cast eyes met mine with a look that was horrible to see.

The silence was the worst of it, the silence and the helplessness. If he had cried out, if he had struggled, it would have been better. But to know that he was alive there, with every nerve and perception at its utmost stretch. Oh! my God! Oh! my God!

My limbs began to ache, and yet I dared not stir a muscle. They ached horribly, or so I thought, and beneath this torture, mental and physical, my mind gave.

I remembered things: remembered how, as a child, I had climbed a tree and reached a place whence I could move neither up nor down, and what I suffered then. Remembered how once in Egypt a foolhardy friend of mine had ascended the Second Pyramid alone, and become thus crucified upon its shining cap, where he remained for a whole half hour with four hundred feet of space beneath him. I could see him now stretching his stockinged foot downwards in a vain attempt to reach the next crack, and drawing it back again; could see his tortured face, a white blot upon the red granite.

Then that face vanished and blackness gathered round me, and in the blackness visions: of the living, resistless avalanche, of the snow-grave into which I had sunk—oh! years and years ago; of Ayesha demanding Leo's life at my hands. Blackness and silence, through which I could only hear the cracking of my muscles.

Suddenly in the blackness a flash, and in the silence a sound. The flash was the flash of a knife which Leo had drawn. He was hacking at the cord with it fiercely, fiercely, to make an end. And the sound was that of the noise he made, a ghastly noise, half shout of defiance and half yell of terror, as at the third stroke it parted.

I saw it part. The tough hide was half cut through, and its severed portion curled upwards and downwards like the upper and lower lips of an angry dog, whilst that which was unsevered stretched out slowly, slowly, till it grew quite thin. Then it snapped, so that the rope flew upwards and struck me across the face like the lash of a whip.

Another instant and I heard a crackling, thudding sound. Leo had struck the ground below. Leo was dead, a mangled mass of flesh and bone as I had pictured him. I could not bear it. My nerve and human dignity came back. I would not wait until, my strength exhausted, I slid from my perch as a wounded bird falls from a tree. No, I would follow him at once, of my own act.

I let my arms fall against my sides, and rejoiced in the relief from pain that the movement gave me. Then balanced upon my heels, I stood upright, took my last look at the sky, muttered my last prayer. For an instant I remained thus poised.

Shouting, "I come," I raised my hands above my head and dived as a bather dives, dived into the black gulf beneath.

Oh! that rush through space! Folk falling thus are supposed to lose consciousness, but I can assert that this is not true. Never were my wits and perceptions more lively than while I travelled from that broken glacier to the ground, and never did a short journey seem to take a longer time. I saw the white floor, like some living thing, leaping up through empty air to meet me, then—finis!

Crash! Why, what was this? I still lived. I was in water, for I could feel its chill, and going down, down, till I thought I should never rise again. But rise I did, though my lungs were nigh to bursting first. As I floated up towards the top I remembered the crash, which told me that I had passed through ice. Therefore I should meet ice at the surface again. Oh! to think that after surviving so much I must be drowned like a kitten and beneath a sheet of ice. My hands touched it. There it was above me shining white like glass. Heaven be praised! My head broke through; in this low and sheltered gorge it was but a film no thicker than a penny formed by the light frost of the previous night. So I rose from the deep and stared about me, treading water with my feet.

Then I saw the gladdest sight that ever my eyes beheld, for on the right, not ten yards away, the water running from his hair and beard, was Leo. Leo alive, for he broke the thin ice with his arms as he struggled towards the shore from the deep river.* He saw me also, and his grey eyes seemed to start out of his head.

"Still living, both of us, and the precipice passed!" he shouted in a ringing, exultant voice. "I told you we were led."

"Aye, but whither?" I answered as I too fought my way through the film of ice.

---

* Usually, as we learned afterwards, the river at his spot was quite shallow; only a foot or two in depth. It was the avalanche that by damming it with fallen heaps of snow had raised its level very many feet. Therefore, to this avalanche, which had threatened to destroy us, we in reality owed our lives, for had the stream stood only at its normal height we must have been dashed to pieces upon the stones.

—L. H. H.

Then it was I became aware that we were no longer alone, for on the bank of the river, some thirty yards from us, stood two figures, a man leaning upon a long staff and a woman. He was a very old man, for his eyes were horny, his snow-white hair and beard hung upon the bent breast and shoulders, and his sardonic, wrinkled features were yellow as wax. They might have been those of a death mask cut in marble. There, clad in an ample, monkish robe, and leaning upon the staff, he stood still as a statue and watched us. I noted it all, every detail, although at the time I did not know that I was doing so, as we broke our way through the ice towards them and afterwards the picture came back to me. Also I saw that the woman, who was very tall, pointed to us.

Nearer the bank, or rather to the rock edge of the river, its surface was free of ice, for here the stream ran very swiftly. Seeing this, we drew close together and swam on side by side to help each other if need were. There was much need, for in the fringe of the torrent the strength that had served me so long seemed to desert me, and I became helpless; numbed, too, with the biting coldness of the water. Indeed, had not Leo grasped my clothes I think that I should have been swept away by the current to perish. Thus aided I fought on a while, till he said—"I am going under. Hold to the rope end."

So I gripped the strip of yak's hide that was still fast about him, and, his hand thus freed, Leo made a last splendid effort to keep us both, cumbered as we were with the thick, soaked garments that dragged us down like lead, from being sucked beneath the surface. Moreover, he succeeded where any other swimmer of less strength must have failed. Still, I believe that we should have drowned, since here the water ran like a mill-race, had not the man upon the shore, seeing our plight and urged thereto by the woman, run with surprising swiftness in one so aged, to a point of rock that jutted some yards into the stream, past which we were being swept, and seating himself, stretched out his long stick towards us.

With a desperate endeavour, Leo grasped it as we went by, rolling over and over each other, and held on. Round we swung into the eddy, found our feet, were knocked down again, rubbed and pounded on the rocks. But still gripping that staff of salvation, to his end of which the old man clung like a limpet to a stone, while the woman clung to him, we recovered ourselves, and, sheltered somewhat by the rock, floundered towards the shore. Lying on his face—for we were still in great danger—

the man extended his arm. We could not reach it; and worse, suddenly the staff was torn from him; we were being swept away.

Then it was that the woman did a noble thing, for springing into the water—yes, up to her armpits—and holding fast to the old man by her left hand, with the right she seized Leo's hair and dragged him shorewards. Now he found his feet for a moment, and throwing one arm about her slender form, steadied himself thus, while with the other he supported me. Next followed a long confused struggle, but the end of it was that three of us, the old man, Leo and I, rolled in a heap upon the bank and lay there gasping.

Presently I looked up. The woman stood over us, water streaming from her garments, staring like one in a dream at Leo's face, smothered as it was with blood running from a deep cut in his head. Even then I noticed how stately and beautiful she was. Now she seemed to awake and, glancing at the robes that clung to her splendid shape, said something to her companion, then turned and ran towards the cliff.

As we lay before him, utterly exhausted, the old man, who had risen, contemplated us solemnly with his dim eyes. He spoke, but we did not understand. Again he tried another language and without success. A third time and our ears were opened, for the tongue he used was Greek; yes, there in Central Asia he addressed us in Greek, not very pure, it is true, but still Greek.

"Are you wizards," he said, "that you have lived to reach this land?"

"Nay," I answered in the same tongue, though in broken words—since of Greek I had thought little for many a year—"for then we should have come otherwise," and I pointed to our hurts and the precipice behind us.

"They know the ancient speech; it is as we were told from the Mountain," he muttered to himself. Then he asked—"Strangers, what seek you?"

Now I grew cunning and did not answer, fearing lest, should he learn the truth, he would thrust us back into the river. But Leo had no such caution, or rather all reason had left him; he was light-headed.

"We seek," he stuttered out—his Greek, which had always been feeble, now was simply barbarous and mixed with various Thibetan dialects—"we seek the land of the Fire Mountain that is crowned with the Sign of Life."

The man stared at us. "So you know," he said, then broke off and added, "and whom do you seek?"

"Her," answered Leo wildly, "the Queen." I think that he meant to say the priestess, or the goddess, but could only think of the Greek for Queen, or rather something resembling it. Or perhaps it was because the woman who had gone looked like a queen.

"Oh!" said the man, "you seek a queen—then you are those for whom we were bidden to watch. Nay, how can I be sure?"

"Is this a time to put questions?" I gasped angrily. "Answer me one rather: who are you?"

"I? Strangers, my title is Guardian of the Gate, and the lady who was with me is the Khania of Kaloon."

At this point Leo began to faint.

"That man is sick," said the Guardian, "and now that you have got your breath again, you must have shelter, both of you, and at once. Come, help me."

So, supporting Leo on either side, we dragged ourselves away from that accursed cliff and Styx-like river up a narrow, winding gorge. Presently it opened out, and there, stretching across the glade, we saw the Gate. Of this all I observed then, for my memory of the details of this scene and of the conversation that passed is very weak and blurred, was that it seemed to be a mighty wall of rock in which a pathway had been hollowed where doubtless once passed the road. On one side of this passage was a stair, which we began to ascend with great difficulty, for Leo was now almost senseless and scarcely moved his legs. Indeed at the head of the first flight he sank down in a heap, nor did our strength suffice to lift him.

While I wondered feebly what was to be done, I heard footsteps, and looking up, saw the woman who had saved him descending the stair, and after her two robed men with a Tartar cast of countenance, very impassive; small eyes and yellowish skin. Even the sight of us did not appear to move them to astonishment. She spoke some words to them, whereon they lifted Leo's heavy frame, apparently with ease, and carried him up the steps.

We followed, and reached a room that seemed to be hewn from the rock above the gateway, where the woman called Khania left us. From it we passed through other rooms, one of them a kind of kitchen, in which a fire burned, till we came to a large chamber, evidently a sleeping place, for in it were wooden bedsteads, mattresses and rugs. Here Leo was laid down, and with the assistance of one of his servants, the old Guardian undressed him, at the same time motioning me to take off my own garments. This I did gladly enough for the first time during many days, though with great pain and difficulty, to find that I was a mass of wounds and bruises.

Presently our host blew upon a whistle, and the other servant appeared bringing hot water in a jar, with which we were washed over. Then the Guardian dressed our hurts with some soothing ointment, and wrapped us round with blankets. After this broth was brought, into which he mixed medicine, and giving me a portion to drink where I lay upon one of the beds, he took Leo's head upon his knee and poured the rest of it down his throat. Instantly a wonderful warmth ran through me, and my aching brain began to swim. Then I remembered no more.

After this we were very, very ill. What may be the exact medical definition of our sickness I do not know, but in effect it was such as follows loss of blood, extreme exhaustion of body, paralysing shock to the nerves and extensive cuts and contusions. These taken together produced a long period of semi-unconsciousness, followed by another period of fever and delirium. All that I can recall of those weeks while we remained the guests of the Guardian of the Gate, may be summed up in one word—dreams, that is until at last I recovered my senses.

The dreams themselves are forgotten, which is perhaps as well, since they were very confused, and for the most part awful; a hotch-potch of nightmares, reflected without doubt from vivid memories of our recent and fearsome sufferings. At times I would wake up from them a little, I suppose when food was administered to me, and receive impressions of whatever was passing in the place. Thus I can recollect that yellow-faced old Guardian standing over me like a ghost in the moonlight, stroking his long beard, his eyes fixed upon my face, as though he would search out the secrets of my soul.

"They are the men," he muttered to himself, "without doubt they are the men," then walked to the window and looked up long and earnestly, like one who studies the stars.

After this I remember a disturbance in the room, and dominating it, as it were, the rich sound of a woman's voice and the rustle of a woman's silks sweeping the stone floor. I opened my eyes and saw that it was she who had helped to rescue us, who had rescued us in fact, a tall and noble-looking lady with a beauteous, weary face and liquid eyes which seemed to burn. From the heavy cloak she wore I thought that she must have just returned from a journey.

She stood above me and looked at me, then turned away with a gesture of indifference, if not of disgust, speaking to the Guardian in a low voice. By way of answer he bowed, pointing to the other bed where Leo lay, asleep, and thither she passed with slow, imperious movements. I saw her bend down and lift the corner of a wrapping which covered his wounded head, and heard her utter some smothered words before she turned round to the Guardian as though to question him further.

But he had gone, and being alone, for she thought me senseless, she drew a rough stool to the side of the bed, and seating herself studied Leo, who lay thereon, with an earnestness that was almost terrible, for her soul seemed to be concentrated in her eyes, and to find expression through them. Long she gazed thus, then rose and began to walk swiftly up and down the chamber, pressing her hands now to her bosom and now to her brow, a certain passionate perplexity stamped upon her face, as though she struggled to remember something and could not.

"Where and when?" she whispered. "Oh! where and when?"

Of the end of that scene I know nothing, for although I fought hard against it, oblivion mastered me. After this I became aware that the regal-looking woman called Khania, was always in the room, and that she seemed to be nursing Leo with great care and tenderness. Sometimes even she nursed me when Leo did not need attention, and she had nothing else to do, or so her manner seemed to suggest. It was as though I excited her curiosity, and she wished me to recover that it might be satisfied.

Again I awoke, how long afterwards I cannot say. It was night, and the room was lighted by the moon only, now shining in a clear sky. Its steady rays entering at the window-place fell on Leo's bed, and by them I saw that the dark, imperial woman was watching at his side. Some sense of her presence must have communicated itself to him, for he began to mutter in his sleep, now in English, now in Arabic. She became intensely interested; as her every movement showed. Then rising suddenly she glided across the room on tiptoe to look at me. Seeing her coming I feigned to be asleep, and so well that she was deceived.

For I was also interested. Who was this lady whom the Guardian had called the Khania of Kaloon? Could it be she whom we sought? Why not? And yet if I saw Ayesha, surely I should know her, surely there would be no room for doubt.

Back she went again to the bed, kneeling down beside Leo, and in the intense silence which followed—for he had ceased his mutterings—I thought that I could hear the beating of her heart. Now she began to speak, very low and in that same bastard Greek tongue, mixed here and there with Mongolian words such as are common to the dialects of Central

Asia. I could not hear or understand all she said, but some sentences I did understand, and they frightened me not a little.

"Man of my dreams," she murmured, "whence come you? Who are you? Why did the Hesea bid me to meet you?" Then some sentences I could not catch. "You sleep; in sleep the eyes are opened. Answer, I bid you; say what is the bond between you and me? Why have I dreamt of you? Why do I know you? Why——?" and the sweet, rich voice died slowly from a whisper into silence, as though she were ashamed to utter what was on her tongue.

As she bent over him a lock of her hair broke loose from its jewelled fillet and fell across his face. At its touch Leo seemed to wake, for he lifted his gaunt, white hand and touched the hair, then said in English—"Where am I? Oh! I remember;" and their eyes met as he strove to lift himself and could not. Then he spoke again in his broken, stumbling Greek, "You are the lady who saved me from the water. Say, are you also that queen whom I have sought so long and endured so much to find?"

"I know not," she answered in a voice as sweet as honey, a low, trembling voice; "but true it is I am a queen—if a Khania be a queen."

"Say, then, Queen, do you remember me?"

"We have met in dreams," she answered, "I think that we have met in a past that is far away. Yes; I knew it when first I saw you there by the river. Stranger with the well remembered face, tell me, I pray you, how you are named?"

"Leo Vincey."

She shook her head, whispering—"I know not the name, yet you I know."

"You know me! How do you know me?" he said heavily, and seemed to sink again into slumber or swoon.

She watched him for a while very intently. Then as though some force that she could not resist drew her, I saw her bend down her head over his sleeping face. Yes; and I saw her kiss him swiftly on the lips, then spring back crimson to the hair, as though overwhelmed with shame at this victory of her mad passion.

Now it was that she discovered me.

Bewildered, fascinated, amazed, I had raised myself upon my bed, not knowing it; I suppose that I might see and hear the better. It was wrong, doubtless, but no common curiosity over-mastered me, who had my share in all this story. More, it was foolish, but illness and wonder had killed my reason.

Yes, she saw me watching them, and such fury seemed to take hold of her that I thought my hour had come.

"Man, have you dared——?" she said in an intense whisper, and snatching at her girdle. Now in her hand shone a knife, and I knew that it was destined for my heart. Then in this sore danger my wit came back to me and as she advanced I stretched out my shaking hand, saying—"Oh! of your pity, give me to drink. The fever burns me, it burns," and I looked round like one bewildered who sees not, repeating, "Give me drink, you who are called Guardian," and I fell back exhausted.

She stopped like a hawk in its stoop, and swiftly sheathed the dagger. Then taking a bowl of milk that stood on a table near her, she held it to my lips, searching my face the while with her flaming eyes, for indeed passion, rage, and fear had lit them till they seemed to flame. I drank the milk in great gulps, though never in my life did I find it more hard to swallow.

"You tremble," she said; "have dreams haunted you?"

"Aye, friend," I answered, "dreams of that fearsome precipice and of the last leap."

"Aught else?" she asked.

"Nay; is it not enough? Oh! what a journey to have taken to befriend a queen."

"To befriend a queen," she repeated puzzled. "What means the man? You swear you have had no other dreams?"

"Aye, I swear by the Symbol of Life and the Mount of the Wavering Flame, and by yourself, O Queen from the ancient days."

Then I sighed and pretended to swoon, for I could think of nothing else to do. As I closed my eyes I saw her face that had been red as dawn turn pale as eve, for my words and all which might lie behind them, had gone home. Moreover, she was in doubt, for I could hear her fingering the handle of the dagger. Then she spoke aloud, words for my ears if they still were open.

"I am glad," she said, "that he dreamed no other dreams, since had he done so and babbled of them it would have been ill-omened, and I do not wish that one who has travelled far to visit us should be hurled to the death-dogs for burial; one, moreover, who although old and hideous, still has the air of a wise and silent man."

Now while I shivered at these unpleasant hints—though what the "death-dogs" in which people were buried might be, I could not conceive—to my intense joy I heard the foot of the Guardian on the stairs, heard him too enter the room and saw him bow before the lady.

"How go these sick men, niece?"* he said in his cold voice.

"They swoon, both of them," she answered.

"Indeed, is it so? I thought otherwise. I thought they woke."

"What have you heard, Shaman (i.e. wizard)?" she asked angrily.

"I? Oh! I heard the grating of a dagger in its sheath and the distant baying of the death-hounds."

"And what have you seen, Shaman?" she asked again, "looking through the Gate you guard?"

"Strange sight, Khania, my niece. But—men awake from swoons."

"Aye," she answered, "so while this one sleeps, bear him to another chamber, for he needs change, and the lord yonder needs more space and untainted air."

The Guardian, whom she called "Shaman" or Magician, held a lamp in his hand, and by its light it was easy to see his face, which I watched out of the corner of my eye. I thought that it wore a very strange expression, one moreover that alarmed me somewhat. From the beginning I had misdoubted me of this old man, whose cast of countenance was vindictive as it was able; now I was afraid of him.

"To which chamber, Khania?" he said with meaning.

"I think," she answered slowly, "to one that is healthful, where he will recover. The man has wisdom," she added as though in explanation, "moreover, having the word from the Mountain, to harm him would be dangerous. But why do you ask?"

He shrugged his shoulders.

"I tell you I heard the death-hounds bay, that is all. Yes, with you I think that he has wisdom, and the bee which seeks honey should suck the flower—before it fades! Also, as you say, there are commands with which it is ill to trifle, even if we cannot guess their meaning."

Then going to the door he blew upon his whistle, and instantly I heard the feet of his servants upon the stairs. He gave them an order, and gently enough they lifted the mattress on which I lay and followed him down sundry passages and past some stairs into another chamber shaped like that we had left, but not so large, where they placed me upon a bed.

---

* I found later that the Khania, Atene, was not Simbri's niece but his great-niece, on the mother's side.

—L. H. H.

The Guardian watched me awhile to see that I did not wake. Next he stretched out his hand and felt my heart and pulse; an examination the results of which seemed to puzzle him, for he uttered a little exclamation and shook his head. After this he left the room, and I heard him bolt the door behind him. Then, being still very weak, I fell asleep in earnest.

When I awoke it was broad daylight. My mind was clear and I felt better than I had done for many a day, signs by which I knew that the fever had left me and that I was on the high road to recovery. Now I remembered all the events of the previous night and was able to weigh them carefully. This, to be sure, I did for many reasons, among them that I knew I had been and still was, in great danger.

I had seen and heard too much, and this woman called Khania guessed that I had seen and heard. Indeed, had it not been for my hints about the Symbol of Life and the Mount of Flame, after I had disarmed her first rage by my artifice, I felt sure that she would have ordered the old Guardian or Shaman to do me to death in this way or the other; sure also that he would not have hesitated to obey her. I had been spared partly because, for some unknown reason, she was afraid to kill me, and partly that she might learn how much I knew, although the "death-hounds had bayed," whatever that might mean. Well, up to the present I was safe, and for the rest I must take my chance. Moreover it was necessary to be cautious, and, if need were, to feign ignorance. So, dismissing the matter of my own fate from my mind, I fell to considering the scene which I had witnessed and what might be its purport.

Was our quest at an end? Was this woman Ayesha? Leo had so dreamed, but he was still delirious, therefore here was little on which to lean. What seemed more to the point was that she herself evidently appeared to think that there existed some tie between her and this sick man. Why had she embraced him? I was sure that she could be no wanton, nor indeed would any woman indulge for its own sake in such folly with a stranger who hung between life and death. What she had done was done because irresistible impulse, born of knowledge, or at least of memories, drove her on, though mayhap the knowledge was imperfect and the memories were undefined. Who save Ayesha could have known anything of Leo in the past? None who lived upon the earth to-day.

And yet, why not, if what Kou-en the abbot and tens of millions of his fellow-worshippers believed were true? If the souls of human beings were in fact strictly limited in number, and became the tenants of an endless succession of physical bodies which they change from time to time as we change our worn-out garments, why should not others have known him? For instance that daughter of the Pharaohs who "caused him through love to break the vows that he had vowed" knew a certain Kallikrates, a priest of "Isis whom the gods cherish and the demons obey;" even Amenartas, the mistress of magic.

Oh! now a light seemed to break upon me, a wonderful light. What if Amenartas and this Khania, this woman with royalty stamped on every feature, should be the same? Would not that "magic of my own people that I have" of which she wrote upon the Sherd, enable her to pierce the darkness of the Past and recognize the priest whom she had bewitched to love her, snatching him out of the very hand of the goddess? What if it were not Ayesha, but Amenartas re-incarnate who ruled this hidden land and once more sought to make the man she loved break through his vows? If so, knowing the evil that must come, I shook even at its shadow. The truth must be learned, but how?

Whilst I wondered the door opened, and the sardonic, inscrutable-old-faced man, whom this Khania had called Magician, and who called the Khania, niece, entered and stood before me.

VII. THE FIRST ORDEAL

The shaman advanced to my side and asked me courteously how I fared.

I answered, "Better. Far better, oh, my host—but how are you named?"

"Simbri," he answered, "and, as I told you by the water, my title is Hereditary Guardian of the Gate. By profession I am the royal Physician in this land."

"Did you say physician or magician?" I asked carelessly, as though I had not caught the word. He gave me a curious look.

"I said physician, and it is well for you and your companion that I have some skill in my art. Otherwise I think, perhaps, you would not have been alive to-day, O my guest—but how are you named?"

"Holly," I said.

"O my guest, Holly."

"Had it not been for the foresight that brought you and the lady Khania to the edge of yonder darksome river, certainly we should not have been alive, venerable Simbri, a foresight that seems to me to savour of magic in such a lonely place. That is why I thought you might have described yourself as a magician, though it is true that you may have been but fishing in those waters."

"Certainly I was fishing, stranger Holly—for men, and I caught two."

"Fishing by chance, host Simbri?"

"Nay, by design, guest Holly. My trade of physician includes the study of future events, for I am the chief of the Shamans or Seers of this land, and, having been warned of your coming quite recently, I awaited your arrival."

"Indeed, that is strange, most courteous also. So here physician and magician mean the same."

"You say it," he answered with a grave bow; "but tell me, if you will, how did you find your way to a land whither visitors do not wander?"

"Oh!" I answered, "perhaps we are but travellers, or perhaps we also have studied—medicine."

"I think that you must have studied it deeply, since otherwise you would not have lived to cross those mountains in search of—now, what did you seek? Your companion, I think, spoke of a queen—yonder, on the banks of the torrent."

"Did he? Did he, indeed? Well, that is strange since he seems to have found one, for surely that royal-looking lady, named Khania, who sprang into the stream and saved us, must be a queen."

"A queen she is, and a great one, for in our land Khania means queen, though how, friend Holly, a man who has lain senseless can have learned this, I do not know. Nor do I know how you come to speak our language."

"That is simple, for the tongue you talk is very ancient, and as it chances in my own country it has been my lot to study and to teach it. It is Greek, but although it is still spoken in the world, how it reached these mountains I cannot say."

"I will tell you," he answered. "Many generations ago a great conqueror born of the nation that spoke this tongue fought his way through the country to the south of us. He was driven back, but a general of his of another race advanced and crossed the mountains, and overcame the people of this land, bringing with him his master's language and his own worship. Here he established his dynasty, and here it remains, for being ringed in with deserts and with pathless mountain snows, we hold no converse with the outer world."

"Yes, I know something of that story; the conqueror was named Alexander, was he not?" I asked.

"He was so named, and the name of the general was Rassen, a native of a country called Egypt, or so our records tell us. His descendants hold the throne to this day, and the Khania is of his blood."

"Was the goddess whom he worshipped called Isis?"

"Nay," he answered, "she was called Hes."

"Which," I interrupted, "is but another title for Isis. Tell me, is her worship continued here? I ask because it is now dead in Egypt, which was its home."

"There is a temple on the Mountain yonder," he replied indifferently, "and in it are priests and priestesses who practise some ancient cult. But the real god of this people now, as long before the day of Rassen their conqueror, is the fire that dwells in this same Mountain, which from time to time breaks out and slays them."

"And does a goddess dwell in the fire?" I asked.

Again he searched my face with his cold eyes, then answered—"Stranger Holly, I know nothing of any goddess. That Mountain is sacred, and to seek to learn its secrets is to die. Why do you ask such questions?"

"Only because I am curious in the matter of old religions, and seeing the symbol of Life upon yonder peak, came hither to study yours, of which indeed a tradition still remains among the learned."

"Then abandon that study, friend Holly, for the road to it runs through the paws of the death-hounds, and the spears of savages. Nor indeed is there anything to learn."

"And what, Physician, are the death-hounds?"

"Certain dogs to which, according to our ancient custom, all offenders against the law or the will of the Khan, are cast to be torn to pieces."

"The will of the Khan! Has this Khania of yours a husband then?"

"Aye," he answered, "her cousin, who was the ruler of half the land. Now they and the land are one. But you have talked enough; I am here to say that your food is ready," and he turned to leave the room.

"One more question, friend Simbri. How came I to this chamber, and where is my companion?"

"You were borne hither in your sleep, and see, the change has bettered you. Do you remember nothing?"

"Nothing, nothing at all," I answered earnestly. "But what of my friend?"

"He also is better. The Khania Atene nurses him."

"Atene?" I said. "That is an old Egyptian name. It means the Disk of the Sun, and a woman who bore it thousands of years ago was famous for her beauty."

"Well, and is not my niece Atene beautiful?"

"How can I tell, O uncle of the Khania," I answered wearily, "who have scarcely seen her?"

Then he departed, and presently his yellow-faced, silent servants brought me my food.

Later in the morning the door opened again, and through it, unattended, came the Khania Atene, who shut and bolted it behind her. This action did not reassure me, still, rising in my bed, I saluted her as best I could, although at heart I was afraid. She seemed to read my doubts for she said—"Lie down, and have no fear. At present you will come by no harm from me. Now, tell me what is the man called Leo to you? Your son? Nay, it cannot be, since—forgive me—light is not born of darkness."

"I have always thought that it was so born, Khania. Yet you are right; he is but my adopted son, and a man whom I love."

"Say, what seek you here?" she asked.

"We seek, Khania, whatsoever Fate shall bring us on yonder Mountain, that which is crowned with flame."

Her face paled at the words, but she answered in a steady voice—"Then there you will find nothing but doom, if indeed you do not find it before you reach its slopes, which are guarded by savage men. Yonder is the College of Hes, and to violate its Sanctuary is death to any man, death in the ever-burning fire."

"And who rules this college, Khania—a priestess?"

"Yes, a priestess, whose face I have never seen, for she is so old that she veils herself from curious eyes."

"Ah! she veils herself, does she?" I answered, as the blood went thrilling through my veins, I who remembered another who also was so old that she veiled herself from curious eyes. "Well, veiled or unveiled, we would visit her, trusting to find that we are welcome."

"That you shall not do," she said, "for it is unlawful, and I will not have your blood upon my hands."

"Which is the stronger," I asked of her, "you, Khania, or this priestess of the Mountain?"

"I am the stronger, Holly, for so you are named, are you not? Look you, at my need I can summon sixty thousand men in war, while she has naught but her priests and the fierce, untrained tribes."

"The sword is not the only power in the world," I answered. "Tell me, now, does this priestess ever visit the country of Kaloon?"

"Never, never, for by the ancient pact, made after the last great struggle long centuries ago between the College and the people of the Plain, it was decreed and sworn to that should she set her foot across the river, this means war to the end between us, and rule for the victor over both. Likewise, save when unguarded they bear their dead to burial, or for some such high purpose, no Khan or Khania of Kaloon ascends the Mountain."

"Which then is the true master—the Khan of Kaloon or the head of the College of Hes?" I asked again.

"In matters spiritual, the priestess of Hes, who is our Oracle and the voice of Heaven. In matters temporal, the Khan of Kaloon."

"The Khan. Ah! you are married, lady, are you not?"

"Aye," she answered, her face flushing. "And I will tell you what you soon must learn, if you have not learned it already, I am the wife of a madman, and he is—hateful to me."

"I have learned the last already, Khania."

She looked at me with her piercing eyes.

"What! Did my uncle, the Shaman, he who is called Guardian, tell you? Nay, you saw, as I knew you saw, and it would have been best to slay you for, oh! what must you think of me?"

I made no answer, for in truth I did not know what to think, also I feared lest further rash admissions should be followed by swift vengeance.

"You must believe," she went on, "that I, who have ever hated men, that I—I swear that it is true—whose lips are purer than those mountain snows, I, the Khania of Kaloon, whom they name Heart-of-Ice, am but a shameless thing." And, covering her face with her hand, she moaned in the bitterness of her distress.

"Nay," I said, "there may be reasons, explanations, if it pleases you to give them."

"Wanderer, there are such reasons; and since you know so much, you shall learn them also. Like that husband of mine, I have become mad. When first I saw the face of your companion, as I dragged him from the river, madness entered me, and I—I——"

"Loved him," I suggested. "Well, such things have happened before to people who were not mad."

"Oh!" she went on, "it was more than love; I was possessed, and that night I knew not what I did. A Power drove me on; a Destiny compelled me, and to the end I am his, and his alone. Yes, I am his, and I swear that he shall be mine;" and with this wild declaration dangerous enough under the conditions, she turned and fled the room.

She was gone, and after the struggle, for such it was, I sank back exhausted. How came it that this sudden passion had mastered her? Who and what was this Khania, I wondered again, and—this was more to the point, who and what would Leo believe her to be? If only I could be with him before he said words or did deeds impossible to recall.

Three days went by, during which time I saw no more of the Khania, who, or so I was informed by Simbri, the Shaman, had returned to her city to make ready for us, her guests. I begged him to allow me to rejoin Leo, but he answered politely, though with much firmness, that my foster-son did better without me. Now, I grew suspicious, fearing lest some harm had come to Leo, though how to discover the truth I knew not. In my anxiety I tried to convey a note to him, written upon a leaf of a water-gained pocket-book, but the yellow-faced servant refused to touch it, and

Simbri said drily that he would have naught to do with writings which he could not read. At length, on the third night I made up my mind that whatever the risk, with leave or without it, I would try to find him.

By this time I could walk well, and indeed was almost strong again. So about midnight, when the moon was up, for I had no other light, I crept from my bed, threw on my garments, and taking a knife, which was the only weapon I possessed, opened the door of my room and started.

Now, when I was carried from the rock-chamber where Leo and I had been together, I took note of the way. First, reckoning from my sleeping-place, there was a passage thirty paces long, for I had counted the footfalls of my bearers. Then came a turn to the left, and ten more paces of passage, and lastly near certain steps running to some place unknown, another sharp turn to the right which led to our old chamber.

Down the long passage I walked stealthily, and although it was pitch dark, found the turn to the left, and followed it till I came to the second sharp turn to the right, that of the gallery from which rose the stairs. I crept round it only to retreat hastily enough, as well I might, for at the door of Leo's room, which she was in the act of locking on the outside, as I could see by the light of the lamp that she held in her hand, stood the Khania herself.

My first thought was to fly back to my own chamber, but I abandoned it, feeling sure that I should be seen. Therefore I determined, if she discovered me, to face the matter out and say that I was trying to find Leo, and to learn how he fared. So I crouched against the wall, and waited with a beating heart. I heard her sweep down the passage, and—yes—begin to mount the stair.

Now, what should I do? To try to reach Leo was useless, for she had locked the door with the key she held. Go back to bed? No, I would follow her, and if we met would make the same excuse. Thus I might get some tidings, or perhaps—a dagger thrust.

So round the corner and up the steps I went, noiselessly as a snake. They were many and winding, like those of a church tower, but at length I came to the head of them, where was a little landing, and opening from it a door. It was a very ancient door; the light streamed through cracks where its panels had rotted, and from the room beyond came the sound of voices, those of the Shaman Simbri and the Khania.

"Have you learned aught, my niece?" I heard him say, and also heard her answer—-"A little. A very little."

Then in my thirst for knowledge I grew bold, and stealing to the door, looked through one of the cracks in its wood. Opposite to me, in the full flood of light thrown by a hanging lamp, her hand resting on a table at which Simbri was seated, stood the Khania. Truly she was a beauteous sight, for she wore robes of royal purple, and on her brow a little coronet of gold, beneath which her curling hair streamed down her shapely neck and bosom. Seeing her I guessed at once that she had arrayed herself thus for some secret end, enhancing her loveliness by every art and grace that is known to woman. Simbri was looking at her earnestly, with fear and doubt written on even his cold, impassive features.

"What passed between you, then?" he asked, peering at her.

"I questioned him closely as to the reason of his coming to this land, and wrung from him the answer that it was to seek some beauteous woman—he would say no more. I asked him if she were more beauteous than I am, and he replied with courtesy—nothing else, I think—that it would be hard to say, but that she had been different. Then I said that though it behooved me not to speak of such a matter, there was no lady in Kaloon whom men held to be so fair as I; moreover, that I was its ruler, and that I and no other had saved him from the water. Aye, and I added that my heart told me I was the woman whom he sought."

"Have done, niece," said Simbri impatiently, "I would not hear of the arts you used—well enough, doubtless. What then?"

"Then he said that it might be so, since he thought that this woman was born again, and studied me a while, asking me if I had ever 'passed through fire.' To this I replied that the only fires I had passed were those of the spirit, and that I dwelt in them now. He said, 'Show me your hair,' and I placed a lock of it in his hand. Presently he let it fall, and from that satchel which he wears about his neck drew out another tress of hair—oh! Simbri, my uncle, the loveliest hair that ever eyes beheld, for it was soft as silk, and reached from my coronet to the ground. Moreover, no raven's wing in the sunshine ever shone as did that fragrant tress.

"'Yours is beautiful,' he said, 'but see, they are not the same.'

"'Mayhap,' I answered, 'since no woman ever wore such locks.'

"'You are right,' he replied, 'for she whom I seek was more than a woman.'

"And then—and then—though I tried him in many ways he would say no more, so, feeling hate against this Unknown rising in my heart, and fearing lest I should utter words that were best unsaid, I left him. Now

I bid you, search the books which are open to your wisdom and tell me of this woman whom he seeks, who she is, and where she dwells. Oh! search them swiftly, that I may find her and—kill her if I can."

"Aye, if you can," answered the Shaman, "and if she lives to kill. But say, where shall we begin our quest? Now, this letter from the Mountain that the head-priest Oros sent to your court a while ago?"—and he selected a parchment from a pile which lay upon the table and looked at her.

"Read," she said, "I would hear it again."

So he read: "From the Hesea of the House of Fire, to Atene, Khania of Kaloon.

"My sister—Warning has reached me that two strangers of a western race journey to your land, seeking my Oracle, of which they would ask a question. On the first day of the next moon, I command that you and with you Simbri, your great-uncle, the wise Shaman, Guardian of the Gate, shall be watching the river in the gulf at the foot of the ancient road, for by that steep path the strangers travel. Aid them in all things and bring them safely to the Mountain, knowing that in this matter I shall hold him and you to account. Myself I will not meet them, since to do so would be to break the pact between our powers, which says that the Hesea of the Sanctuary visits not the territory of Kaloon, save in war. Also their coming is otherwise appointed."

"It would seem," said Simbri, laying down the parchment, "that these are no chance wanderers, since Hes awaits them."

"Aye, they are no chance wanderers, since my heart awaited one of them also. Yet the Hesea cannot be that woman, for reasons which are known to you."

"There are many women on the Mountain," suggested the Shaman in a dry voice, "if indeed any woman has to do with this matter."

"I at least have to do with it, and he shall not go to the Mountain."

"Hes is powerful, my niece, and beneath these smooth words of hers lies a dreadful threat. I say that she is mighty from of old and has servants in the earth and air who warned her of the coming of these men, and will warn her of what befalls them. I know it, who hate her, and to your royal house of Rassen it has been known for many a generation. Therefore thwart her not lest ill befall us all, for she is a spirit and terrible. She says that it is appointed that they shall go——"

"And I say it is appointed that he shall not go. Let the other go if he desires."

"Atene, be plain, what will you with the man called Leo—that he should become your lover?" asked the Shaman.

She stared him straight in the eyes, and answered boldly—"Nay, I will that he should become my husband."

"First he must will it too, who seems to have no mind that way. Also, how can a woman have two husbands?"

She laid her hand upon his shoulder and said—"I have no husband. You know it well, Simbri. I charge you by the close bond of blood between us, brew me another draught——"

"That we may be bound yet closer in a bond of murder! Nay, Atene, I will not; already your sin lies heavy on my head. You are very fair; take the man in your own net, if you may, or let him be, which is better far."

"I cannot let him be. Would that I were able. I must love him as I must hate the other whom he loves, yet some power hardens his heart against me. Oh! great Shaman, you that peep and mutter, you who can read the future and the past, tell me what you have learned from your stars and divinations."

"Already I have sought through many a secret, toilsome hour and learned this, Atene," he answered. "You are right, the fate of yonder man is intertwined with yours, but between you and him there rises a mighty wall that my vision cannot pierce nor my familiars climb. Yet I am taught that in death you and he—aye, and I also, shall be very near together."

"Then come death," she exclaimed with sullen pride, "for thence at least I'll pluck out my desire."

"Be not so sure," he answered, "for I think that the Power follows us even down this dark gulf of death. I think also that I feel the sleepless eyes of Hes watching our secret souls."

"Then blind them with the dust of illusions—as you can. To-morrow, also, saying nothing of their sex, send a messenger to the Mountain and tell the Hesea that two old strangers have arrived—mark you, old—but that they are very sick, that their limbs were broken in the river, and that when they have healed again, I will send them to ask the question of her Oracle—that is, some three moons hence. Perchance she may believe you, and be content to wait; or if she does not, at least no more words. I must sleep or my brain will burst. Give me that medicine which brings dreamless rest, for never did I need it more, who also feel eyes upon me," and she glanced towards the door.

Then I left, and not too soon, for as I crept down the darksome passage, I heard it open behind me.

VIII. THE DEATH-HOUNDS

It may have been ten o'clock on the following morning, or a little past it, when the Shaman Simbri came into my room and asked me how I had slept.

"Like a log," I answered, "like a log. A drugged man could not have rested more soundly."

"Indeed, friend Holly, and yet you look fatigued."

"My dreams troubled me somewhat," I answered. "I suffer from such things. But surely by your face, friend Simbri, you cannot have slept at all, for never yet have I seen you with so weary an air."

"I am weary," he said, with a sigh. "Last night I spent up on my business—watching at the Gates."

"What gates?" I asked. "Those by which we entered this kingdom, for, if so, I would rather watch than travel them."

"The Gates of the Past and of the Future. Yes, those two which you entered, if you will; for did you not travel out of a wondrous Past towards a Future that you cannot guess?"

"But both of which interest you," I suggested.

"Perhaps," he answered, then added, "I come to tell you that within an hour you are to start for the city, whither the Khania has but now gone on to make ready for you."

"Yes; only you told me that she had gone some days ago. Well, I am sound again and prepared to march, but say, how is my foster-son?"

"He mends, he mends. But you shall see him for yourself. It is the Khania's will. Here come the slaves bearing your robes, and with them I leave you."

So with their assistance I dressed myself, first in good, clean underlinen, then in wide woollen trousers and vest, and lastly in a fur-lined camel-hair robe dyed black that was very comfortable to wear, and in appearance not unlike a long overcoat. A flat cap of the same material and a pair of boots made of untanned hide completed my attire.

Scarcely was I ready when the yellow-faced servants, with many bows, took me by the hand and led me down the passages and stairs of the

Gate-house to its door. Here, to my great joy, I found Leo, looking pale and troubled, but otherwise as well as I could expect after his sickness. He was attired like myself, save that his garments were of a finer quality, and the overcoat was white, with a hood to it, added, I suppose, to protect the wound in his head from cold and the sun. This white dress I thought became him very well, also about it there was nothing grotesque or even remarkable. He sprang to me and seized my hand, asking how I fared and where I had been hidden away, a greeting of which, as I could see, the warmth was not lost upon Simbri, who stood by.

I answered, well enough now that we were together again, and for the rest I would tell him later.

Then they brought us palanquins, carried, each of them, by two ponies, one of which was harnessed ahead and the other behind between long shaft-like poles. In these we seated ourselves, and at a sign from Simbri slaves took the leading ponies by the bridle and we started, leaving behind us that grim old Gate-house through which we were the first strangers to pass for many a generation.

For a mile or more our road ran down a winding, rocky gorge, till suddenly it took a turn, and the country of Kaloon lay stretched before us. At our feet was a river, probably the same with which we had made acquaintance in the gulf, where, fed by the mountain snows, it had its source. Here it flowed rapidly, but on the vast, alluvial lands beneath became a broad and gentle stream that wound its way through the limitless plains till it was lost in the blue of the distance.

To the north, however, this smooth, monotonous expanse was broken by that Mountain which had guided us from afar, the House of Fire. It was a great distance from us, more than a hundred miles, I should say, yet even so a most majestic sight in that clear air. Many leagues from the base of its peak the ground began to rise in brown and rugged hillocks, from which sprang the holy Mountain itself, a white and dazzling point that soared full twenty thousand feet into the heavens.

Yes, and there upon the nether lip of its crater stood the gigantic pillar, surmounted by a yet more gigantic loop of virgin rock, whereof the blackness stood out grimly against the blue of the sky beyond and the blinding snow beneath.

We gazed at it with awe, as well we might, this beacon of our hopes that for aught we knew might also prove their monument, feeling even then that yonder our fate would declare itself. I noted further that all those with us did it reverence by bowing their heads as they caught sight of the peak, and by laying the first finger of the right hand across the first finger of the left, a gesture, as we afterwards discovered, designed to avert its evil influence. Yes, even Simbri bowed, a yielding to inherited superstition of which I should scarcely have suspected him.

"Have you ever journeyed to that Mountain?" asked Leo of him.

Simbri shook his head and answered evasively.

"The people of the Plain do not set foot upon the Mountain. Among its slopes beyond the river which washes them, live hordes of brave and most savage men, with whom we are oftentimes at war; for when they are hungry they raid our cattle and our crops. Moreover, there, when the Mountain labours, run red streams of molten rock, and now and again hot ashes fall that slay the traveller."

"Do the ashes ever fall in your country?" asked Leo.

"They have been known to do so when the Spirit of the Mountain is angry, and that is why we fear her."

"Who is this Spirit?" said Leo eagerly.

"I do not know, lord," he answered with impatience. "Can men see a spirit?"

"You look as though you might, and had, not so long ago," replied Leo, fixing his gaze on the old man's waxen face and uneasy eyes. For now their horny calm was gone from the eyes of Simbri, which seemed as though they had beheld some sight that haunted him.

"You do me too much honour, lord," he replied; "my skill and vision do not reach so far. But see, here is the landing-stage, where boats await us, for the rest of our journey is by water."

These boats proved to be roomy and comfortable, having flat bows and sterns, since, although sometimes a sail was hoisted, they were designed for towing, not to be rowed with oars. Leo and I entered the largest of them, and to our joy were left alone except for the steersman.

Behind us was another boat, in which were attendants and slaves, and some men who looked like soldiers, for they carried bows and swords. Now the ponies were taken from the palanquins, that were packed away, and ropes of green hide, fastened to iron rings in the prows of the boats, were fixed to the towing tackle with which the animals had been reharnessed. Then we started, the ponies, two arranged tandem fashion to each punt, trotting along a well-made towing path that was furnished with wooden bridges wherever canals or tributary streams entered the main river.

"Thank Heaven," said Leo, "we are together again at last! Do you remember, Horace, that when we entered the land of Kor it was thus, in a boat? The tale repeats itself."

"I can quite believe it," I answered. "I can believe anything. Leo, I say that we are but gnats meshed in a web, and yonder Khania is the spider and Simbri the Shaman guards the net. But tell me all you remember of what has happened to you, and be quick, for I do not know how long they may leave us alone."

"Well," he said, "of course I remember our arrival at that Gate after the lady and the old man had pulled us out of the river, and, Horace, talking of spiders reminds me of hanging at the end of that string of yak's hide. Not that I need much reminding, for I am not likely to forget it. Do you know I cut the rope because I felt that I was going mad, and wished to die sane. What happened to you? Did you slip?"

"No; I jumped after you. It seemed best to end together, so that we might begin again together."

"Brave old Horace!" he said affectionately, the tears starting to his grey eyes.

"Well, never mind all that," I broke in; "you see you were right when you said that we should get through, and we have. Now for your tale."

"It is interesting, but not very long," he answered, colouring. "I went to sleep, and when I woke it was to find a beautiful woman leaning over me, and Horace—at first I thought that it was—you know who, and that she kissed me; but perhaps it was all a dream."

"It was no dream," I answered. "I saw it."

"I am sorry to hear it—very sorry. At any rate there was the beautiful woman—the Khania—for I saw her plenty of times afterwards, and talked to her in my best modern Greek—by the way, Ayesha knew the old Greek; that's curious."

"She knew several of the ancient tongues, and so did other people. Go on."

"Well, she nursed me very kindly, but, so far as I know, until last night there was nothing more affectionate, and I had sense enough to refuse to talk about our somewhat eventful past. I pretended not to understand, said that we were explorers, etc., and kept asking her where you were, for I forgot to say I found that you had gone. I think that she grew rather angry with me, for she wanted to know something, and, as you can guess, I wanted to know a good deal. But I could get nothing out of her except that she was the Khania—a person in authority. There was no doubt about that, for when one of those slaves or servants came in and interrupted her while she was trying to draw the facts out of me, she called to some of her people to throw him out of the window, and he only saved himself by going down the stairs very quickly.

"Well, I could make nothing of her, and she could make little of me, though why she should be so tenderly interested in a stranger, I don't know—unless, unless—oh! who is she, Horace?"

"If you will go on I will tell you what I think presently. One tale at a time."

"Very good. I got quite well and strong, comparatively speaking, till the climax last night, which upset me again. After that old prophet, Simbri, had brought me my supper, just as I was thinking of going to sleep, the Khania came in alone, dressed like a queen. I can tell you she looked really royal, like a princess in a fairy book, with a crown on, and her chestnut black hair flowing round her.

"Well, Horace, then she began to make love to me in a refined sort of way, or so I thought, looked at me and sighed, saying that we had known each other in the past—very well indeed I gathered—and implying that she wished to continue our friendship. I fenced with her as best I could; but a man feels fairly helpless lying on his back with a very handsome and very imperial-looking lady standing over him and paying him compliments.

"The end of it was that, driven to it by her questions and to stop that sort of thing, I told her that I was looking for my wife, whom I had lost, for, after all, Ayesha is my wife, Horace. She smiled and suggested that I need not look far; in short, that the lost wife was already found—in herself, who had come to save me from death in the river. Indeed, she spoke with such conviction that I grew sure that she was not merely amusing herself, and felt very much inclined to believe her, for, after all, Ayesha may be changed now.

"Then while I was at my wits' end I remembered the lock of hair—all that remains to us of her," and Leo touched his breast. "I drew it out and compared it with the Khania's, and at the sight of it she became quite different, jealous, I suppose, for it is longer than hers, and not in the least like.

"Horace, I tell you that the touch of that lock of hair—for she did touch it—appeared to act upon her nature like nitric acid upon sham gold.

It turned it black; all the bad in her came out. In her anger her voice sounded coarse; yes, she grew almost vulgar, and, as you know, when Ayesha was in a rage she might be wicked as we understand it, and was certainly terrible, but she was never either coarse or vulgar, any more than lightning is.

"Well, from that moment I was sure that whoever this Khania may be, she had nothing to do with Ayesha; they are so different that they never could have been the same—like the hair. So I lay quiet and let her talk, and coax, and threaten on, until at length she drew herself up and marched from the room, and I heard her lock the door behind her. That's all I have to tell you, and quite enough too, for I don't think that the Khania has done with me, and, to say the truth, I am afraid of her."

"Yes," I said, "quite enough. Now sit still, and don't start or talk loud, for that steersman is probably a spy, and I can feel old Simbri's eyes fixed upon our backs. Don't interrupt either, for our time alone may be short."

Then I set to work and told him everything I knew, while he listened in blank astonishment.

"Great Heavens! what a tale," he exclaimed as I finished. "Now, who is this Hesea who sent the letter from the Mountain? And who, who is the Khania?"

"Who does your instinct tell you that she is, Leo?"

"Amenartas?" he whispered doubtfully. "The woman who wrote the Sherd, whom Ayesha said was the Egyptian princess—my wife two thousand years ago? Amenartas re-born?"

I nodded. "I think so. Why not? As I have told you again and again, I have always been certain of one thing, that if we were allowed to see the next act of the piece, we should find Amenartas, or rather the spirit of Amenartas, playing a leading part in it; you will remember I wrote as much in that record.

"If the old Buddhist monk Kou-en could remember his past, as thousands of them swear that they do, and be sure of his identity continued from that past, why should not this woman, with so much at stake, helped as she is by the wizardry of the Shaman, her uncle, faintly remember hers?

"At any rate, Leo, why should she not still be sufficiently under its influence to cause her, without any fault or seeking of her own, to fall madly in love at first sight with a man whom, after all, she has always loved?"

"The argument seems sound enough, Horace, and if so I am sorry for the Khania, who hasn't much choice in the matter—been forced into it, so to speak."

"Yes, but meanwhile your foot is in a trap again. Guard yourself, Leo, guard yourself. I believe that this is a trial sent to you, and doubtless there will be more to follow. But I believe also that it would be better for you to die than to make any mistake."

"I know it well," he answered; "and you need not be afraid. Whatever this Khania may have been to me in the past—if she was anything at all—that story is done with. I seek Ayesha, and Ayesha alone, and Venus herself shall not tempt me from her."

Then we began to speak with hope and fear of that mysterious Hesea who had sent the letter from the Mountain, commanding the Shaman Simbri to meet us: the priestess or spirit whom he declared was "mighty from of old" and had "servants in the earth and air."

Presently the prow of our barge bumped against the bank of the river, and looking round I saw that Simbri had left the boat in which he sat and was preparing to enter ours. This he did, and, placing himself gravely on a seat in front of us, explained that nightfall was coming on, and he wished to give us his company and protection through the dark.

"And to see that we do not give him the slip in it," muttered Leo.

Then the drivers whipped up their ponies, and we went on again.

"Look behind you," said Simbri presently, "and you will see the city where you will sleep to-night."

We turned ourselves, and there, about ten miles away, perceived a flat-roofed town of considerable, though not of very great size. Its position was good, for it was set upon a large island that stood a hundred feet or more above the level of the plain, the river dividing into two branches at the foot of it, and, as we discovered afterwards, uniting again beyond.

The vast mound upon which this city was built had the appearance of being artificial, but very possibly the soil whereof it was formed had been washed up in past ages during times of flood, so that from a mudbank in the centre of the broad river it grew by degrees to its present proportions. With the exception of a columned and towered edifice that crowned the city and seemed to be encircled by gardens, we could see no great buildings in the place.

"How is the city named?" asked Leo of Simbri.

"Kaloon," he answered, "as was all this land even when my forefathers, the conquerors, marched across the mountains and took it more than two thousand years ago. They kept the ancient title, but the territory of the Mountain they called Hes, because they said that the loop upon yonder peak was the symbol of a goddess of this name whom their general worshipped."

"Priestesses still live there, do they not?" said Leo, trying in his turn to extract the truth.

"Yes, and priests also. The College of them was established by the conquerors, who subdued all the land. Or rather, it took the place of another College of those who fashioned the Sanctuary and the Temple, whose god was the fire in the Mountain, as it is that of the people of Kaloon to-day."

"Then who is worshipped there now?"

"The goddess Hes, it is said; but we know little of the matter, for between us and the Mountain folk there has been enmity for ages. They kill us and we kill them, for they are jealous of their shrine, which none may visit save by permission, to consult the Oracle and to make prayer or offering in times of calamity, when a Khan dies, or the waters of the river sink and the crops fail, or when ashes fall and earthquakes shake the land, or great sickness comes. Otherwise, unless they attack us, we leave them alone, for though every man is trained to arms, and can fight if need be, we are a peaceful folk, who cultivate the soil from generation to generation, and thus grow rich. Look round you. Is it not a scene of peace?"

We stood up in the boat and gazed about us at the pastoral prospect. Everywhere appeared herds of cattle feeding upon meadow lands, or troops of mules and horses, or square fields sown with corn and outlined by trees. Village folk, also, clad in long, grey gowns, were labouring on the land, or, their day's toil finished, driving their beasts homewards along roads built upon the banks of the irrigation dykes, towards the hamlets that were placed on rising knolls amidst tall poplar groves.

In its sharp contrast with the arid deserts and fearful mountains amongst which we had wandered for so many years, this country struck us as most charming, and indeed, seen by the red light of the sinking sun on that spring day, even as beautiful with the same kind of beauty which is to be found in Holland. One could understand too that these landowners and peasant-farmers would by choice be men of peace, and what a temptation their wealth must offer to the hungry, half-savage tribes of the mountains.

Also it was easy to guess when the survivors of Alexander's legions under their Egyptian general burst through the iron band of snow-clad hills and saw this sweet country, with its homes, its herds, and its ripening grass, that they must have cried with one voice, "We will march and fight and toil no more. Here we will sit us down to live and die." Thus doubtless they did, taking them wives from among the women of the people of the land which they had conquered—perhaps after a single battle.

Now as the light faded the wreaths of smoke which hung over the distant Fire-mountain began to glow luridly. Redder and more angry did they become while the darkness gathered, till at length they seemed to be charged with pulsing sheets of flame propelled from the womb of the volcano, which threw piercing beams of light through the eye of the giant loop that crowned its brow. Far, far fled those beams, making a bright path across the land, and striking the white crests of the bordering wall of mountains. High in the air ran that path, over the dim roofs of the city of Kaloon, over the river, yes, straight above us, over the mountains, and doubtless—though there we could not follow them—across the desert to that high eminence on its farther side where we had lain bathed in their radiance. It was a wondrous and most impressive sight, one too that filled our companions with fear, for the steersmen in our boats and the drivers on the towing-path groaned aloud and began to utter prayers. "What do they say?" asked Leo of Simbri.

"They say, lord, that the Spirit of the Mountain is angry, and passes down yonder flying light that is called the Road of Hes to work some evil to our land. Therefore they pray her not to destroy them."

"Then does that light not always shine thus?" he asked again.

"Nay, but seldom. Once about three months ago, and now to-night, but before that not for years. Let us pray that it portends no misfortune to Kaloon and its inhabitants."

For some minutes this fearsome illumination continued, then it ceased as suddenly as it had begun, and there remained of it only the dull glow above the crest of the peak.

Presently the moon rose, a white, shining ball, and by its rays we perceived that we drew near to the city. But there was still something left for us to see before we reached its shelter. While we sat quietly in the boat—for the silence was broken only by the lapping of the still waters against its sides and the occasional splash of the slackened tow-line upon their surface—we heard a distant sound as of a hunt in full cry.

Nearer and nearer it came, its volume swelling every moment, till it was quite close at last. Now echoing from the trodden earth of the towing-path—not that on which our ponies travelled, but the other on the west bank of the river—was heard the beat of the hoofs of a horse galloping furiously. Presently it appeared, a fine, white animal, on the back of which sat a man. It passed us like a flash, but as he went by the man lifted himself and turned his head, so that we saw his face in the moonlight; saw also the agony of fear that was written on it and in his eyes.

He had come out of the darkness. He was gone into the darkness, but after him swelled that awful music. Look! a dog appeared, a huge, red dog, that dropped its foaming muzzle to the ground as it galloped, then lifted it and uttered a deep-throated, bell-like bay. Others followed, and yet others: in all there must have been a hundred of them, every one baying as it took the scent.

"The death-hounds!" I muttered, clasping Leo by the arm.

"Yes," he answered, "they are running that poor devil. Here comes the huntsman."

As he spoke there appeared a second figure, splendidly mounted, a cloak streaming from his shoulders, and in his hand a long whip, which he waved. He was big but loosely jointed, and as he passed he turned his face also, and we saw that it was that of a madman. There could be no doubt of it; insanity blazed in those hollow eyes and rang in that savage, screeching laugh.

"The Khan! The Khan!" said Simbri, bowing, and I could see that he was afraid.

Now he too was gone, and after him came his guards. I counted eight of them, all carrying whips, with which they flogged their horses.

"What does this mean, friend Simbri?" I asked, as the sounds grew faint in the distance.

"It means, friend Holly," he answered, "that the Khan does justice in his own fashion—hunting to death one that has angered him."

"What then is his crime? And who is that poor man?"

"He is a great lord of this land, one of the royal kinsmen, and the crime for which he has been condemned is that he told the Khania he loved her, and offered to make war upon her husband and kill him, if she would promise herself to him in marriage. But she hated the man, as she hates all men, and brought the matter before the Khan. That is all the story."

"Happy is that prince who has so virtuous a wife!" I could not help saying unctuously, but with meaning, and the old wretch of a Shaman turned his head at my words and began to stroke his white beard.

It was but a little while afterwards that once more we heard the baying of the death-hounds. Yes, they were heading straight for us, this time across country. Again the white horse and its rider appeared, utterly exhausted, both of them, for the poor beast could scarcely struggle on to the towing-path. As it gained it a great red hound with a black ear gripped its flank, and at the touch of the fangs it screamed aloud in terror as only a horse can. The rider sprang from its back, and, to our horror, ran to the river's edge, thinking evidently to take refuge in our boat. But before ever he reached the water the devilish brutes were upon him.

What followed I will not describe, but never shall I forget the scene of those two heaps of worrying wolves, and of the maniac Khan, who yelled in his fiendish joy, and cheered on his death-hounds to finish their red work.

IX. THE COURT OF KALOON

Horrified, sick at heart, we continued our journey. No wonder that the Khania hated such a mad despot. And this woman was in love with Leo, and this lunatic Khan, her husband, was a victim to jealousy, which he avenged after the very unpleasant fashion that we had witnessed. Truly an agreeable prospect for all of us! Yet, I could not help reflecting, as an object lesson that horrid scene had its advantages.

Now we reached the place where the river forked at the end of the island, and disembarked upon a quay. Here a guard of men commanded by some Household officer, was waiting to receive us. They led us through a gate in the high wall, for the town was fortified, up a narrow, stone-paved street which ran between houses apparently of the usual Central Asian type, and, so far as I could judge by moonlight, with no pretensions to architectural beauty, and not large in size.

Clearly our arrival was expected and excited interest, for people were gathered in knots about the street to watch us pass; also at the windows of the houses and even on their flat roofs. At the top of the long street was a sort of market place, crossing which, accompanied by a curious crowd who made remarks about us that we could not understand, we reached a gate in an inner wall. Here we were challenged, but at a word from Simbri it opened, and we passed through to find ourselves in gardens. Following a road or drive, we came to a large, rambling house or palace, surmounted by high towers and very solidly built of stone in a heavy, bastard Egyptian style.

Beyond its doorway we found ourselves in a courtyard surrounded by a kind of verandah from which short passages led to different rooms. Down one of these passages we were conducted by the officer to an apartment, or rather a suite, consisting of a sitting and two bed-chambers, which were panelled, richly furnished in rather barbaric fashion, and well-lighted with primitive oil lamps.

Here Simbri left us, saying that the officer would wait in the outer room to conduct us to the dining-hall as soon as we were ready. Then we entered the bed-chambers, where we found servants, or slaves, quiet-mannered, obsequious men. These valets changed our foot-gear, and taking off our heavy travelling robes, replaced them with others fashioned like civilized frock-coats, but made of some white material and trimmed with a beautiful ermine fur.

Having dressed us in these they bowed to show that our toilette was finished, and led us to the large outer room where the officer awaited us. He conducted us through several other rooms, all of them spacious and apparently unoccupied, to a great hall lit with many lamps and warmed—for the nights were still cold—with large peat fires. The roof of this hall was flat and supported by thick, stone columns with carved capitals, and its walls were hung with worked tapestries, that gave it an air of considerable comfort.

At the head of the hall on a dais stood a long, narrow table, spread with a cloth and set with platters and cups of silver. Here we waited till butlers with wands appeared through some curtains which they drew. Then came a man beating a silver gong, and after him a dozen or more courtiers, all dressed in white robes like ourselves, followed by perhaps as many ladies, some of them young and good-looking, and for the most part of a fair type, with well-cut features, though others were rather yellow-skinned. They bowed to us and we to them.

Then there was a pause while we studied one another, till a trumpet blew and heralded by footmen in a kind of yellow livery, two figures were seen advancing down the passage beyond the curtains, preceded by the Shaman Simbri and followed by other officers. They were the Khan and the Khania of Kaloon.

No one looking at this Khan as he entered his dining-hall clad in festal white attire would have imagined him to be the same raving human brute whom we had just seen urging on his devilish hounds to tear a fellow-creature and a helpless horse to fragments and devour them. Now he seemed a heavy, loutish man, very strongly built and not ill-looking, but with shifty eyes, evidently a person of dulled intellect, whom one would have thought incapable of keen emotions of any kind. The Khania need not be described. She was as she had been in the chambers of the Gate, only more weary looking; indeed her eyes had a haunted air and it was easy to see that the events of the previous night had left their mark upon her mind. At the sight of us she flushed a little, then beckoned to us to advance, and said to her husband—"My lord, these are the strangers of whom I have told you."

His dull eyes fell upon me first, and my appearance seemed to amuse him vaguely, at any rate he laughed rudely, saying in barbarous Greek mixed with words from the local patois—"What a curious old animal! I have never seen you before, have I?"

"No, great Khan," I answered, "but I have seen you out hunting this night. Did you have good sport?"

Instantly he became wide awake, and answered, rubbing his hands—"Excellent. He gave us a fine run, but my little dogs caught him at last, and then——" and he snapped his powerful jaws together.

"Cease your brutal talk," broke in his wife fiercely, and he slunk away from her and in so doing stumbled against Leo, who was waiting to be presented to him.

The sight of this great, golden-bearded man seemed to astonish him, for he stared at him, then asked—"Are you the Khania's other friend whom she went to see in the mountains of the Gate? Then I could not understand why she took so much trouble, but now I do. Well, be careful, or I shall have to hunt you also."

Now Leo grew angry and was about to reply, but I laid my hand upon his arm and said in English—"Don't answer; the man is mad."

"Bad, you mean," grumbled Leo; "and if he tries to set his cursed dogs on me, I will break his neck."

Then the Khania motioned to Leo to take a seat beside her, placing me upon her other hand, between herself and her uncle, the Guardian, while the Khan shuffled to a chair a little way down the table, where he called two of the prettiest ladies to keep him company.

Such was our introduction to the court of Kaloon. As for the meal that followed, it was very plentiful, but coarse, consisting for the most part of fish, mutton, and sweetmeats, all of them presented upon huge silver platters. Also much strong drink was served, a kind of spirit distilled from grain, of which nearly all present drank more than was good for them. After a few words to me about our journey, the Khania turned to Leo and talked to him for the rest of the evening, while I devoted myself to the old Shaman Simbri.

Put briefly, the substance of what I learned from him then and afterwards was as follows—Trade was unknown to the people of Kaloon, for the reason that all communication with the south had been cut off for ages, the bridges that once existed over the chasm having been allowed to rot away. Their land, which was very large and densely inhabited, was ringed round with unclimbable mountains, except to the north, where stood the great Fire-peak. The slopes of this Peak and an unvisited expanse of country behind that ran up to the confines of a desert, were the home of ferocious mountain tribes, untamable Highlanders, who killed every stranger they caught. Consequently, although the precious and other metals were mined to a certain extent and manufactured into articles of use and ornament, money did not exist among the peoples either of the Plain or of the Mountain, all business being transacted on the principle of barter, and even the revenue collected in kind.

Amongst the tens of thousands of the aborigines of Kaloon dwelt a mere handful of a ruling class, who were said to be—and probably were—descended from the conquerors that appeared in the time of Alexander. Their blood, however, was now much mixed with that of the first inhabitants, who, to judge from their appearance and the yellow hue of their descendants must have belonged to some branch of the great Tartar race. The government, if so it could be called, was, on the whole, of a mild though of a very despotic nature, and vested in an hereditary Khan or Khania, according as a man or a woman might be in the most direct descent.

Of religions there were two, that of the people, who worshipped the Spirit of the Fire Mountain, and that of the rulers, who believed in magic, ghosts and divinations. Even this shadow of a religion, if so it can be called, was dying out, like its followers, for generation by generation, the white lords grew less in number or became absorbed in the bulk of the people.

Still their rule was tolerated. I asked Simbri why, seeing that they were so few. He shrugged his shoulders and answered, because it suited the country of which the natives had no ambition. Moreover, the present Khania, our hostess, was the last of the direct line of rulers, her husband and cousin having less of the blood royal in his veins, and as such the people were attached to her.

Also, as is commonly the case with bold and beautiful women, she was popular among them, especially as she was just and very liberal to the poor. These were many, as the country was over-populated, which accounted for its wonderful state of cultivation. Lastly they trusted to her skill and courage to defend them from the continual attacks of the Mountain tribes who raided their crops and herds. Their one grievance against her was that she had no child to whom the khanship could descend, which meant that after her death, as had happened after that of her father, there would be struggles for the succession.

"Indeed," added Simbri, with meaning, and glancing at Leo, out of the corners of his eyes, "the folk say openly that it would be a good thing if the Khan, who oppresses them and whom they hate, should die, so that the Khania might take another husband while she is still young. Although he is mad, he knows this, and that is why he is so jealous of any lord who looks at her, as, friend Holly, you saw to-night. For should such an one gain her favour, Rassen thinks that it would mean his death."

"Also he may be attached to his wife," I suggested, speaking in a whisper.

"Perhaps so," answered Simbri; "but if so, she loves not him, nor any of these men," and he glanced round the hall.

Certainly they did not look lovable, for by this time most of them were half drunk, while even the women seemed to have taken as much as was good for them. The Khan himself presented a sorry spectacle, for he was leaning back in his chair, shouting something about his hunting, in a thick voice. The arm of one of his pretty companions was round his neck, while the other gave him to drink from a gold cup; some of the contents of which had been spilt down his white robe.

Just then Atene looked round and saw him and an expression of hatred and contempt gathered on her beautiful face.

"See," I heard her say to Leo, "see the companion of my days, and learn what it is to be Khania of Kaloon."

"Then why do you not cleanse your court?" he asked.

"Because, lord, if I did so there would be no court left. Swine will to their mire and these men and women, who live in idleness upon the toil of the humble folk, will to their liquor and vile luxury. Well, the end is near, for it is killing them, and their children are but few; weakly also, for the ancient blood grows thin and stale. But you are weary and would rest. To-morrow we will ride together," and calling to an officer, she bade him conduct us to our rooms.

So we rose, and, accompanied by Simbri, bowed to her and went, she standing and gazing after us, a royal and pathetic figure in the midst of all that dissolute revelry. The Khan rose also, and in his cunning fashion understood something of the meaning of it all.

"You think us gay," he shouted; "and why should we not be who do not know how long we have to live? But you yellow-haired fellow, you must not let Atene look at you like that. I tell you she is my wife, and if you do, I shall certainly have to hunt you."

At this drunken sally the courtiers roared with laughter, but taking Leo by the arm Simbri hurried him from the hall.

"Friend," said Leo, when we were outside, "it seems to me that this Khan of yours threatens my life."

"Have no fear, lord," answered the Guardian; "so long as the Khania does not threaten it you are safe. She is the real ruler of this land, and I stand next to her."

"Then I pray you," said Leo, "keep me out of the way of that drunken man, for, look you, if I am attacked I defend myself."

"And who can blame you?" Simbri replied with one of his slow, mysterious smiles.

Then we parted, and having placed both our beds in one chamber, slept soundly enough, for we were very tired, till we were awakened in the morning by the baying of those horrible death-hounds, being fed, I suppose, in a place nearby.

Now in this city of Kaloon it was our weary destiny to dwell for three long months, one of the most hateful times, perhaps, that we ever passed in all our lives. Indeed, compared to it our endless wanderings amid the Central Asia snows and deserts were but pleasure pilgrimages, and our stay at the monastery beyond the mountains a sojourn in Paradise. To set out its record in full would be both tedious and useless, so I will only tell briefly of our principal adventures.

On the morrow of our arrival the Khania Atene sent us two beautiful white horses of pure and ancient blood, and at noon we mounted them and went out to ride with her accompanied by a guard of soldiers. First she led us to the kennels where the death-hounds were kept, great flagged courts surrounded by iron bars, in which were narrow, locked gates. Never had I seen brutes so large and fierce; the mastiffs of Thibet were but as lap-dogs compared to them. They were red and black, smooth-coated and with a blood-hound head, and the moment they saw us they came ravening and leaping at the bars as an angry wave leaps against a rock.

These hounds were in the charge of men of certain families, who had tended them for generations. They obeyed their keepers and the Khan readily enough, but no stranger might venture near them. Also these brutes were the executioners of the land, for to them all murderers and other criminals were thrown, and with them, as we had seen, the Khan hunted any who had incurred his displeasure. Moreover, they were used for a more innocent purpose, the chasing of certain great bucks which were preserved in woods and swamps of reeds. Thus it came about that they were a terror to the country, since no man knew but what in the end he might be devoured by them. "Going to the dogs" is a term full of meaning in any land, but in Kaloon it had a significance that was terrible.

After we had looked at the hounds, not without a prophetic shudder, we rode round the walls of the town, which were laid out as a kind of boulevard, where the inhabitants walked and took their pleasure in the evenings. On these, however, there was not much to see except the river beneath and the plain beyond, moreover, though they were thick and high there were places in them that must be passed carefully, for, like everything else with which the effete ruling class had to do, they had been allowed to fall into disrepair.

The town itself was an uninteresting place also, for the most part peopled by hangers-on of the Court. So we were not sorry when we crossed the river by a high-pitched bridge, where in days to come I was destined to behold one of the strangest sights ever seen by mortal man, and rode out into the country. Here all was different, for we found ourselves among the husbandmen, who were the descendants of the original owners of the land and lived upon its produce. Every available inch of soil seemed to be cultivated by the aid of a wonderful system of irrigation. Indeed water was lifted to levels where it would not flow naturally, by means of wheels turned with mules, or even in some places carried up by the women, who bore poles on their shoulders to which were balanced buckets.

Leo asked the Khania what happened if there was a bad season. She replied grimly that famine happened, in which thousands of people perished, and that after the famine came pestilence. These famines were periodical, and were it not for them, she added, the people would long ago have been driven to kill each other like hungry rats, since having no outlet and increasing so rapidly, the land, large as it was, could not hold them all.

"Will this be a good year?" I asked.

"It is feared not," she answered, "for the river has not risen well and but few rains have fallen. Also the light that shone last night on the Fire-mountain is thought a bad omen, which means, they say, that the Spirit of the Mountain is angry and that drought will follow. Let us hope they will not say also that this is because strangers have visited the land, bringing with them bad luck."

"If so," said Leo with a laugh, "we shall have to fly to the Mountain to take refuge there."

"Do you then wish to take refuge in death?" she asked darkly. "Of this be sure, my guests, that never while I live shall you be allowed to cross the river which borders the slopes of yonder peak."

"Why not, Khania?"

"Because, my lord Leo—that is your name, is it not?—such is my will, and while I rule here my will is law. Come, let us turn homewards."

That night we did not eat in the great hall, but in the room which adjoined our bed-chambers. We were not left alone, however, for the Khania and her uncle, the Shaman, who always attended her, joined our meal. When we greeted them wondering, she said briefly that it was arranged thus because she refused to expose us to more insults. She added that a festival had begun which would last for a week, and that she did not wish us to see how vile were the ways of her people.

That evening and many others which followed it—we never dined in the central hall again—passed pleasantly enough, for the Khania made Leo tell her of England where he was born, and of the lands that he had visited, their peoples and customs. I spoke also of the history of Alexander, whose general Rassen, her far-off forefather, conquered the country of Kaloon, and of the land of Egypt, whence the latter came, and so it went on till midnight, while Atene listened to us greedily, her eyes fixed always on Leo's face.

Many such nights did we spend thus in the palace of the city of Kaloon where, in fact, we were close prisoners. But oh! the days hung heavy on our hands. If we went into the courtyard or reception rooms of the palace, the lords and their followers gathered round us and pestered us with questions, for, being very idle, they were also very curious.

Also the women, some of whom were fair enough, began to talk to us on this pretext or on that, and did their best to make love to Leo; for, in contrast with their slim, delicate-looking men, they found this deep-chested, yellow-haired stranger to their taste. Indeed they troubled him much with gifts of flowers and messages sent by servants or soldiers, making assignations with him, which of course he did not keep.

If we went out into the streets, matters were as bad, for then the people ceased from their business, such as it was, and followed us about, staring at us till we took refuge again in the palace gardens.

There remained, therefore, only our rides in the country with the

Khania, but after three or four of them, these came to an end owing to the jealousy of the Khan, who vowed that if we went out together any more he would follow with the death-hounds. So we must ride alone, if at all, in the centre of a large guard of soldiers sent to see that we did not attempt to escape, and accompanied very often by a mob of peasants, who with threats and entreaties demanded that we should give back the rain which they said we had taken from them. For now the great drought had begun in earnest.

Thus it came about that at length our only resource was making pretence to fish in the river, where the water was so clear and low that we could catch nothing, watching the while the Fire-mountain, that loomed in the distance mysterious and unreachable, and vainly racking our brains for plans to escape thither, or at least to communicate with its priestess, of whom we could learn no more.

For two great burdens lay upon our souls. The burden of desire to continue our search and to meet with its reward which we were sure that we should pluck amid the snows of yonder peak, if we could but come there; and the burden of approaching catastrophe at the hands of the Khania Atene. She had made no love to Leo since that night in the Gateway, and, indeed, even if she had wished to, this would have been difficult, since I took care that he was never left for one hour alone. No duenna could have clung to a Spanish princess more closely than I did to Leo. Yet I could see well that her passion was no whit abated; that it grew day by day, indeed, as the fire swells in the heart of a volcano, and that soon it must break loose and spread its ruin round. The omen of it was to be read in her words, her gestures, and her tragic eyes.

X. IN THE SHAMAN'S CHAMBER

One night Simbri asked us to dine with him in his own apartments in the highest tower of the palace—had we but known it, for us a fateful place indeed, for here the last act of the mighty drama was destined to be fulfilled. So we went, glad enough of any change. When we had eaten Leo grew very thoughtful, then said suddenly—"Friend Simbri, I wish to ask a favour of you—that you will beg the Khania to let us go our ways."

Instantly the Shaman's cunning old face became like a mask of ivory.

"Surely you had better ask your favours of the lady herself, lord; I do not think that any in reason will be refused to you," he replied.

"Let us stop fencing," said Leo, "and consider the facts. It has seemed to me that the Khania Atene is not happy with her husband."

"Your eyes are very keen, lord, and who shall say that they have deceived you?"

"It has seemed, further," went on Leo, reddening, "that she has been so good as to look on me with—some undeserved regard."

"Ah! perhaps you guessed that in the Gate-house yonder, if you have not forgotten what most men would remember."

"I remember certain things, Simbri, that have to do with her and you."

The Shaman only stroked his beard and said: "Proceed!"

"There is little to add, Simbri, except that I am not minded to bring scandal on the name of the first lady in your land."

"Nobly said, lord, nobly said, though here they do not trouble much about such things. But how if the matter could be managed without scandal? If, for instance, the Khania chose to take another husband the whole land would rejoice, for she is the last of her royal race."

"How can she take another husband when she has one living?"

"True; indeed that is a question which I have considered, but the answer to it is that men die. It is the common lot, and the Khan has been drinking very heavily of late."

"You mean that men can be murdered," said Leo angrily. "Well, I will have nothing to do with such a crime. Do you understand me?"

As the words passed his lips I heard a rustle and turned my head. Behind us were curtains beyond which the Shaman slept, kept his instruments of divination and worked out his horoscopes. Now they had been drawn, and between them, in her royal array, stood the Khania still as a statue.

"Who was it that spoke of crime?" she asked in a cold voice. "Was it you, my lord Leo?"

Rising from his chair, he faced her and said—"Lady, I am glad that you have heard my words, even if they should vex you."

"Why should it vex me to learn that there is one honest man in this court who will have naught to do with murder? Nay, I honour you for those words. Know also that no such foul thoughts have come near to me. Yet, Leo Vincey, that which is written—is written."

"Doubtless, Khania; but what is written?"

"Tell him, Shaman."

Now Simbri passed behind the curtain and returned thence with a roll from which he read: "The heavens have declared by their signs infallible that before the next new moon, the Khan Rassen will lie dead at the hands of the stranger lord who came to this country from across the mountains."

"Then the heavens have declared a lie," said Leo contemptuously.

"That is as you will," answered Atene; "but so it must befall, not by my hand or those of my servants, but by yours. And then?"

"Why by mine? Why not by Holly's? Yet, if so, then doubtless I shall suffer the punishment of my crime at the hands of his mourning widow," he replied exasperated.

"You are pleased to mock me, Leo Vincey, well knowing what a husband this man is to me."

Now I felt that the crisis had come, and so did Leo, for he looked her in the face and said—"Speak on, lady, say all you wish; perhaps it will be better for us both."

"I obey you, lord. Of the beginning of this fate I know nothing, but I read from the first page that is open to me. It has to do with this present life of mine. Learn, Leo Vincey, that from my childhood onwards you have haunted me. Oh! when first I saw you yonder by the river, your face was not strange to me, for I knew it—I knew it well in dreams. When I was a little maid and slept one day amidst the flowers by the river's brim, it came first to me—ask my uncle here if this be not so, though it is true that your face was younger then. Afterwards again and again I saw it in my sleep and learned to know that you were mine, for the magic of my heart taught me this.

"Then passed the long years while I felt that you were drawing near to me, slowly, very slowly, but ever drawing nearer, wending onward and outward through the peoples of the world; across the hills, across the plains, across the sands, across the snows, on to my side. At length came the end, for one night not three moons ago, whilst this wise man, my uncle, and I sat together here studying the lore that he has taught me and striving to wring its secrets from the past, a vision came to me.

"Look you, I was lost in a charmed sleep which looses the spirit from the body and gives it strength to stray afar and to see those things that have been and that are yet to be. Then I saw you and your companion clinging to a point of broken ice, over the river of the gulf. I do not lie; it is written here upon the scroll. Yes, it was you, the man of my dreams, and no other, and we knew the place and hurried thither and waited by the water, thinking that perhaps beneath it you lay dead.

"Then, while we waited, lo! two tiny figures appeared far above upon the icy tongue that no man may climb, and oh! you know the rest. Spellbound we stood and saw you slip and hang, saw you sever the thin cord and rush downwards, yes, and saw that brave man, Holly, leap headlong after you.

"But mine was the hand that drew you from the torrent, where otherwise you must have drowned, you the love of the long past and of to-day, aye, and of all time. Yes, you and no other, Leo Vincey. It was this spirit that foresaw your danger and this hand which delivered you from death, and—and would you refuse them now—when I, the Khania of Kaloon, proffer them to you?"

So she spoke, and leaned upon the table, looking up into his face with lips that trembled and with appealing eyes.

"Lady," said Leo, "you saved me, and again I thank you, though perhaps it would have been better if you had let me drown. But, forgive me the question, if all this tale be true, why did you marry another man?"

Now she shrank back as though a knife had pricked her.

"Oh! blame me not," she moaned, "it was but policy which bound me to this madman, whom I ever loathed. They urged me to it; yes, even you, Simbri, my uncle, and for that deed accursed be your head—urged me, saying that it was necessary to end the war between Rassen's faction and my own. That I was the last of the true race, moreover, which must be carried on; saying also that my dreams and my rememberings were but sick phantasies. So, alas! alas! I yielded, thinking to make my people great."

"And yourself, the greatest of them, if all I hear is true," commented Leo bluntly, for he was determined to end this thing. "Well, I do not blame you, Khania, although now you tell me that I must cut a knot you tied by taking the life of this husband of your own choice, for so forsooth it is decreed by fate, that fate which you have shaped. Yes, I must do what you will not do, and kill him. Also your tale of the decree of the heavens and of that vision which led you to the precipice to save us is false. Lady, you met me by the river because the 'mighty' Hesea, the Spirit of the Mountain, so commanded you."

"How know you that?" Atene said, springing up and facing him, while the jaw of old Simbri dropped and the eyelids blinked over his glazed eyes.

"In the same way that I know much else. Lady, it would have been better if you had spoken all the truth."

Now Atene's face went ashen and her cheeks sank in.

"Who told you?" she whispered. "Was it you, Magician?" and she turned upon her uncle like a snake about to strike. "Oh! if so, be sure that I shall learn it, and though we are of one blood and have loved each other, I will pay you back in agony."

"Atene, Atene," Simbri broke in, holding up his claw-like hands, "you know well it was not I."

"Then it was you, you ape-faced wanderer, you messenger of the evil gods? Oh! why did I not kill you at the first? Well, that fault can be remedied."

"Lady," I said blandly, "am I also a magician?"

"Aye," she answered, "I think that you are, and that you have a mistress who dwells in fire."

"Then, Khania," I said, "such servants and such mistresses are ill to meddle with. Say, what answer has the Hesea sent to your report of our coming to this land?"

"Listen," broke in Leo before she could reply. "I go to ask a certain question of the Oracle on yonder mountain peak. With your will or without it I tell you that I go, and afterwards you can settle which is the stronger—the Khania of Kaloon or the Hesea of the House of Fire."

Atene listened and for a while stood silent, perhaps because she had no answer. Then she said with a little laugh—"Is that your will? Well, I think that yonder are none whom you would wish to wed. There is fire and to spare, but no lovely, shameless spirit haunts it to drive men mad with evil longings;" and as though at some secret thought, a spasm of pain crossed her face and caught her breath. Then she went on in the same cold voice—"Wanderers, this land has its secrets, into which no foreigner must pry. I say to you yet again that while I live you set no foot upon that Mountain. Know also, Leo Vincey, I have bared my heart to you, and I have been told in answer that this long quest of yours is not for me, as I was sure in my folly, but, as I think, for some demon wearing the shape of woman, whom you will never find. Now I make no prayer to you; it is not fitting, but you have learned too much.

"Therefore, consider well to-night and before next sundown answer. Having offered, I do not go back, and tomorrow you shall tell me whether you will take me when the time comes, as come it must, and rule this land and be great and happy in my love, or whether, you and your familiar together, you will—die. Choose then between the vengeance of Atene and her love, since I am not minded to be mocked in my own land as a wanton who sought a stranger and was—refused."

Slowly, slowly, in an intense whisper she spoke the words, that fell one by one from her lips like drops of blood from a death wound, and there followed silence. Never shall I forget the scene. There the old wizard watched us through his horny eyes, that blinked like those of some night bird. There stood the imperial woman in her royal robes, with icy rage written on her face and vengeance in her glance. There, facing her, was the great form of Leo, quiet, alert, determined, holding back his doubts and fears with the iron hand of will. And there to the right was I, noting all things and wondering how long I, "the familiar," who had earned Atene's hate, would be left alive upon the earth.

Thus we stood, watching each other, till suddenly I noted that the flame of the lamp above us flickered and felt a draught strike upon my face. Then I looked round, and became aware of another presence. For yonder in the shadow showed the tall form of a man. See! it shambled forward silently, and I saw that its feet were naked. Now it reached the ring of the lamplight and burst into a savage laugh.

It was the Khan.

Atene, his wife, looked up and saw him, and never did I admire that passionate woman's boldness more, who admired little else about her save her beauty, for her face showed neither anger nor fear, but contempt only. And yet she had some cause to be afraid, as she well knew.

"What do you here, Rassen?" she asked, "creeping on me with your naked feet? Get you back to your drink and the ladies of your court."

But he still laughed on, an hyena laugh.

"What have you heard?" she said, "that makes you so merry?"

"What have I heard?" Rassen gurgled out between his screams of hideous glee. "Oho! I have heard the Khania, the last of the true blood, the first in the land, the proud princess who will not let her robes be soiled by those of the 'ladies of the court' and my wife, my wife, who asked me to marry her—mark that, you strangers—because I was her cousin and a rival ruler, and the richest lord in all the land, and thereby she thought she would increase her power—I have heard her offer herself to a nameless wanderer with a great yellow beard, and I have heard him, who hates and would escape from her"—here he screamed with laughter—"refuse her in such a fashion as I would not refuse the lowest woman in the palace.

"I have heard also—but that I always knew—that I am mad; for, strangers, I was made mad by a hate-philtre which that old Rat," and he pointed to Simbri, "gave me in my drink—yes, at my marriage feast. It worked well, for truly there is no one whom I hate more than the Khania Atene. Why, I cannot bear her touch, it makes me sick. I loathe to be in the same room with her; she taints the air; there is a smell of sorceries about her.

"It seems that it takes you thus also, Yellow-beard? Well, if so, ask the old Rat for a love drink; he can mix it, and then you will think her sweet and sound and fair, and spend some few months jollily enough. Man, don't be a fool, the cup that is thrust into your hands looks goodly. Drink, drink deep. You'll never guess the liquor's bad—till to-morrow—though it be mixed with a husband's poisoned blood," and again Rassen screamed in his unholy mirth.

To all these bitter insults, venomed with the sting of truth, Atene listened without a word. Then, she turned to us and bowed.

"My guests," she said, "I pray you pardon me for all I cannot help. You have strayed to a corrupt and evil land, and there stands its crown and flower. Khan Rassen, your doom is written, and I do not hasten it, because once for a little while we were near to each other, though you have been naught to me for this many a year save a snake that haunts my house. Were it otherwise, the next cup you drank should still your madness, and that vile tongue of yours which gives its venom voice. My uncle, come with me. Your hand, for I grow weak with shame and woe."

The old Shaman hobbled forward, but when he came face to face with the Khan he stopped and looked him up and down with his dim eyes.

Then he said—"Rassen, I saw you born, the son of an evil woman, and your father none knew but I. The flame flared that night upon the Fire-mountain, and the stars hid their faces, for none of them would own you, no, not even those of the most evil influence. I saw you wed and rise drunken from your marriage feast, your arm about a wanton's neck. I have seen you rule, wasting the land for your cruel pleasure, turning the fertile fields into great parks for your game, leaving those who tilled them to starve upon the road or drown themselves in ditches for very misery. And soon, soon I shall see you die in pain and blood, and then the chain will fall from the neck of this noble lady whom you revile, and another more worthy shall take your place and rear up children to fill your throne, and the land shall have rest again."

Now I listened to these words—and none who did not hear them can guess the fearful bitterness with which they were spoken—expecting every moment that the Khan would draw the short sword at his side and cut the old man down. But he did not; he cowered before him like a dog before some savage master, the weight of whose whip he knows. Yes, answering nothing, he shrank into the corner and cowered there, while Simbri, taking Atene by the hand, went from the room. At its massive, iron-bound door he turned and pointing to the crouching figure with his staff, said—"Khan Rassen, I raised you up, and now I cast you down. Remember me when you lie dying—in blood and pain."

Their footsteps died away, and the Khan crept from his corner, looking about him furtively.

"Have that Rat and the other gone?" he asked of us, wiping his damp brow with his sleeve; and I saw that fear had sobered him and that for awhile the madness had left his eyes.

I answered that they had gone.

"You think me a coward," he went on passionately, "and it is true, I am afraid of him and her—as you, Yellow-beard, will be afraid when your turn comes. I tell you that they sapped my strength and crazed me with their drugged drink, making me the thing I am, for who can war against their wizardries? Look you now. Once I was a prince, the lord of half this land, noble of form and upright of heart, and I loved her accursed beauty as all must love it on whom she turns her eyes. And she turned them on me, she sought me in marriage; it was that old Rat who bore her message.

"So I stayed the great war and married the Khania and became the

Khan; but better had it been for me if I had crept into her kitchen as a scullion, than into her chamber as a husband. For from the first she hated me, and the more I loved, the more she hated, till at our wedding feast she doctored me with that poison which made me loathe her, and thus divorced us; which made me mad also, eating into my brain like fire."

"If she hated you so sorely, Khan," I asked, "why did she not mix a stronger draught and have done with you?"

"Why? Because of policy, for I ruled half the land. Because it suited her also that I should live on, a thing to mock at, since while I was alive no other husband could be forced upon her by the people. For she is not a woman, she is a witch, who desires to live alone, or so I thought until to-night"—and he glowered at Leo.

"She knew also that although I must shrink from her, I still love her in my heart, and can still be jealous, and therefore that I should protect her from all men. It was she who set me on that lord whom my dogs tore awhile ago, because he was powerful and sought her favour and would not be denied. But now," and again he glowered at Leo, "now I know why she has always seemed so cold. It is because there lived a man to melt whose ice she husbanded her fire."

Then Leo, who all this while had stood silent, stepped forward.

"Listen, Khan," he said. "Did the ice seem like melting a little while ago?"

"No—unless you lied. But that was only because the fire is not yet hot enough. Wait awhile until it burns up, and melt you must, for who can match his will against Atene?"

"And what if the ice desires to flee the fire? Khan, they said that I should kill you, but I do not seek your blood. You think that I would rob you of your wife, yet I have no such thought towards her. We desire to escape this town of yours, but cannot, because its gates are locked, and we are prisoners, guarded night and day. Hear me, then. You have the power to set us free and to be rid of us."

The Khan looked at him cunningly. "And if I set you free, whither would you go? You could tumble down yonder gorge, but only the birds can climb its heights."

"To the Fire-mountain, where we have business."

Rassen stared at him.

"Is it I who am mad, or are you, who wish to visit the Fire-mountain? Yet that is nothing to me, save that I do not believe you. But if so you might return again and bring others with you. Perchance, having its lady, you wish this land also by right of conquest. It has foes up yonder."

"It is not so," answered Leo earnestly. "As one man to another, I tell you it is not so. I ask no smile of your wife and no acre of your soil. Be wise and help us to be gone, and live on undisturbed in such fashion as may please you."

The Khan stood still awhile, swinging his long arms vacantly, till something seemed to come into his mind that moved him to merriment, for he burst into one of his hideous laughs.

"I am thinking," he said, "what Atene would say if she woke up to find her sweet bird flown. She would search for you and be angry with me."

"It seems that she cannot be angrier than she is," I answered. "Give us a night's start and let her search never so closely, she shall not find us."

"You forget, Wanderer, that she and her old Rat have arts. Those who knew where to meet you might know where to seek you. And yet, and yet, it would be rare to see her rage. 'Oh, Yellow-beard, where are you, Yellow-beard?' he went on, mimicking his wife's voice. 'Come back and let me melt your ice, Yellow-beard.'"

Again he laughed; then said suddenly—"When can you be ready?"

"In half an hour," I answered.

"Good. Go to your chambers and prepare. I will join you there presently."

So we went.

XI. THE HUNT AND THE KILL

We reached our rooms, meeting no one in the passages, and there made our preparations. First we changed our festal robes for those warmer garments in which we had travelled to the city of Kaloon. Then we ate and drank what we could of the victuals which stood in the antechamber, not knowing when we should find more food, and filled two satchels such as these people sling about their shoulders, with the remains of the meat and liquor and a few necessaries. Also we strapped our big hunting knives about our middles and armed ourselves with short spears that were made for the stabbing of game.

"Perhaps he has laid a plot to murder us, and we may as well defend ourselves while we can," suggested Leo.

I nodded, for the echoes of the Khan's last laugh still rang in my ears. It was a very evil laugh.

"Likely enough," I said. "I do not trust that insane brute. Still, he wishes to be rid of us."

"Yes, but as he said, live men may return, whereas the dead do not."

"Atene thinks otherwise," I commented.

"And yet she threatened us with death," answered Leo.

"Because her shame and passion make her mad," I replied, after which we were silent.

Presently the door opened, and through it came the Khan, muffled in a great cloak as though to disguise himself.

"Come," he said, "if you are ready." Then, catching sight of the spears we held, he added: "You will not need those things. You do not go a-hunting."

"No," I answered, "but who can say—we might be hunted."

"If you believe that perhaps you had best stay where you are till the Khania wearies of Yellow-beard and opens the gates for you," he replied, eyeing me with his cunning glance.

"I think not," I said, and we started, the Khan leading the way and motioning us to be silent.

We passed through the empty rooms on to the verandah, and from the verandah down into the courtyard, where he whispered to us to keep in the shadow. For the moon shone very clearly that night, so clearly, I remember, that I could see the grass which grew between the joints of the pavement, and the little shadows thrown by each separate blade upon the worn surface of its stones. Now I wondered how we should pass the gate, for there a guard was stationed, which had of late been doubled by order of the Khania. But this gate we left upon our right, taking a path that led into the great walled garden, where Rassen brought us to a door hidden behind a clump of shrubs, which he unlocked with a key he carried.

Now we were outside the palace wall, and our road ran past the kennels. As we went by these, the great, sleepless death-hounds, that wandered to and fro like prowling lions, caught our wind and burst into a sudden chorus of terrific bays. I shivered at the sound, for it was fearful in that silence, also I thought that it would arouse the keepers. But the Khan went to the bars and showed himself, whereon the brutes, which knew him, ceased their noise.

"Fear not," he said as he returned, "the huntsmen know that they are starved to-night, for to-morrow certain criminals will be thrown to them."

Now we had reached the palace gates. Here the Khan bade us hide in an archway and departed. We looked at each other, for the same thought was in both our minds—that he had gone to fetch the murderers who were to make an end of us. But in this we did him wrong, for presently we heard the sound of horses' hoofs upon the stones, and he returned leading the two white steeds that Atene had given us.

"I saddled them with my own hands," he whispered. "Who can do more to speed the parting guest? Now mount, hide your faces in your cloaks as I do, and follow me."

So we mounted, and he trotted before us like a running footman, such as the great lords of Kaloon employed when they went about their business or their pleasure. Leaving the main street, he led us through a quarter of the town that had an evil reputation, and down its tortuous by-ways. Here we met a few revellers, while from time to time night-birds flitted from the doorways and, throwing aside their veils, looked at us, but as we made no sign drew back again, thinking that we passed to some assignation. We reached the deserted docks upon the river's edge and came to a little quay, alongside of which a broad ferryboat was fastened.

"You must put your horses into it and row across," Rassen said, "for the bridges are guarded, and without discovering myself I cannot bid the soldiers to let you pass."

So with some little trouble we urged the horses into the boat, where I held them by their bridles while Leo took the oars.

"Now go your ways, accursed wanderers," cried the Khan as he thrust us from the quay, "and pray the Spirit of the Mountain that the old Rat and his pupil—your love, Yellow-beard, your love—are not watching you in their magic glass. For if so we may meet again."

Then as the stream caught us, sweeping the boat out towards the centre of the river, he began to laugh that horrible laugh of his, calling after us—"Ride fast, ride fast for safety, strangers; there is death behind."

Leo put out his strength and backed water, so that the punt hung upon the edge of the stream.

"I think that we should do well to land again and kill that man, for he means mischief," he said.

He spoke in English, but Rassen must have caught the ring of his voice and guessed its meaning with the cunning of the mad. At least he shouted—"Too late, fools," and with a last laugh turned, ran so swiftly up the quay that his cloak flew out upon the air behind him, and vanished into the shadows at its head.

"Row on," I said, and Leo bent himself to the oars.

But the ferry-boat was cumbersome and the current swift, so that we were swept down a long way before we could cross it. At length we reached still water near the further shore, and seeing a landing-place, managed to beach the punt and to drag our horses to the bank. Then leaving the craft to drift, for we had no time to scuttle her, we looked to our girths and bridles, and mounted, heading towards the far column of glowing smoke which showed like a beacon above the summit of the House of Fire.

At first our progress was very slow, for here there seemed to be no path, and we were obliged to pick our way across the fields, and to search for bridges that spanned such of the water-ditches as were too wide for us to jump. More than an hour was spent in this work, till we came to a village wherein none were stirring, and here struck a road which seemed to run towards the mountain, though, as we learned afterwards, it took us very many miles out of our true path. Now for the first time we were able to canter, and pushed on at some speed, though not too fast, for we wished to spare our horses and feared lest they might fall in the uncertain light.

A while before dawn the moon sank behind the Mountain, and the gloom grew so dense that we were forced to stop, which we did, holding the horses by their bridles and allowing them to graze a little on some young corn. Then the sky turned grey, the light faded from the column of smoke that was our guide, the dawn came, blushing red upon the vast snows of the distant peak, and shooting its arrows through the loop above the pillar. We let the horses drink from a channel that watered the corn, and, mounting them, rode onward slowly.

Now with the shadows of the night a weight of fear seemed to be lifted off our hearts and we grew hopeful, aye, almost joyous. That hated city was behind us. Behind us were the Khania with her surging, doom-driven passions and her stormy loveliness, the wizardries of her horny-eyed mentor, so old in years and secret sin, and the madness of that strange being, half-devil, half-martyr, at once cruel and a coward—the Khan, her husband, and his polluted court. In front lay the fire, the snow and the mystery they hid, sought for so many empty years. Now we would solve it or we would die. So we pressed forward joyfully to meet our fate, whatever it might be.

For many hours our road ran deviously through cultivated land, where the peasants at their labour laid down their tools and gathered into knots to watch us pass, and quaint, flat-roofed villages, whence the women snatched up their children and fled at the sight of us. They believed us to be lords from the court who came to work them some harm in person or in property, and their terror told us how the country smarted beneath the rod of the oppressor. By mid-day, although the peak seemed to be but little nearer, the character of the land had changed. Now it sloped gently upwards, and therefore could not be irrigated.

Evidently all this great district was dependent on the fall of timely rains, which had not come that spring. Therefore, although the population was still dense and every rod of the land was under the plough or spade, the crops were failing. It was pitiful to see the green, uneared corn already turning yellow because of the lack of moisture, the beasts searching the starved pastures for food and the poor husbandmen wandering about their fields or striving to hoe the iron soil.

Here the people seemed to know us as the two foreigners whose coming had been noised abroad, and, the fear of famine having made them bold, they shouted at us as we went by to give them back the rain which we had stolen, or so we understood their words. Even the women and the children in the villages prostrated themselves before us, pointing first to the Mountain and then to the hard, blue sky, and crying to us to send them rain. Once, indeed, we were threatened by a mob of peasants armed with spades and reaping-hooks, who seemed inclined to bar our path, so that we were obliged to put our horses to a gallop and pass through them with a rush. As we went forward the country grew ever more arid and its inhabitants more scarce, till we saw no man save a few wandering herds who drove their cattle from place to place in search of provender.

By evening we guessed that we had reached that border tract which was harried by the Mountain tribes, for here strong towers built of stone were dotted about the heaths, doubtless to serve as watch-houses or places of refuge. Whether they were garrisoned by soldiers I do not know, but I doubt it, for we saw none. It seems probable indeed that these forts were relics of days when the land of Kaloon was guarded from attack by rulers of a very different character to that of the present Khan and his immediate predecessors.

At length even the watch-towers were left behind, and by sundown we found ourselves upon a vast uninhabited plain, where we could see no living thing. Now we made up our minds to rest our horses awhile, proposing to push forward again with the moon, for having the wrath of the Khania behind us we did not dare to linger. By this evening doubtless she would have discovered our escape, since before sundown, as she had decreed, Leo must make his choice and give his answer. Then, as we were sure, she would strike swiftly. Perhaps her messengers were already at their work rousing the country to capture us, and her soldiers following on our path.

We unsaddled the horses and let them refresh themselves by rolling on the sandy soil, and graze after a fashion upon the coarse tufts of withering herbage which grew around. There was no water here; but this did not so much matter, for both they and we had drunk at a little muddy pool we found not more than an hour before. We were finishing our meal of the food that we had brought with us, which, indeed, we needed sorely after our sleepless night and long day's journey, when my horse, which was knee-haltered close at hand, lay down to roll again. This it could not do with ease because of the rope about its fore-leg, and I watched its efforts idly, till at length, at the fourth attempt, after hanging for a few seconds upon its back, its legs sticking straight into the air, it fell over slowly towards me as horses do.

"Why are its hoofs so red? Has it cut itself?" asked Leo in an indifferent voice.

As it chanced I also had just noticed this red tinge, and for the first time, since it was most distinct about the animal's frogs, which until it rolled thus I had not seen. So I rose to look at them, thinking that probably the evening light had deceived us, or that we might have passed through some ruddy-coloured mud. Sure enough they were red, as though a dye had soaked into the horn and the substance of the frogs. What was more, they gave out a pungent, aromatic smell that was unpleasant, such a smell as might arise from blood mixed with musk and spices.

"It is very strange," I said. "Let us look at your beast, Leo."

So we did, and found that its hoofs had been similarly-treated.

"Perhaps it is a native mixture to preserve the horn," suggested Leo.

I thought awhile, then a terrible idea struck me.

"I don't want to frighten you," I said, "but I think that we had better saddle up and get on."

"Why?" he asked.

"Because I believe that villain of a Khan has doctored our horses."

"What for? To make them go lame?"

"No, Leo, to make them leave a strong scent upon dry ground."

He turned pale. "Do you mean—those hounds?"

I nodded. Then wasting no more time in words, we saddled up in frantic haste. Just as I fastened the last strap of my saddle I thought that a faint sound reached my ear.

"Listen," I said. Again it came, and now there was no doubt about it. It was the sound of baying dogs.

"By heaven! the death-hounds," said Leo.

"Yes," I answered quietly enough, for at this crisis my nerves hardened and all fear left me, "our friend the Khan is out a-hunting. That is why he laughed."

"What shall we do?" asked Leo. "Leave the horses?"

I looked at the Peak. Its nearest flanks were miles and miles away.

"Time enough to do that when we are forced. We can never reach that mountain on foot, and after they had run down the horses, they would hunt us by spoor or gaze. No, man, ride as you never rode before."

We sprang to our saddles, but before we gave rein I turned and looked behind me. It will be remembered that we had ridden up a long slope which terminated in a ridge, about three miles away, the border of the great plain whereon we stood. Now the sun had sunk behind that ridge so that although it was still light the plain had fallen into shadow. Therefore, while no distant object could be seen upon the plain, anything crossing the ridge remained visible enough in that clear air, at least to persons of keen sight.

This is what we saw. Over the ridge poured a multitude of little objects, and amongst the last of these galloped a man mounted on a great horse, who led another horse by the bridle.

"All the pack are out," said Leo grimly, "and Rassen has brought a second mount with him. Now I see why he wanted us to leave the spears, and I think," he shouted as we began to gallop, "that before all is done the Shaman may prove himself a true prophet."

Away we sped through the gathering darkness, heading straight for the Peak. While we went I calculated our chances. Our horses, as good as any in the land, were still strong and fresh, for although we had ridden far we had not over-pressed them, and their condition was excellent. But doubtless the death-hounds were fresh also, for, meaning to run us down at night when he thought that he might catch us sleeping, Rassen would have brought them along easily, following us by inquiry among the peasants and only laying them on our spoor after the last village had been left behind.

Also he had two mounts, and for aught we knew—though afterwards this proved not to be the case, for he wished to work his wickedness alone and unseen—he might be followed by attendants with relays. Therefore it would appear that unless we reached some place whither he did not dare to follow, before him—that is the slopes of the Peak many miles away, he must run us down. There remained the chance also that the dogs would tire and refuse to pursue the chase.

This, however, seemed scarcely probable, for they were extraordinarily swift and strong, and so savage that when once they had scented blood, in which doubtless our horses' hoofs were steeped, they would fall dead from exhaustion sooner than abandon the trail. Indeed, both the Khania and Simbri had often told us as much. Another chance—they might lose the scent, but seeing its nature, again this was not probable. Even an English pack will carry the trail of a red herring breast high without a fault for hours, and here was something stronger—a cunning compound of which the tell-tale odour would hold for days. A last chance. If we were forced to abandon our horses, we, their riders, might possibly escape, could we find any place to hide in on that great plain. If not, we should be seen as well as scented, and then——No, the odds were all against us, but so they had often been before; meanwhile we had three miles start, and perhaps help would come to us from the Mountain, some help unforeseen. So we set our teeth and sped away like arrows while the light lasted.

Very soon it failed, and whilst the moon was hidden behind the mountains the night grew dark.

Now the hounds gained on us, for in the gloom, which to them was nothing, we did not dare to ride full speed, fearing lest our horses should stumble and lame themselves, or fall. Then it was for the second time since we had dwelt in this land of Kaloon that of a sudden the fire flamed upon the Peak. When we had seen it before, it had appeared to flash across the heavens in one great lighthouse ray, concentrated through the loop above the pillar, and there this night also the ray ran far above us like a lance of fire. But now that we were nearer to its fount we found ourselves bathed in a soft, mysterious radiance like that of the phosphorescence on a summer sea, reflected downwards perhaps from the clouds and massy rock roof of the column loop and diffused by the snows beneath.

This unearthly glimmer, faint as it was, helped us much, indeed but for it we must have been overtaken, for here the ground was very rough, full of holes also made by burrowing marmots. Thus in our extremity help did come to us from the Mountain, until at length the moon rose, when as quickly as they had appeared the volcanic fires vanished, leaving behind them nothing but the accustomed pillar of dull red smoke.

It is a commonplace to speak of the music of hounds at chase, but often I have wondered how that music sounds in the ears of the deer or the fox fleeing for its life.

Now, when we filled the place of the quarry, it was my destiny to solve this problem, and I assert with confidence that the progeny of earth can produce no more hideous noise. It had come near to us, and in the desolate silence of the night the hellish harmonies of its volume seemed terrific, yet I could discern the separate notes of which it was composed, especially one deep, bell-like bay.

I remembered that I had heard this bay when we sat in the boat upon the river and saw that poor noble done to death for the crime of loving the Khania. As the hunt passed us then I observed that it burst from the throat of the leading hound, a huge brute, red in colour, with a coal-black ear, fangs that gleamed like ivory, and a mouth which resembled a hot oven. I even knew the name of the beast, for afterwards the Khan, whose peculiar joy it was, had pointed it out to me. He called it Master, because no dog in the pack dared fight it, and told me that it could kill an armed man alone.

Now, as its baying warned us, Master was not half a mile away!

The coming of the moonlight enabled us to gallop faster, especially as here the ground was smooth, being covered with a short, dry turf, and for the next two hours we gained upon the pack. Yes, it was only two hours, or perhaps less, but it seemed a score of centuries. The slopes of the Peak were now not more than ten miles ahead, but our horses were giving out at last. They had borne us nobly, poor beasts, though we were no light weights, yet their strength had its limits. The sweat ran from them, their sides panted like bellows, they breathed in gasps, they stumbled and would scarcely answer to the flogging of our spear-shafts. Their gallop sank to a jolting canter, and I thought that soon they must come to a dead stop.

We crossed the brow of a gentle rise, from which the ground, that was sprinkled with bush and rocks, sloped downwards to where, some miles below us, the river ran, bounding the enormous flanks of the Mountain. When we had travelled a little way down this slope we were obliged to turn in order to pass between two heaps of rock, which brought us side on to its brow. And there, crossing it not more than three hundred yards away, we saw the pack. There were fewer of them now; doubtless many had fallen out of the hunt, but many still remained. Moreover, not far behind them rode the Khan, though his second mount was gone, or more probably he was riding it, having galloped the first to a standstill.

Our poor horses saw them also, and the sight lent them wings, for all the while they knew that they were running for their lives. This we could tell from the way they quivered whenever the baying came near to them, not as horses tremble with the pleasureable excitement of the hunt, but in an extremity of terror, as I have often seen them do when a prowling tiger roars close to their camp. On they went as though they were fresh from the stable, nor did they fail again until another four miles or so were covered and the river was but a little way ahead, for we could hear the rush of its waters.

Then slowly but surely the pack overtook us. We passed a clump of bush, but when we had gone a couple of hundred yards or so across the open plain beyond, feeling that the horses were utterly spent, I shouted to Leo—"Ride round back to the bush and hide there." So we did, and scarcely had we reached it and dismounted when the hounds came past. Yes, they went within fifty yards of us, lolloping along upon our spoor and running all but mute, for now they were too weary to waste their breath in vain. "Run for it," I said to Leo as soon as they had gone by, "for they will be back on the scent presently," and we set off to the right across the line that the hounds had taken, so as not to cut our own spoor.

About a hundred yards away was a rock, which fortunately we were able to reach before the pack swung round upon the horses' tracks, and therefore they did not view us. Here we stayed until following the loop, they came to the patch of bush and passed behind it. Then we ran forward again as far as we could go. Glancing backwards as we went, I saw our two poor, foundered beasts plunging away across the plain, happily almost in the same line along which we had ridden from the rise. They were utterly done, but freed from our weights and urged on by fear, could still gallop and keep ahead of the dogs, though we knew that this would not be for very long. I saw also that the Khan, guessing what we had done in our despair, was trying to call his hounds off the horses, but as yet without avail, for they would not leave the quarry which they had viewed.

All this came to my sight in a flash, but I remember the picture well. The mighty, snow-clad Peak surmounted by its column of glowing smoke and casting its shadow for mile upon mile across the desert flats; the plain with its isolated rocks and grey bushes; the doomed horses struggling across it with convulsive bounds; the trailing line of great dogs that loped after them, and amongst these, looking small and lonely in that vast place, the figure of the Khan and his horse, of which the black hide was beflecked with foam. Then above, the blue and tender sky, where the round moon shone so clearly that in her quiet, level light no detail, even the smallest, could escape the eye.

Now youth and even middle age were far behind me, and although a very strong man for my years, I could not run as I used to do. Also I was most weary, and my limbs were stiff and chafed with long riding, so I made but slow progress, and to worsen matters I struck my left foot against a stone and hurt it much. I implored Leo to go on and leave me, for we thought that if we could once reach the river our scent would be lost in the water; at any rate that it would give us a chance of life. Just then too, I heard the belling bay of the hound Master, and waited for the next. Yes, it was nearer to us. The Khan had made a cast and found our line. Presently we must face the end.

"Go, go!" I said. "I can keep them back for a few minutes and you may escape. It is your quest, not mine. Ayesha awaits you, not me, and I am weary of life. I wish to die and have done with it."

Thus I gasped, not all at once, but in broken words, as I hobbled along clinging to Leo's arm. But he only answered in a low voice—"Be quiet, or they will hear you," and on he went, dragging me with him.

We were quite near the water now, for we could see it gleaming below us, and oh! how I longed for one deep drink. I remember that this was the uppermost desire in my mind, to drink and drink. But the hounds were nearer still to us, so near that we could hear the pattering of their feet on the dry ground mingled with the thud of the hoofs of the Khan's galloping horse. We had reached some rocks upon a little rise, just where the bank began, when Leo said suddenly—"No use, we can't make it. Stop and let's see the thing through."

So we wheeled round, resting our backs against the rock. There, about a hundred yards off, were the death-hounds, but Heaven be praised! only three of them. The rest had followed the flying horses, and doubtless when they caught them at last, which may have been far distant, had stopped to gorge themselves upon them. So they were out of the fight. Only three, and the Khan, a wild figure, who galloped with them; but those three, the black and red brute, Master, and two others almost as fierce and big.

"It might be worse," said Leo. "If you will try to tackle the dogs, I'll do my best with the Khan," and stooping down he rubbed his palms in the grit, for they were wet as water, an example which I followed. Then we gripped the spears in our right hands and the knives in our left, and waited.

The dogs had seen us now and came on, growling and baying fearfully. With a rush they came, and I am not ashamed to own that I felt terribly afraid, for the brutes seemed the size of lions and more fierce. One, it was the smallest of them, outstripped the others, and, leaping up the little rise, sprang straight at my throat.

Why or how I do not know, but on the impulse of the moment I too sprang to meet it, so that its whole weight came upon the point of my spear, which was backed by my weight. The spear entered between its forelegs and such was the shock that I was knocked backwards. But when I regained my feet I saw the dog rolling on the ground before me and gnashing at the spear shaft, which had been twisted from my hand.

The other two had jumped at Leo, but failed to get hold, though one of them tore away a large fragment from his tunic. Foolishly enough, he hurled his spear at it but missed, for the steel passed just under its belly and buried itself deep in the ground. The pair of them did not come on again at once. Perhaps the sight of their dying companion made them pause. At any rate, they stood at a little distance snarling, where, as our spears were gone, they were safe from us.

Now the Khan had ridden up and sat upon his horse glowering at us, and his face was like the face of a devil. I had hoped that he might fear to attack, but the moment I saw his eyes, I knew that this would not be. He was quite mad with hate, jealousy, and the long-drawn excitement of the hunt, and had come to kill or be killed. Sliding from the saddle, he drew his short sword—for either he had lost his spear or had brought none—and made a hissing noise to the two dogs, pointing at me with the sword. I saw them spring and I saw him rush at Leo, and after that who can tell exactly what happened?

My knife went home to the hilt in the body of one dog—and it came to the ground and lay there—for its hindquarters were paralysed, howling, snarling and biting at me. But the other, the fiend called Master, got me by the right arm beneath the elbow, and I felt my bones crack in its mighty jaws, and the agony of it, or so I suppose, caused me to drop the knife, so that I was weaponless. The brute dragged me from the rock and began to shake and worry me, although I kicked it in the stomach with all my strength. I fell to my knees and, as it chanced, my left hand came upon a stone of about the size of a large orange, which I gripped. I gained my feet again and pounded at its skull with the stone, but still it did not leave go, and this was well for me, for its next hold would have been on my throat.

We twisted and tumbled to and fro, man and dog together. At one turn I thought that I saw Leo and the Khan rolling over and over each other upon the ground; at another, that he, the Khan, was sitting against a stone looking at me, and it came into my mind that he must have killed Leo and was watching while the dog worried me to death.

Then just as things began to grow black, something sprang forward and I saw the huge hound lifted from the earth. Its jaws opened, my arm came free and fell against my side. Yes! the brute was whirling round in the air. Leo held it by its hind legs and with all his great strength whirled it round and round.

Thud!

He had dashed its head against the rock, and it fell and lay still, a huddled heap of black and red. Oddly enough, I did not faint; I suppose that the pain and the shock to my nerves kept me awake, for I heard Leo say in a matter-of-fact voice between his gasps for breath—"Well, that's over, and I think that I have fulfilled the Shaman's prophecy. Let's look and make sure."

Then he led me with him to one of the rocks, and there, resting supinely against it, sat the Khan, still living but unable to move hand or foot. The madness had quite left his face and he looked at us with melancholy eyes, like the eyes of a sick child.

"You are brave men," he said, slowly, "strong also, to have killed those hounds and broken my back. So it has come about as was foretold by the old Rat. After all, I should have hunted Atene, not you, though now she lives to avenge me, for her own sake, not mine. Yellow-beard, she hunts you too and with deadlier hounds than these, those of her thwarted passions. Forgive me and fly to the Mountain, Yellow-beard, whither I go before you, for there one dwells who is stronger than Atene."

Then his jaw dropped and he was dead.

"He is gone," I panted, "and the world hasn't lost much."

"Well, it didn't give him much, did it, poor devil, so don't let's speak ill of him," answered Leo, who had thrown himself exhausted to the ground. "Perhaps he was all right before they made him mad. At any rate he had pluck, for I don't want to tackle such another."

"How did you manage it?" I asked.

"Dodged in beneath his sword, closed with him, threw him and smashed him up over that lump of stone. Sheer strength, that's all. A cruel business, but it was his life or mine, and there you are. It's lucky I finished it in time to help you before that oven-mouthed brute tore your throat out. Did you ever see such a dog? It looks as large as a young donkey. Are you much hurt, Horace?"

"Oh, my forearm is chewed to a pulp, but nothing else, I think. Let us get down to the water; if I can't drink soon I shall faint. Also the rest of the pack is somewhere about, fifty or more of them."

"I don't think they will trouble us, they have got the horses, poor beasts. Wait a minute and I will come."

Then he rose, found the Khan's sword, a beautiful and ancient weapon, and with a single cut of its keen edge, killed the second dog that I had wounded, which was still yowling and snarling at us. After this he collected the two spears and my knife, saying that they might be useful, and without trouble caught the Khan's horse, which stood with hanging head close by, so tired that even this desperate fight had not frightened it away.

"Now," he said, "up you go, old fellow. You are not fit to walk any farther;" and with his help I climbed into the saddle.

Then slipping the rein over his arm he led the horse, which walked stiffly, on to the river, that ran within a quarter of a mile of us, though to me, tortured as I was by pain and half delirious with exhaustion, the journey seemed long enough.

Still we came there somehow, and, forgetting my wounds, I tumbled from the horse, threw myself flat and drank and drank, more, I think, than ever I did before. Not in all my life have I tasted anything so delicious as was that long draught of water. When I had satisfied my thirst, I dipped my head and made shift to jerk my wounded arm into it, for its coolness seemed to still the pain. Presently Leo rose, the water running from his face and beard, and said—"What shall we do now? The river seems to be wide, over a hundred yards, and it is low, but there may be deep water in the middle. Shall we try to cross, in which case we might drown, or stop where we are till daylight and take our chance of the death-hounds?"

"I can't go another foot," I murmured faintly, "much less try to ford an unknown river."

Now, about thirty yards from the shore was an island covered with reeds and grasses.

"Perhaps we could reach that," he said. "Come, get on to my back, and we will try."

I obeyed with difficulty, and we set out, he feeling his way with the handle of the spear. The water proved to be quite shallow; indeed, it never came much above his knees, so that we reached the island without trouble. Here Leo laid me down on the soft rushes, and, returning to the mainland, brought over the black horse and the remaining weapons, and having unsaddled the beast, knee-haltered and turned it loose, whereon it immediately lay down, for it was too spent to feed.

Then he set to work to doctor my wounds. Well it proved for me that the sleeve of my garment was so thick, for even through it the flesh of my forearm was torn to ribbons, moreover a bone seemed to be broken. Leo collected a double handful of some soft wet moss and, having washed the arm, wrapped it round with a handkerchief, over which he laid the moss. Then with a second handkerchief and some strips of linen torn from our undergarments he fastened a couple of split reeds to serve as rough splints to the wounded limb. While he was doing this I suppose that I slept or swooned. At any rate, I remember no more.

Sometime during that night Leo had a strange dream, of which he told me the next morning. I suppose that it must have been a dream as certainly I saw or was aware of nothing. Well, he dreamed—I use his own words as nearly as possible—that again he heard those accursed death-hounds in full cry. Nearer and nearer they came, following our spoor to the edge of the river—all the pack that had run down the horses. At the water's brink they halted and were mute. Then suddenly a puff of wind brought the scent of us upon the island to one of them which lifted up its head and uttered a single bay. The rest clustered about it, and all at once they made a dash at the water.

Leo could see and hear everything. He felt that after all our doom was now at hand, and yet, held in the grip of nightmare, if nightmare it were, he was quite unable to stir or even to cry out to wake and warn me.

Now followed the marvel of this vision. Giving tongue as they came, half swimming and half plunging, the hounds drew near to the island where we slept. Then, suddenly Leo saw that we were no longer alone. In front of us, on the brink of the water, stood the figure of a woman clad in some dark garment. He could not describe her face or appearance, for her back was towards him.

All he knew was that she stood there, like a guard, holding some object in her raised hand, and that suddenly the advancing hounds caught sight of her. In an instant it was as though they were paralysed by fear—for their bays turned to fearful howlings. One or two of those that were nearest to the island seemed to lose their footing and be swept away by the stream. The rest struggled back to the bank, and fled wildly like whipped curs.

Then the dark, commanding figure, which in his dream Leo took to be the guardian Spirit of the Mountain, vanished. That it left no footprints behind it I can vouch, for in the morning we looked to see.

When, awakened by the sharp pangs in my arm, I opened my eyes again, the dawn was breaking. A thin mist hung over the river and the island, and through it I could see Leo sleeping heavily at my side and the shape of the black horse, which had risen and was grazing close at hand. I lay still for a while remembering all that we had undergone and wondering that I should live to wake, till presently above the murmuring of the water I heard a sound which terrified me, the sound of voices. I sat up and peered through the reeds, and there upon the bank, looking enormous in the mist, I saw two figures mounted upon horses, those of a woman and a man.

They were pointing to the ground as though they examined spoor in the sand. I heard the man say something about the dogs not daring to enter the territory of the Mountain, a remark which came back to my mind again after Leo had told me his dream. Then I remembered how we were placed.

"Wake!" I whispered to Leo. "Wake, we are pursued."

He sprang to his feet, rubbing his eyes and snatching at a spear. Now those upon the bank saw him, and a sweet voice spoke through the mist, saying—"Lay down that weapon, my guest, for we are not come to harm you."

It was the voice of the Khania Atene, and the man with her was the old Shaman Simbri.

"What shall we do now, Horace?" asked Leo with something like a groan, for in the whole world there were no two people whom he less wished to see.

"Nothing," I answered, "it is for them to play."

"Come to us," called the Khania across the water. "I swear that we mean no harm. Are we not alone?"

"I do not know," answered Leo, "but it seems unlikely. Where we are we stop until we are ready to march again."

Atene spoke to Simbri. What she said we could not hear, for she whispered, but she appeared to be arguing with him and persuading him to some course of which he strongly disapproved. Then suddenly both of them put their horses at the water and rode to us through the shallows. Reaching the island, they dismounted, and we stood staring at each other. The old man seemed very weary in body and oppressed in mind, but the Khania was strong and beautiful as ever, nor had passion and fatigue left any trace upon her inscrutable face. It was she who broke the silence, saying—"You have ridden fast and far since last we met, my guests, and left an evil token to mark the path you took. Yonder among the rocks one lies dead. Say, how came he to his end, who has no wound upon him?"

"By these," answered Leo, stretching out his hands.

"I knew it," she answered, "and I blame you not, for fate decreed that death for him, and now it is fulfilled. Still, there are those to whom you must answer for his blood, and I only can protect you from them."

"Or betray me to them," said Leo. "Khania, what do you seek?"

"That answer which you should have given me this twelve hours gone. Remember, before you speak, that I alone can save your life—aye, and will do it and clothe you with that dead madman's crown and mantle."

"You shall have your answer on yonder Mountain," said Leo, pointing to the peak above us, "where I seek mine."

She paled a little and replied, "To find that it is death, for, as I have told you, the place is guarded by savage folk who know no pity."

"So be it. Then Death is the answer that we seek. Come, Horace, let us go to meet him."

"I swear to you," she broke in, "that there dwells not the woman of your dreams. I am that woman, yes, even I, as you are the man of mine."

"Then, lady, prove it yonder upon the Mountain," Leo answered.

"There dwells there no woman," Atene went on hurriedly, "nothing dwells there. It is the home of fire and—a Voice."

"What voice?"

"The Voice of the Oracle that speaks from the fire. The Voice of a Spirit whom no man has ever seen, or shall see."

"Come, Horace," said Leo, and he moved towards the horse.

"Men," broke in the old Shaman, "would you rush upon your doom? Listen; I have visited yonder haunted place, for it was I who according to custom brought thither the body of the Khan Atene's father for burial, and I warn you to set no foot within its temples."

"Which your mistress said that we should never reach," I commented, but Leo only answered—"We thank you for your warning," and added, "Horace, watch them while I saddle the horse, lest they do us a mischief."

So I took the spear in my uninjured hand and stood ready. But they made no attempt to hurt us, only fell back a little and began to talk in hurried whispers. It was evident to me that they were much perturbed. In a few minutes the horse was saddled and Leo assisted me to mount it. Then he said—"We go to accomplish our fate, whatever it may be, but before we part, Khania, I thank you for the kindness you have shown us, and pray you to be wise and forget that we have ever been. Through no will of mine your husband's blood is on my hands, and that alone must separate us for ever. We are divided by the doors of death and destiny. Go back to your people, and pardon me if most unwillingly I have brought you doubt and trouble. Farewell."

She listened with bowed head, then replied, very sadly—"I thank you for your gentle words, but, Leo Vincey, we do not part thus easily. You have summoned me to the Mountain, and even to the Mountain I shall follow you. Aye, and there I will meet its Spirit, as I have always known I must and as the Shaman here has always known I must. Yes, I will match my strength and magic against hers, as it is decreed that I shall do. To the victor be that crown for which we have warred for ages."

Then suddenly Atene sprang to her saddle, and turning her horse's head rode it back through the water to the shore, followed by old Simbri, who lifted up his crooked hands as though in woe and fear, muttering as he went—"You have entered the forbidden river and now, Atene, the day of decision is upon us all—upon us and her—that predestined day of ruin and of war."

"What do they mean?" asked Leo of me.

"I don't know," I answered; "but I have no doubt we shall find out soon enough and that it will be something unpleasant. Now for this river."

Before we had struggled through it I thought more than once that the day of drowning was upon us also, for in places there were deep rapids which nearly swept us away. But Leo, who waded, leading the Khan's horse by the bridle, felt his path and supported himself with the spear shaft, so that in the end we reached the other bank safely.

Beyond it lay a breadth of marshy lands, that doubtless were overflowed when the torrent was in flood. Through these we pushed our way as fast as we could, for we feared lest the Khania had gone to fetch her escort, which we thought she might have left behind the rise, and would return with it presently to hunt us down. At that time we did not know what we learned afterwards, that with its bordering river the soil of the Mountain was absolutely sacred and, in practice, inviolable. True, it had been invaded by the people of Kaloon in several wars, but on each occasion their army was destroyed or met with terrible disaster. Little wonder then they had come to believe that the House of Fire was under the protection of some unconquerable Spirit.

Leaving the marsh, we reached a bare, rising plain, which led to the first slope of the Mountain three or four miles away. Here we expected every moment to be attacked by the savages of whom we had heard so much, but no living creature did we see. The place was a desert streaked with veins of rock that once had been molten lava. I do not remember much else about it; indeed, the pain in my arm was so sharp that I had no eyes for physical features. At length the rise ended in a bare, broad donga, quite destitute of vegetation, of which the bottom was buried in lava and a debris of rocks washed down by the rain or melting snows from slopes above. This donga was bordered on the farther side by a cliff, perhaps fifty feet in height, in which we could see no opening.

Still we descended the place, that was dark and rugged; pervaded, moreover, by an extraordinary gloom, and as we went perceived that its lava floor was sprinkled over with a multitude of white objects. Soon we came to the first of these and found that it was the skeleton of a human being. Here was a veritable Valley of Dead Bones, thousands upon thousands of them; a gigantic graveyard. It seemed as though some great army had perished here.

Indeed, we found afterwards that this was the case, for on one of those occasions in the far past when the people of Kaloon had attacked the Mountain tribes, they were trapped and slaughtered in this gully, leaving their bones as a warning and a token. Among these sad skeletons we wandered disconsolately, seeking a path up the opposing cliff, and finding none, until at length we came to a halt, not knowing which way to turn. Then it was that we met with our first strange experience on the Mountain.

The gulf and its mouldering relics depressed us, so that for awhile we were silent, and, to tell the truth, somewhat afraid. Yes, even the horse seemed afraid, for it snorted a little, hung its head and shivered. Close by us lay a pile of bones, the remains evidently of a number of wretched creatures that, dead or living, had been hurled down from the cliff above, and on the top of the pile was a little huddled heap, which we took for more bones.

"Unless we can find a way out of this accursed charnel-house before long, I think that we shall add to its company," I said, staring round me.

As the words left my lips it seemed to me that from the corner of my eye I saw the heap on the top of the bones stir. I looked round. Yes, it was stirring. It rose, it stood up, a human figure, apparently that of a woman—but of this I could not be sure—wrapped from head to foot in white and wearing a hanging veil over its face, or rather a mask with cut eye-holes. It advanced towards us while we stared at it, till the horse, catching sight of the thing, shied violently and nearly threw me. When at a distance of about ten paces it paused and beckoned with its hand, that was also swathed in white like the arm of a mummy.

"What the devil are you?" shouted Leo, and his voice echoed drearily among those naked rocks. But the creature did not answer, it only continued to beckon.

Leo walked up to it to assure himself that we were not the victims of some hallucination. As he came it glided back to its heap of bones and stood there like a ghost of one dead arisen from amidst these grinning evidences of death, or rather a swathed corpse, for that is what it resembled. Leo followed with the intention of touching it to assure himself of its reality, whereon it lifted its white-wrapped arm and struck him lightly on the breast. Then as he recoiled it pointed with its hand, first upwards as though to the Peak or the sky, and next at the wall of rock which faced us.

He returned to me saying, “What shall we do?”

“Follow, I suppose. It may be a messenger from above,” and I nodded toward the mountain crest.

“From below, more likely,” Leo muttered, “for I don’t like the look of this guide.”

Still he motioned with his hand to the creature to proceed. Apparently it understood, for it turned to the left and began to pick its way amongst the stones and skeletons swiftly and without noise. We followed for several hundred yards till it reached a shallow cleft in the rock. This cleft we had seen already, but as it appeared to end at a depth of about thirty feet, we passed on. The figure entered here and vanished.

“It must be a shadow,” said Leo doubtfully.

“Nonsense,” I answered, “shadows don’t strike one. Go on.”

So he led the horse up the cleft, to find that at the end it turned sharply to the right and that the form was standing there awaiting us. Forward it went again and we after it down a little gorge that grew ever gloomier till it terminated in what might have been a cave, or a gallery cut in the rock.

Here our guide came back to us apparently with the intention of taking the horse by the bridle, but at this nearer sight of it the brute snorted and reared up, so that it almost fell backwards upon me. As it found its feet again the figure struck it on the head in the same passionless, inhuman way that it had struck Leo, whereon the horse trembled and burst into a sweat as though with fear, making no further attempt to escape or to disobey. Then it took one side of the bridle in its swathed hand and, Leo clinging to the other, we plunged into the tunnel.

Our position was not pleasant, for we knew not whither we were being led by this horrible conductor, and suspected that it might be to meet our deaths in the darkness. Moreover, I guessed that the path was narrow and bordered by some gulf, for as we went I heard stones fall, apparently to a considerable depth, while the poor horse lifted its feet gingerly and snorted in abject fear. At length we saw daylight, and never was I more glad of its advent, although it showed us that there was a gulf on our right, and that the path we travelled could not measure more than ten feet in width.

Now we were out of the tunnel, that evidently had saved us a wide detour, and standing for the first time upon the actual slope of the

Mountain, which stretched upwards for a great number of miles till it reached the snow-line above. Here also we saw evidences of human life, for the ground was cultivated in patches and herds of mountain sheep and cattle were visible in the distance.

Presently we entered a gully, following a rough path that led along the edge of a raging torrent. It was a desolate place, half a mile wide or more, having hundreds of fantastic lava boulders strewn about its slopes. Before we had gone a mile I heard a shrill whistle, and suddenly from behind these boulders sprang a number of men, quite fifty of them. All we could note at the time was that they were brawny, savage-looking fellows, for the most part red haired and bearded, although their complexions were rather dark, who wore cloaks of white goat skins and carried spears and shields. I should imagine that they were not unlike the ancient Picts and Scots as they appeared to the invading Romans. At us they came uttering their shrill, whistling cries, evidently with the intention of spearing us on the spot.

"Now for it," said Leo, drawing his sword, for escape was impossible; they were all round us. "Good-bye, Horace."

"Good-bye," I answered rather faintly, understanding what the Khania and the old Shaman had meant when they said that we should be killed before we ascended the first slope of the Mountain.

Meanwhile our ghastly-looking guide had slipped behind a great boulder, and even then it occurred to me that her part in the tragedy being played, she, if it were a woman at all, was withdrawing herself while we met our miserable fate. But here I did her injustice, for she had, I suppose, come to save us from this very fate which without her presence we must most certainly have suffered. When the savages were within a few yards suddenly she appeared on the top of the boulder, looking like a second Witch of Endor, and stretched out her arm. Not a word did she speak, only stretched out her draped arm, but the effect was remarkable and instantaneous.

At the sight of her down on to their faces went those wild men, every one of them, as though a lightning stroke had in an instant swept them out of existence. Then she let her arm fall and beckoned, whereon a great fellow who, I suppose, was the leader of the band, rose and crept towards her with bowed head, submissive as a beaten dog. To him she made signs, pointing to us, pointing to the far-off Peak, crossing and uncrossing her white-wrapped arms, but so far as I could hear, speaking no word. It was evident that the chief understood her, however, for he said something in a guttural language. Then he uttered his shrill whistle, whereon the band rose and departed thence at full speed, this way and the other, so that in another minute they had vanished as quickly as they came.

Now our guide motioned to us to proceed, and led the way upward as calmly as though nothing had happened.

For over two hours we went on thus till our path brought us from the ravine on to a grassy declivity, across which it wound its way. Here, to our astonishment, we found a fire burning, and hanging above the fire an earthenware pot, which was on the boil, although we could see no man tending it. The figure signalled to me to dismount, pointing to the pot in token that we were to eat the food which doubtless she had ordered the wild men to prepare for us, and very glad was I to obey her. Provision had been made for the horse also, for near the fire lay a great bundle of green forage.

While Leo off-saddled the beast and spread the provender for it, taking with me a spare earthen vessel that lay ready, I went to the edge of the torrent to drink and steep my wounded arm in its ice-cold stream. This relieved it greatly, though by now I was sure from various symptoms that the brute Master's fangs had fortunately only broken or injured the small bone, a discovery for which I was thankful enough. Having finished attending to it as well as I was able, I filled the jar with water.

On my way back a thought struck me, and going to where our mysterious guide stood still as Lot's wife after she had been turned into a pillar of salt, I offered it to her, hoping that she would unveil her face and drink. Then for the first time she showed some sign of being human, or so I thought, for it seemed to me that she bowed ever so little in acknowledgment of the courtesy. If so—and I may have been mistaken—this was all, for the next instant she turned her back on me to show that it was declined. So she would not, or for aught I knew, could not drink. Neither would she eat, for when Leo tried her afterwards with food she refused it in like fashion.

Meanwhile he had taken the pot off the fire, and as soon as its contents grew cool enough we fell on them eagerly, for we were starving. After we had eaten and drunk, Leo re-dressed my arm as best he could and we rested awhile. Indeed, I think that, being very tired, we began to doze, for I was awakened by a shadow falling on us and looked up to see our corpse-like guide standing close by and pointing first to the sun, then at the horse, as though to show us that we had far to travel. So we saddled up and went on again somewhat refreshed, for at least we were no longer ravenous.

All the rest of that day we journeyed on up the grassy slopes, seeing no man, although occasionally we heard the wild whistle which told us that we were being watched by the Mountain savages. By sundown the character of the country had changed, for the grass was replaced with rocks, amongst which grew stunted firs. We had left the lower slopes and were beginning to climb the Mountain itself.

The sun sank and we went on through the twilight. The twilight died and we went on through the dark, our path lit only by the stars and the faint radiance of the glowing pillar of smoke above the Peak, which was reflected on to us from the mighty mantle of its snows. Forward we toiled, whilst a few paces ahead of us walked our unwearying guide. If she had seemed weird and inhuman before, now she appeared a very ghost, as, clad in her graveyard white, upon which the faint light shimmered, never speaking, never looking back, she glided on noiselessly between the black rocks and the twisted, dark-green firs and junipers.

Soon we lost all count of the road. We turned this way and turned that way, we passed an open patch and through the shadows of a grove, till at length as the moon rose we entered a ravine, and following a path that ran down it, came to a place which is best described as a large amphitheatre cut by the hand of nature out of the rock of the Mountain. Evidently it was chosen as a place of defence, for its entrance was narrow and tortuous, built up at the end also, so that only one person could pass its gateway at a time. Within an open space and at its farther side stood low, stone houses built against the rock. In front of these houses, the moonlight shining full upon them, were gathered several hundred men and women arranged in a semicircle and in alternate companies, who appeared to be engaged in the celebration of some rite.

It was wild enough. In front of them, and in the exact centre of the semi-circle, stood a gigantic, red-bearded man, who was naked except for a skin girdle about his loins. He was swinging himself backwards and forwards, his hands resting upon his hips, and as he swung, shouting something like "Ho, haha, ho!" When he bent towards the audience it bent towards him, and every time he straightened himself it echoed his final shout of "Ho!" in a volume of sound that made the precipices ring. Nor was this all, for perched upon his hairy head, with arched back and waving tail, stood a great white cat.

Anything stranger, and indeed more fantastic than the general effect of this scene, lit by the bright moonlight and set in that wild arena, it was never my lot to witness. The red-haired, half-naked men and women, the gigantic priest, the mystical white cat, that, gripping his scalp with its claws, waved its tail and seemed to take a part in the performance; the unholy chant and its volleying chorus, all helped to make it extraordinarily impressive. This struck us the more, perhaps, because at the time we could not in the least guess its significance, though we imagined that it must be preliminary to some sacrifice or offering. It was like the fragment of a nightmare preserved by the awakened senses in all its mad, meaningless reality.

Now round the open space where these savages were celebrating their worship, or whatever it might be, ran a rough stone wall about six feet in height, in which wall was a gateway. Towards this we advanced quite unseen, for upon our side of the wall grew many stunted pines. Through these pines our guide led us, till in the thickest of them, some few yards from the open gateway and a little to the right of it, she motioned to us to stop.

Then she went to a low place in the wall and stood there as though she were considering the scene beyond. It seemed to us, indeed, that she saw what she had not expected and was thereby perplexed or angered. Presently she appeared to make up her mind, for again she motioned to us to remain where we were, enjoining silence upon us by placing her swathed hand upon the mask that hid her face. Next moment she was gone. How she went, or whither, I cannot say; all we knew was that she was no longer there.

"What shall we do now?" whispered Leo to me.

"Stay where we are till she comes back again or something happens," I answered.

So there being nothing else to be done, we stayed, hoping that the horse would not betray us by neighing, or that we might not be otherwise discovered, since we were certain that if so we should be in danger of death. Very soon, however, we forgot the anxieties of our own position in the study of the wild scene before us, which now began to develop a fearful interest.

It would seem that what has been described was but preliminary to the drama itself, and that this drama was the trial of certain people for their lives. This we could guess, for after awhile the incantation ceased and the crowd in front of the big man with the cat upon his head opened out, while behind him a column of smoke rose into the air, as though light had been set to some sunk furnace.

Into the space that had thus been cleared were now led seven persons, whose hands were tied behind them. They were of both sexes and included an old man and a woman with a tall and handsome figure, who appeared to be quite young, scarcely more than a girl indeed. These seven were ranged in a line where they stood, clearly in great fear, for the old man fell upon his knees and one of the women began to sob. Thus they were left awhile, perhaps to allow the fire behind them to burn up, which it soon did with great fierceness, throwing a vivid light upon every detail of the spectacle.

Now all was ready, and a man brought a wooden tray to the red-bearded priest, who was seated on a stool, the white cat upon his knees, whither we had seen it leap from his head a little while before. He took the tray by its handles and at a word from him the cat jumped on to it and sat there. Then amidst the most intense silence he rose and uttered some prayer, apparently to the cat, which sat facing him. This done he turned the tray round so that the creature's back was now towards him, and, advancing to the line of prisoners, began to walk up and down in front of them, which he did several times, at each turn drawing a little nearer.

Holding out the tray, he presented it at the face of the prisoner on the left, whereon the cat rose, arched its back and began to lift its paws up and down. Presently he moved to the next prisoner and held it before him awhile, and so on till he came to the fifth, that young woman of whom I have spoken. Now the cat grew very angry, for in the death-like stillness we could hear it spitting and growling. At length it seemed to lift its paws and strike the girl upon the face, whereon she screamed aloud, a terrible scream. Then all the audience broke out into a shout, a single word, which we understood, for we had heard one very like it used by the people of the Plain. It was "Witch! Witch! Witch!"

Executioners who were waiting for the victim to be chosen in this ordeal by cat, rushed forward and seizing the girl began to drag her towards the fire. The prisoner who was standing by her and whom we rightly guessed to be her husband, tried to protect her, but his arms being bound, poor fellow, he could do nothing. One of the executioners knocked him down with a stick. For a moment his wife escaped and threw herself upon him, but the brutes lifted her up again, haling her towards the fire, whilst all the audience shouted wildly.

"I can't stand this," said Leo, "it's murder—coldblooded murder," and he drew his sword.

"Best leave the beasts alone," I answered doubtfully, though my own blood was boiling in my veins.

Whether he heard or not I do not know, for the next thing I saw was Leo rushing through the gate waving the Khan's sword and shouting at the top of his voice. Then I struck my heels into the ribs of the horse and followed after him. In ten seconds we were among them. As we came the savages fell back this way and that, staring at us amazed, for at first I think they took us for apparitions. Thus Leo on foot and I galloping after him, we came to the place.

The executioners and their victim were near the fire now—a very great fire of resinous pine logs built in a pit that measured about eight feet across. Close to it sat the priest upon his stool, watching the scene with a cruel smile, and rewarding the cat with little gobbets of raw meat, that he took from a leathern pouch at his side, occupations in which he was so deeply engaged that he never saw us until we were right on to him.

Shouting, "Leave her alone, you blackguards," Leo rushed at the executioners, and with a single blow of his sword severed the arm of one of them who gripped the woman by the nape of the neck.

With a yell of pain and rage the man sprang back and stood waving the stump towards the people and staring at it wildly. In the confusion that followed I saw the victim slip from the hands of her astonished would-be murderers and run into the darkness, where she vanished. Also I saw the witch-doctor spring up, still holding the tray on which the cat was sitting, and heard him begin to shout a perfect torrent of furious abuse at Leo, who in reply waved his sword and cursed him roundly in English and many other languages.

Then of a sudden the cat upon the tray, infuriated, I suppose, by the noise and the interruption of its meal, sprang straight at Leo's face. He appeared to catch it in mid-air with his left hand and with all his strength dashed it to the ground, where it lay writhing and screeching. Then, as though by an afterthought, he stooped, picked the devilish creature up again and hurled it into the heart of the fire, for he was mad with rage and knew not what he did.

At the sight of that awful sacrilege—for such it was to them who worshipped this beast—a gasp of horror rose from the spectators, followed by a howl of execration. Then like a wave of the sea they rushed at us. I saw Leo cut one man down, and next instant I was off the horse and being dragged towards the furnace. At the edge of it I met Leo in like plight, but fighting furiously, for his strength was great and they were half afraid of him.

"Why couldn't you leave the cat alone?" I shouted at him in idiotic remonstrance, for my brain had gone, and all I knew was that we were about to be thrown into the fiery pit. Already I was over it; I felt the flames singe my hair and saw its red caverns awaiting me, when of a sudden the brutal hands that held me were unloosed and I fell backwards to the ground, where I lay staring upwards.

This was what I saw. Standing in front of the fire, her draped form quivering as though with rage, was our ghostly-looking guide, who pointed with her hand at the gigantic, red-headed witch-doctor. But she was no longer alone, for with her were a score or more of men clad in white robes and armed with swords; black-eyed, ascetic-looking men, with clean-shaved heads and faces, for their scalps shone in the firelight.

At the sight of them terror had seized that multitude which, mad as goaded bulls but a few seconds before, now fled in every direction like sheep frightened by a wolf. The leader of the white-robed priests, a man with a gentle face, which when at rest was clothed in a perpetual smile, was addressing the medicine-man, and I understood something of his talk.

"Dog," he said in effect, speaking in a smooth, measured voice that yet was terrible, "accursed dog, beast-worshipper, what were you about to do to the guests of the mighty Mother of the Mountain? Is it for this that you and your idolatries have been spared so long? Answer, if you have anything to say. Answer quickly, for your time is short."

With a groan of fear the great fellow flung himself upon his knees, not to the head-priest who questioned him, but before the quivering shape of our guide, and to her put up half-articulate prayers for mercy.

"Cease," said the high-priest, "she is the Minister who judges and the Sword that strikes. I am the Ears and the Voice. Speak and tell me—were you about to cast those men, whom you were commanded to receive hospitably, into yonder fire because they saved the victim of your devilries and killed the imp you cherished? Nay, I saw it all. Know that it was but a trap set to catch you, who have been allowed to live too long."

But still the wretch writhed before the draped form and howled for mercy.

"Messenger," said the high-priest, "with thee the power goes. Declare thy decree."

Then our guide lifted her hand slowly and pointed to the fire. At once the man turned ghastly white, groaned and fell back, as I think, quite dead, slain by his own terror.

Now many of the people had fled, but some remained, and to these the priest called in cold tones, bidding them approach. They obeyed, creeping towards him.

"Look," he said, pointing to the man, "look and tremble at the justice of Hes the Mother. Aye, and be sure that as it is with him, so shall it be with every one of you who dares to defy her and to practise sorcery and murder. Lift up that dead dog who was your chief."

Some of them crept forward and did his bidding.

"Now, cast him into the bed which he had made ready for his victims."

Staggering forward to the edge of the flaming pit, they obeyed, and the great body fell with a crash amongst the burning boughs and vanished there.

"Listen, you people," said the priest, "and learn that this man deserved his dreadful doom. Know you why he purposed to kill that woman whom the strangers saved? Because his familiar marked her as a witch, you think. I tell you it was not so. It was because she being fair, he would have taken her from her husband, as he had taken many another, and she refused him. But the Eye saw, the Voice spoke, and the Messenger did judgment. He is caught in his own snare, and so shall you be, every one of you who dares to think evil in his heart or to do it with his hands.

"Such is the just decree of the Hesea, spoken by her from her throne amidst the fires of the Mountain."

One by one the terrified tribesmen crept away. When the last of them were gone the priest advanced to Leo and saluted him by placing his hand upon his forehead.

"Lord," he said, in the same corrupt Grecian dialect which was used by the courtiers of Kaloon, "I will not ask if you are hurt, since from the moment that you entered the sacred river and set foot within this land you and your companion were protected by a power invisible and could not be harmed by man or spirit, however great may have seemed your danger. Yet vile hands have been laid upon you, and this is the command of the Mother whom I serve, that, if you desire it, every one of those men who touched you shall die before your eyes. Say, is that your will?"

"Nay," answered Leo; "they were mad and blind, let no blood be shed for us. All we ask of you, friend—but, how are you called?"

"Name me Oros," he answered.

"Friend Oros—a good title for one who dwells upon the Mountain—all we ask is food and shelter, and to be led swiftly into the presence of her whom you name Mother, that Oracle whose wisdom we have travelled far to seek."

He bowed and answered: "The food and shelter are prepared and to-morrow, when you have rested, I am commanded to conduct you whither you desire to be. Follow me, I pray you"; and he preceded us past the fiery pit to a building that stood about fifty yards away against the rock wall of the amphitheatre.

It would seem that it was a guest-house, or at least had been made ready to serve that purpose, as in it lamps were lit and a fire burned, for here the air was cold. The house was divided into two rooms, the second of them a sleeping place, to which he led us through the first.

"Enter," he said, "for you will need to cleanse yourselves, and you"—here he addressed himself to me—"to be treated for that hurt to your arm which you had from the jaws of the great hound."

"How know you that?" I asked.

"It matters not if I do know and have made ready," Oros answered gravely.

This second room was lighted and warmed like the first, moreover, heated water stood in basins of metal and on the beds were laid clean linen garments and dark-coloured hooded robes, lined with rich fur. Also upon a little table were ointments, bandages, and splints, a marvellous thing to see, for it told me that the very nature of my hurt had been divined. But I asked no more questions; I was too weary; moreover, I knew that it would be useless.

Now the priest Oros helped me to remove my tattered robe, and, undoing the rough bandages upon my arm, washed it gently with warm water, in which he mixed some spirit, and examined it with the skill of a trained doctor.

"The fangs rent deep," he said, "and the small bone is broken, but you will take no harm, save for the scars which must remain." Then, having treated the wounds with ointment, he wrapped the limb with such a delicate touch that it scarcely pained me, saying that by the morrow the swelling would have gone down and he would set the bone. This indeed happened.

After it was done he helped me to wash and to clothe myself in the clean garments, and put a sling about my neck to serve as a rest for my arm. Meanwhile Leo had also dressed himself, so that we left the chamber together very different men to the foul, blood-stained wanderers who had entered there. In the outer room we found food prepared for us, of which we ate with a thankful heart and without speaking. Then, blind with weariness, we returned to the other chamber and, having removed our outer garments, flung ourselves upon the beds and were soon plunged in sleep.

At some time in the night I awoke suddenly, at what hour I do not know, as certain people wake, I among them, when their room is entered, even without the slightest noise. Before I opened my eyes I felt that some one was with us in the place. Nor was I mistaken. A little lamp still burned in the chamber, a mere wick floating in oil, and by its light I saw a dim, ghost-like form standing near the door. Indeed I thought almost that it was a ghost, till presently I remembered, and knew it for our corpse-like guide, who appeared to be looking intently at the bed on which Leo lay, or so I thought, for the head was bent in that direction.

At first she was quite still, then she moaned aloud, a low and terrible moan, which seemed to well from the very heart.

So the thing was not dumb, as I had believed. Evidently it could suffer, and express its suffering in a human fashion. Look! it was wringing its padded hands as in an excess of woe. Now it would seem that Leo began to feel its influence also, for he stirred and spoke in his sleep, so low at first that I could only distinguish the tongue he used, which was Arabic. Presently I caught a few words.

"Ayesha," he said, "Ayesha!"

The figure glided towards him and stopped. He sat up in the bed still fast asleep, for his eyes were shut. He stretched out his arms, as though seeking one whom he would embrace, and spoke again in a low and passionate voice—"Ayesha, through life and death I have sought thee long. Come to me, my goddess, my desired."

The figure glided yet nearer, and I could see that it was trembling, and now its arms were extended also.

At the bedside she halted, and Leo laid himself down again. Now the coverings had fallen back, exposing his breast, where lay the leather satchel he always wore, that which contained the lock of Ayesha's hair. He was fast asleep, and the figure seemed to fix its eyes upon this satchel. Presently it did more, for, with surprising deftness those white-wrapped fingers opened its clasp, yes, and drew out the long tress of shining hair. Long and earnestly she gazed at it, then gently replaced the relic, closed the satchel and for a little while seemed to weep. While she stood thus the dreaming Leo once more stretched out his arms and spoke, saying, in the same passion-laden voice—"Come to me, my darling, my beautiful, my beautiful!"

At those words, with a little muffled scream, like that of a scared night-bird, the figure turned and flitted through the doorway.

When I was quite certain that she had gone, I gasped aloud.

What might this mean, I wondered, in a very agony of bewilderment. This could certainly be no dream: it was real, for I was wide awake. Indeed, what did it all mean? Who was the ghastly, mummy-like thing which had guided us unharmed through such terrible dangers; the Messenger that all men feared, who could strike down a brawny savage with a motion of its hand? Why did it creep into the place thus at dead of night, like a spirit revisiting one beloved? Why did its presence cause me to awake and Leo to dream? Why did it draw out the tress; indeed, how knew it that this tress was hidden there? And why—oh! why, at those tender and passionate words did it flit away at last like some scared bat?

The priest Oros had called our guide Minister, and Sword, that is, one who carries out decrees. But what if they were its own decrees? What if this thing should be she whom we sought, Ayesha herself? Why should I tremble at the thought, seeing that if so, our quest was ended, we had achieved? Oh! it must be because about this being there was something terrible, something un-human and appalling. If Ayesha lived within those mummy-cloths, then it was a different Ayesha whom we had known and worshipped. Well could I remember the white-draped form of She-Who-Must-Be-Obeyed, and how, long before she revealed her glorious face to us, we guessed the beauty and the majesty hidden beneath that veil by which her radiant life and loveliness incarnate could not be disguised.

But what of this creature? I would not pursue the thought. I was mistaken. Doubtless she was what the priest Oros had said—some half-supernatural being to whom certain powers were given, and, doubtless, she had come to spy on us in our rest that she might make report to the giver of those powers.

Comforting myself thus I fell asleep again, for fatigue overcame even such doubts and fears. In the morning, when they were naturally less vivid, I made up my mind that, for various reasons, it would be wisest to say nothing of what I had seen to Leo. Nor, indeed, did I do so until some days had gone by.

When I awoke the full light was pouring into the chamber, and by it I saw the priest Oros standing at my bedside. I sat up and asked him what time it was, to which he answered with a smile, but in a low voice, that it lacked but two hours of mid-day, adding that he had come to set my arm. Now I saw why he spoke low, for Leo was still fast asleep.

"Let him rest on," he said, as he undid the wrappings on my arm, "for he has suffered much, and," he continued significantly, "may still have more to suffer."

"What do you mean, friend Oros?" I asked sharply. "I thought you told us that we were safe upon this Mountain."

"I told you, friend——" and he looked at me.

"Holly is my name——"

"—friend Holly, that your bodies are safe. I said nothing of all the rest of you. Man is more than flesh and blood. He is mind and spirit as well, and these can be injured also."

"Who is there that would injure them?" I asked.

"Friend," he answered, gravely, "you and your companion have come to a haunted land, not as mere wanderers, for then you would be dead ere now, but of set purpose, seeking to lift the veil from mysteries which have been hid for ages. Well, your aim is known and it may chance that it will be achieved. But if this veil is lifted, it may chance also that you will find what shall send your souls shivering to despair and madness. Say, are you not afraid?"

"Somewhat," I answered. "Yet my foster-son and I have seen strange things and lived. We have seen the very Light of Life roll by in majesty; we have been the guests of an Immortal, and watched Death seem to conquer her and leave us untouched. Think you then that we will turn cowards now? Nay, we march on to fulfil our destinies."

At these words Oros showed neither curiosity nor surprise; it was as though I told him only what he knew.

"Good," he replied, smiling, and with a courteous bow of his shaven head, "within an hour you shall march on—to fulfil your destinies. If I have warned you, forgive me, for I was bidden so to do, perhaps to try your mettle. Is it needful that I should repeat this warning to the lord——" and again he looked at me.

"Leo Vincey," I said.

"Leo Vincey, yes, Leo Vincey," he repeated, as though the name were familiar to him but had slipped his mind. "But you have not answered my question. Is it needful that I should repeat the warning?"

"Not in the least; but you can do so if you wish when he awakes."

"Nay, I think with you, that it would be but waste of words, for—forgive the comparison;—what the wolf dares"—and he looked at me—"the tiger does not flee from," and he nodded towards Leo. "There, see how much better are the wounds upon your arm, which is no longer swollen. Now I will bandage it, and within some few weeks the bone will be as sound again as it was before you met the Khan Rassen hunting in the Plains. By the way, you will see him again soon, and his fair wife with him."

"See him again? Do the dead, then, come to life upon this Mountain?"

"Nay, but certain of them are brought hither for burial. It is the privilege of the rulers of Kaloon; also, I think, that the Khania has questions to ask of its Oracle."

"Who is its Oracle?" I asked with eagerness.

"The Oracle," he replied darkly, "is a Voice. It was ever so, was it not?"

"Yes; I have heard that from Atene, but a voice implies a speaker. Is this speaker she whom you name Mother?"

"Perhaps, friend Holly."

"And is this Mother a spirit?"

"It is a point that has been much debated. They told you so in the Plains, did they not? Also the Tribes think it on the Mountain. Indeed, the thing seems reasonable, seeing that all of us who live are flesh and spirit. But you will form your own judgment and then we can discuss the matter. There, your arm is finished. Be careful now not to strike it or to fall, and look, your companion awakes."

Something over an hour later we started upon our upward journey. I was again mounted on the Khan's horse, which having been groomed and fed was somewhat rested, while to Leo a litter had been offered. This he declined, however, saying that he had now recovered and would not be carried like a woman. So he walked by the side of my horse, using his spear as a staff. We passed the fire-pit—now full of dead, white ashes, among which were mixed those of the witch-finder and his horrible cat—preceded by our dumb guide, at the sight of whom, in her pale wrappings, the people of the tribe who had returned to their village prostrated themselves, and so remained until she was gone by.

One of them, however, rose again and, breaking through our escort of priests, ran to Leo, knelt before him and kissed his hand. It was that young woman whose life he had saved, a noble-looking girl, with masses of red hair, and by her was her husband, the marks of his bonds still showing on his arms. Our guide seemed to see this incident, though how she did so I do not know. At any rate she turned and made some sign which the priest interpreted.

Calling the woman to him he asked her sternly how she dared to touch the person of this stranger with her vile lips. She answered that it was because her heart was grateful. Oros said that for this reason she was forgiven; moreover, that in reward for what they had suffered he was commanded to lift up her husband to be the ruler of that tribe during the pleasure of the Mother. He gave notice, moreover, that all should obey the new chief in his place, according to their customs, and if he did any evil, make report that he might suffer punishment. Then waving the pair aside, without listening to their thanks or the acclamations of the crowd, he passed on.

As we went down the ravine by which we had approached the village on the previous night, a sound of chanting struck our ears. Presently the path turned, and we saw a solemn procession advancing up that dismal, sunless gorge. At the head of it rode none other than the beautiful Khania, followed by her great-uncle, the old Shaman, and after these came a company of shaven priests in their white robes, bearing between them a bier, upon which, its face uncovered, lay the body of the Khan, draped in a black garment. Yet he looked better thus than he had ever done, for now death had touched this insane and dissolute man with something of the dignity which he lacked in life.

Thus then we met. At the sight of our guide's white form, the horse which the Khania rode reared up so violently that I thought it would have thrown her. But she mastered the animal with her whip and voice, and called out—"Who is this draped hag of the Mountain that stops the path of the Khania Atene and her dead lord? My guests, I find you in ill company, for it seems that you are conducted by an evil spirit to meet an evil fate. That guide of yours must surely be something hateful and hideous, for were she a wholesome woman she would not fear to show her face."

Now the Shaman plucked his mistress by the sleeve, and the priest Oros, bowing to her, prayed her to be silent and cease to speak such ill-omened words into the air, which might carry them she knew not whither. But some instinctive hate seemed to bubble up in Atene, and she would not be silent, for she addressed our guide using the direct "thou," a manner of speech that we found was very usual on the Mountain though rare upon the Plains.

"Let the air carry them whither it will," she cried. "Sorceress, strip off thy rags, fit only for a corpse too vile to view. Show us what thou art, thou flitting night-owl, who thinkest to frighten me with that livery of death, which only serves to hide the death within."

"Cease, I pray lady, cease," said Oros, stirred for once out of his imperturbable calm. "She is the Minister, none other, and with her goes the Power."

"Then it goes not against Atene, Khania of Kaloon," she answered, "or so I think. Power, forsooth! Let her show her power. If she has any it is not her own, but that of the Witch of the Mountain, who feigns to be a spirit, and by her sorceries has drawn away my guests"—and she pointed to us—"thus bringing my husband to his death."

"Niece, be silent!" said the old Shaman, whose wrinkled face was white with terror, whilst Oros held up his hands as though in supplication to some unseen Strength, saying—"O thou that hearest and seest, be merciful, I beseech thee, and forgive this woman her madness, lest the blood of a guest should stain the hands of thy servants, and the ancient honour of our worship be brought low in the eyes of men."

Thus he prayed, but although his hands were uplifted, it seemed to me that his eyes were fixed upon our guide, as ours were. While he spoke, I saw her hand raised, as she had raised it when she slew or rather sentenced the witch-doctor. Then she seemed to reflect, and stayed it in mid air, so that it pointed at the Khania. She did not move, she made no sound, only she pointed, and the angry words died upon Atene's lips, the fury left her eyes, and the colour her face. Yes, she grew white and silent as the corpse upon the bier behind her. Then, cowed by that invisible power, she struck her horse so fiercely that it bounded by us onward towards the village, at which the funeral company were to rest awhile.

As the Shaman Simbri followed the Khania, the priest Oros caught his horse's bridle and said to him—"Magician, we have met before, for instance, when your lady's father was brought to his funeral. Warn her, then, you that know something of the truth and of her power to speak more gently of the ruler of this land. Say to her, from me, that had she not been the ambassadress of death, and, therefore, inviolate, surely ere now she would have shared her husband's bier. Farewell, tomorrow we will speak again," and, loosing the Shaman's bridle, Oros passed on.

Soon we had left the melancholy procession behind us and, issuing from the gorge, turned up the Mountain slope towards the edge of the bright snows that lay not far above. It was as we came out of this darksome valley, where the overhanging pine trees almost eclipsed the light, that suddenly we missed our guide.

"Has she gone back to—to reason with the Khania?" I asked of Oros.

"Nay!" he answered, with a slight smile, "I think that she has gone forward to give warning that the Hesea's guests draw near."

"Indeed," I answered, staring hard at the bare slope of mountain, up which not a mouse could have passed without being seen. "I understand—she has gone forward," and the matter dropped. But what I did not understand was—how she had gone. As the Mountain was honeycombed with caves and galleries, I suppose, however, that she entered one of them.

All the rest of that day we marched upwards, gradually drawing nearer to the snow-line, as we went gathering what information we could from the priest Oros. This was the sum of it—From the beginning of the world, as he expressed it, that is, from thousands and thousands of years ago, this Mountain had been the home of a peculiar fire-worship, of which the head heirophant was a woman. About twenty centuries before, however, the invading general named Rassen, had made himself Khan of Kaloon. Rassen established a new priestess on the Mountain, a worshipper of the Egyptian goddess, Hes, or Isis. This priestess had introduced certain modifications in the ancient doctrines, superseding the cult of fire, pure and simple, by a new faith, which, while holding to some of the old ceremonies, revered as its head the Spirit of Life or Nature, of whom they looked upon their priestess as the earthly representative.

Of this priestess Oros would only tell us that she was "ever present," although we gathered that when one priestess died or was "taken to the fire," as he put it, her child, whether in fact or by adoption, succeeded her and was known by the same names, those of "Hes" or the "Hesea" and "Mother." We asked if we should see this Mother, to which he answered that she manifested herself very rarely. As to her appearance and attributes he would say nothing, except that the former changed from time to time and that when she chose to use it she had "all power."

The priests of her College, he informed us, numbered three hundred, never more nor less, and there were also three hundred priestesses. Certain of those who desired it were allowed to marry, and from among their children were reared up the new generation of priests and priestesses. Thus they were a people apart from all others, with distinct racial characteristics. This, indeed, was evident, for our escort were all exceedingly like to each other, very handsome and refined in appearance, with dark eyes, clean-cut features and olive-hued skins; such a people as might well have descended from Easterns of high blood, with a dash of that of the Egyptians and Greeks thrown in.

We asked him whether the mighty looped pillar that towered from the topmost cup of the Mountain was the work of men. He answered, No; the hand of Nature had fashioned it, and that the light shining through it came from the fires which burned in the crater of the volcano. The first priestess, having recognized in this gigantic column the familiar Symbol of Life of the Egyptian worship, established her altars beneath its shadow.

For the rest, the Mountain with its mighty slopes and borderlands was peopled by a multitude of half-savage folk, who accepted the rule of the Hesea, bringing her tribute of all things necessary, such as food and metals. Much of the meat and grain however the priests raised themselves on sheltered farms, and the metals they worked with their own hands. This rule, however, was of a moral nature, since for centuries the College had sought no conquests and the Mother contented herself with punishing crime in some such fashion as we had seen. For the petty wars between the Tribes and the people of the Plain they were not responsible, and those chiefs who carried them on were deposed, unless they had themselves been attacked. All the Tribes, however, were sworn to the defence of the Hesea and the College, and, however much they might quarrel amongst themselves, if need arose, were ready to die for her to the last man. That war must one day break out again between the priests of the Mountain and the people of Kaloon was recognized; therefore they endeavoured to be prepared for that great and final struggle.

Such was the gist of his history, which, as we learned afterwards, proved to be true in every particular.

Towards sundown we came to a vast cup extending over many thousand acres, situated beneath the snow-line of the peak and filled with rich soil washed down, I suppose, from above. So sheltered was the place by its configuration and the over-hanging mountain that, facing south-west as it did, notwithstanding its altitude it produced corn and other temperate crops in abundance. Here the College had its farms, and very well cultivated these seemed to be. This great cup, which could not be seen from below, we entered through a kind of natural gateway, that might be easily defended against a host.

There were other peculiarities, but it is not necessary to describe them further than to say that I think the soil benefited by the natural heat of the volcano, and that when this erupted, as happened occasionally, the lava streams always passed to the north and south of the cup of land. Indeed, it was these lava streams that had built up the protecting cliffs.

Crossing the garden-like lands, we came to a small town beautifully built of lava rock. Here dwelt the priests, except those who were on duty, no man of the Tribes or other stranger being allowed to set foot within the place.

Following the main street of this town, we arrived at the face of the precipice beyond, and found ourselves in front of a vast archway, closed with massive iron gates fantastically wrought. Here, taking my horse with them, our escort left us alone with Oros. As we drew near the great gates swung back upon their hinges. We passed them—with what sensations I cannot describe—and groped our way down a short corridor which ended in tall, iron-covered doors. These also rolled open at our approach, and next instant we staggered back amazed and half-blinded by the intense blaze of light within.

Imagine, you who read, the nave of the vastest cathedral with which you are acquainted. Then double or treble its size, and you will have some conception of that temple in which we found ourselves. Perhaps in the beginning it had been a cave, who can say? but now its sheer walls, its multitudinous columns springing to the arched roof far above us, had all been worked on and fashioned by the labour of men long dead; doubtless the old fire-worshippers of thousands of years ago.

You will wonder how so great a place was lighted, but I think that never would you guess. Thus—by twisted columns of living flame! I counted eighteen of them, but there may have been others. They sprang from the floor at regular intervals along the lines of what in a cathedral would be the aisles. Right to the roof they sprang, of even height and girth, so fierce was the force of the natural gas that drove them, and there were lost, I suppose, through chimneys bored in the thickness of the rock. Nor did they give off smell or smoke, or in that great, cold place, any heat which could be noticed, only an intense white light like that of molten iron, and a sharp hissing noise as of a million angry snakes.

The huge temple was utterly deserted, and, save for this sybilant, pervading sound, utterly silent; an awesome, an overpowering place.

"Do these candles of yours ever go out?" asked Leo of Oros, placing his hand before his dazzled eyes.

"How can they," replied the priest, in his smooth, matter-of-fact voice, "seeing that they rise from the eternal fire which the builders of this hall worshipped? Thus they have burned from the beginning, and thus they will burn for ever, though, if we wish it, we can shut off their light.* Be pleased to follow me: you will see greater things."

So in awed silence we followed, and, oh! how small and miserable we three human beings looked alone in that vast temple illuminated by this lightning radiance. We reached the end of it at length, only to find that to right and left ran transepts on a like gigantic scale and lit in the same

---

* This, as I ascertained afterwards, was done by thrusting a broad stone of great thickness over the apertures through which the gas or fire rushed and thus cutting off the air. These stones were worked to and fro by means of pulleys connected with iron rods.

—L. H. H.

amazing fashion. Here Oros bade us halt, and we waited a little while, till presently, from either transept arose a sound of chanting, and we perceived two white-robed processions advancing towards us from their depths.

On they came, very slowly, and we saw that the procession to the right was a company of priests, and that to the left a company of priestesses, a hundred or so of them in all.

Now the men ranged themselves in front of us, while the women ranged themselves behind, and at a signal from Oros, all of them still chanting some wild and thrilling hymn, once more we started forward, this time along a narrow gallery closed at the end with double wooden doors. As our procession reached these they opened, and before us lay the crowning wonder of this marvellous fane, a vast, ellipse-shaped apse. Now we understood. The plan of the temple was the plan of the looped pillar which stood upon the brow of the Peak, and as we rightly guessed, its dimensions were the same.

At intervals around this ellipse the fiery columns flared, but otherwise the place was empty.

No, not quite, for at the head of the apse, almost between two of the flame columns, stood a plain, square altar of the size of a small room, in front of which, as we saw when we drew nearer, were hung curtains of woven silver thread. On this altar was placed a large statue of silver, that, backed as it was by the black rock, seemed to concentrate and reflect from its burnished surface the intense light of the two blazing pillars.

It was a lovely thing, but to describe it is hard indeed. The figure, which was winged, represented a draped woman of mature years, and pure but gracious form, half hidden by the forward-bending wings. Sheltered by these, yet shown between them, appeared the image of a male child, clasped to its bearer's breast with her left arm, while the right was raised toward the sky. A study of Motherhood, evidently, but how shall I write of all that was conveyed by those graven faces?

To begin with the child. It was that of a sturdy boy, full of health and the joy of life. Yet he had been sleeping, and in his sleep some terror had over-shadowed him with the dark shades of death and evil. There was fear in the lines of his sweet mouth and on the lips and cheeks, that seemed to quiver. He had thrown his little arm about his mother's neck, and, pressing close against her breast, looked up to her for safety, his right hand and outstretched finger pointing downwards and behind him, as though to indicate whence the danger came. Yet it was passing, already half-forgotten, for the upturned eyes expressed confidence renewed, peace of soul attained.

And the mother. She did not seem to mock or chide his fears, for her lovely face was anxious and alert. Yet upon it breathed a very atmosphere of unchanging tenderness and power invincible; care for the helpless, strength to shelter it from every harm. The great, calm eyes told their story, the parted lips were whispering some tale of hope, sure and immortal; the raised hand revealed whence that hope arose. All love seemed to be concentrated in the brooding figure, so human, yet so celestial; all heaven seemed to lie an open path before those quivering wings. And see, the arching instep, the upward-springing foot, suggested that thither those wings were bound, bearing their God-given burden far from the horror of the earth, deep into the bosom of a changeless rest above.

The statue was only that of an affrighted child in its mother's arms; its interpretation made clear even to the dullest by the simple symbolism of some genius—Humanity saved by the Divine.

While we gazed at its enchanting beauty, the priests and priestesses, filing away to right and left, arranged themselves alternately, first a man and then a woman, within the ring of the columns of fire that burned around the loop-shaped shrine. So great was its circumference that the whole hundred of them must stand wide apart one from another, and, to our sight, resembled little lonely children clad in gleaming garments, while their chant of worship reached us only like echoes thrown from a far precipice. In short, the effect of this holy shrine and its occupants was superb yet overwhelming, at least I know that it filled me with a feeling akin to fear.

Oros waited till the last priest had reached his appointed place. Then he turned and said, in his gentle, reverent tones—"Draw nigh, now, O Wanderers well-beloved, and give greeting to the Mother," and he pointed towards the statue.

"Where is she?" asked Leo, in a whisper, for here we scarcely dared to speak aloud. "I see no one."

"The Hesea dwells yonder," he answered, and, taking each of us by the hand, he led us forward across the great emptiness of the apse to the altar at its head.

As we drew near the distant chant of the priests gathered in volume, assuming a glad, triumphant note, and it seemed to me—though this, perhaps was fancy—that the light from the twisted columns of flame grew even brighter.

At length we were there, and, Oros, loosing our hands, prostrated himself thrice before the altar. Then he rose again, and, falling behind us, stood in silence with bent head and folded fingers. We stood silent also, our hearts filled with mingled hope and fear like a cup with wine.

Were our labours ended? Had we found her whom we sought, or were we, perchance, but enmeshed in the web of some marvellous mummery and about to make acquaintance with the secret of another new and mystical worship? For years and years we had searched, enduring every hardness of flesh and spirit that man can suffer, and now we were to learn whether we had endured in vain. Yes, and Leo would learn if the promise was to be fulfilled to him, or whether she whom he adored had become but a departed dream to be sought for only beyond the gate of Death. Little wonder that he trembled and turned white in the agony of that great suspense.

Long, long was the time. Hours, years, ages, aeons, seemed to flow over us as we stood there before glittering silver curtains that hid the front of the black altar beneath the mystery of the sphinx-like face of the glorious image which was its guardian, clothed with that frozen smile of eternal love and pity. All the past went before us as we struggled in those dark waters of our doubt. Item by item, event by event, we rehearsed the story which began in the Caves of Kor, for our thoughts, so long attuned, were open to each other and flashed from soul to soul.

Oh! now we knew, they were open also to another soul. We could see nothing save the Altar and the Effigy, we could only hear the slow chant of the priests and priestesses and the snake-like hiss of the rushing fires. Yet we knew that our hearts were as an open book to One who watched beneath the Mother's shadowing wings.

Now the curtains were open. Before us appeared a chamber hollowed from the thickness of the altar, and in its centre a throne, and on the throne a figure clad in waves of billowy white flowing from the head over the arms of the throne down to its marble steps. We could see no more in the comparative darkness of that place, save that beneath the folds of the drapery the Oracle held in its hand a loop-shaped, jewelled sceptre.

Moved by some impulse, we did as Oros had done, prostrating ourselves, and there remained upon our knees. At length we heard a tinkling as of little bells, and, looking up, saw that the sistrum-shaped sceptre was stretched towards us by the draped arm which held it. Then a thin, clear voice spoke, and I thought that it trembled a little. It spoke in Greek, but in a much purer Greek than all these people used.

"I greet you, Wanderers, who have journeyed so far to visit this most ancient shrine, and although doubtless of some other faith, are not ashamed to do reverence to that unworthy one who is for this time its Oracle and the guardian of its mysteries. Rise now and have no fear of me; for have I not sent my Messenger and servants to conduct you to this Sanctuary?"

Slowly we rose, and stood silent, not knowing what to say.

"I greet you, Wanderers," the voice repeated. "Tell me thou"—and the sceptre pointed towards Leo—"how art thou named?"

"I am named Leo Vincey," he answered.

"Leo Vincey! I like the name, which to me well befits a man so goodly. And thou, the companion of—Leo Vincey?"

"I am named Horace Holly."

"So. Then tell me, Leo Vincey and Horace Holly, what came ye so far to seek?"

We looked at each other, and I said—"The tale is long and strange. O—but by what title must we address thee?"

"By the name which I bear here, Hes."

"O Hes," I said, wondering what name she bore elsewhere.

"Yet I desire to hear that tale," she went on, and to me her voice sounded eager. "Nay, not all to-night, for I know that you both are weary; a little of it only. In sooth, Strangers, there is a sameness in this home of contemplations, and no heart can feed only on the past, if such a thing there be. Therefore I welcome a new history from the world without. Tell it me, thou, Leo, as briefly as thou wilt, so that thou tell the truth, for in the Presence of which I am a Minister, may nothing else be uttered."

"Priestess," he said, in his curt fashion, "I obey. Many years ago when I was young, my friend and foster-father and I, led by records of the past, travelled to a wild land, and there found a certain divine woman who had conquered time."

"Then that woman must have been both aged and hideous."

"I said, Priestess, that she had conquered time, not suffered it, for the gift of immortal youth was hers. Also she was not hideous; she was beauty itself."

"Therefore stranger, thou didst worship her for her beauty's sake, as a man does."

"I did not worship her; I loved her, which is another thing. The priest Oros here worships thee, whom he calls Mother. I loved that immortal woman."

"Then thou shouldst love her still. Yet, not so, since love is very mortal."

"I love her still," he answered, "although she died."

"Why, how is that? Thou saidst she was immortal."

"Perchance she only seemed to die; perchance she changed. At least I lost her, and what I lost I seek, and have sought this many a year."

"Why dost thou seek her in my Mountain, Leo Vincey?"

"Because a vision led me to ask counsel of its Oracle. I am come hither to learn tidings of my lost love, since here alone these may be found."

"And thou, Holly, didst thou also love an immortal woman whose immortality, it seems, must bow to death?"

"Priestess," I answered, "I am sworn to this quest, and where my foster-son goes I follow. He follows beauty that is dead——"

"And thou dost follow him. Therefore both of you follow beauty as men have ever done, being blind and mad."

"Nay," I answered, "if they were blind, beauty would be naught to them who could not see it, and if they were mad, they would not know it when it was seen. Knowledge and vision belong to the wise, O Hes."

"Thou art quick of wit and tongue, Holly, as——" and she checked herself, then of a sudden, said, "Tell me, did my servant the Khania of

Kaloon entertain both of you hospitably in her city, and speed you on your journey hither, as I commanded her?"

"We knew not that she was thy servant," I replied. "Hospitality we had and to spare, but we were sped from her Court hitherward by the death-hounds of the Khan, her husband. Tell us, Priestess, what thou knowest of this journey of ours."

"A little," she answered carelessly. "More than three moons ago my spies saw you upon the far mountains, and, creeping very close to you at night, heard you speak together of the object of your wanderings, then, returning thence swiftly, made report to me. Thereon I bade the Khania Atene, and that old magician her great-uncle, who is Guardian of the Gate, go down to the ancient gates of Kaloon to receive you and bring you hither with all speed. Yet for men who burned to learn the answer to a riddle, you have been long in coming."

"We came as fast as we might, O Hes," said Leo; "and if thy spies could visit those mountains, where no man was, and find a path down that hideous precipice, they must have been able also to tell thee the reason of our delay. Therefore I pray, ask it not of us."

"Nay, I will ask it of Atene herself, and she shall surely answer me, for she stands without," replied the Hesea in a cold voice. "Oros, lead the Khania hither and be swift."

The priest turned and walking quickly to the wooden doors by which we had entered the shrine, vanished there.

"Now," said Leo to me nervously in the silence that followed, and speaking in English, "now I wish we were somewhere else, for I think that there will be trouble."

"I don't think, I am sure," I answered; "but the more the better, for out of trouble may come the truth, which we need sorely." Then I stopped, reflecting that the strange woman before us said that her spies had overheard our talk upon the mountains, where we had spoken nothing but English.

As it proved, I was wise, for quite quietly the Hesea repeated after me—"Thou hast experience, Holly, for out of trouble comes the truth, as out of wine."

Then she was silent, and, needless to say, I did not pursue the conversation.

The doors swung open, and through them came a procession clad in black, followed by the Shaman Simbri, who walked in front of a bier, upon which lay the body of the Khan, carried by eight priests. Behind it was Atene, draped in a black veil from head to foot, and after her marched another company of priests. In front of the altar the bier was set down and the priests fell back, leaving Atene and her uncle standing alone before the corpse.

"What seeks my vassal, the Khania of Kaloon?" asked the Hesea in a cold voice.

Now Atene advanced and bent the knee, but with little graciousness.

"Ancient Mother, Mother from of old, I do reverence to thy holy Office, as my forefathers have done for many a generation," and again she curtseyed. "Mother, this dead man asks of thee that right of sepulchre in the fires of the holy Mountain which from the beginning has been accorded to the royal departed who went before him."

"It has been accorded as thou sayest," answered the Hesea, "by those priestesses who filled my place before me, nor shall it be refused to thy dead lord—or to thee Atene—when thy time comes."

"I thank thee, O Hes, and I pray that this decree may be written down, for the snows of age have gathered on thy venerable head and soon thou must leave us for awhile. Therefore bid thy scribes that it be written down, so that the Hesea who rules after thee may fulfil it in its season."

"Cease," said the Hesea, "cease to pour out thy bitterness at that which should command thy reverence, oh! thou foolish child, who dost not know but that to-morrow the fire shall claim the frail youth and beauty which are thy boast. I bid thee cease, and tell me how did death find this lord of thine?"

"Ask those wanderers yonder, that were his guests, for his blood is on their heads and cries for vengeance at thy hands."

"I killed him," said Leo, "to save my own life. He tried to hunt us down with his dogs, and there are the marks of them," and he pointed to my arm. "The priest Oros knows, for he dressed the hurts."

"How did this chance?" asked the Hesea of Atene.

"My lord was mad," she answered boldly, "and such was his cruel sport."

"So. And was thy lord jealous also? Nay, keep back the falsehood I see rising to thy lips. Leo Vincey, answer thou me. Yet, I will not ask thee to lay bare the secrets of a woman who has offered thee her love. Thou, Holly, speak, and let it be the truth."

"It is this, O Hes," I answered. "Yonder lady and her uncle the Shaman

Simbri saved us from death in the waters of the river that bounds the precipices of Kaloon. Afterwards we were ill, and they treated us kindly, but the Khania became enamoured of my foster-son."

Here the figure of the Priestess stirred beneath its gauzy wrappings, and the Voice asked—"And did thy foster-son become enamoured of the Khania, as being a man he may well have done, for without doubt she is fair?"

"He can answer that question for himself, O Hes. All I know is that he strove to escape from her, and that in the end she gave him a day to choose between death and marriage with her, when her lord should be dead. So, helped by the Khan, her husband, who was jealous of him, we fled towards this Mountain, which we desired to reach. Then the Khan set his hounds upon us, for he was mad and false-hearted. We killed him and came on in spite of this lady, his wife, and her uncle, who would have prevented us, and were met in a Place of Bones by a certain veiled guide, who led us up the Mountain and twice saved us from death. That is all the story."

"Woman, what hast thou to say?" asked the Hesea in a menacing voice.

"But little," Atene answered, without flinching. "For years I have been bound to a madman and a brute, and if my fancy wandered towards this man and his fancy wandered towards me—well, Nature spoke to us, and that is all. Afterwards it seems that he grew afraid of the vengeance of Rassen, or this Holly, whom I would that the hounds had torn bone from bone, grew afraid. So they strove to escape the land, and perchance wandered to thy Mountain. But I weary of this talk, and ask thy leave to rest before to-morrow's rite."

"Thou sayest, Atene," said the Hesea, "that Nature spoke to this man and to thee, and that his heart is thine; but that, fearing thy lord's vengeance, he fled from thee, he who seems no coward. Tell me, then, is that tress he hides in the satchel on his breast thy gage of love to him?"

"I know nothing of what he hides in the satchel," answered the Khania sullenly.

"And yet, yonder in the Gatehouse when he lay so sick he set the lock against thine own—ah, dost remember now?"

"So, O Hes, already he has told thee all our secrets, though they be such as most men hide within their breasts;" and she looked contemptuously at Leo.

"I told her nothing of the matter, Khania," Leo said in an angry voice.

"Nay, thou toldest me nothing, Wanderer; my watching wisdom told me. Oh, didst thou think, Atene, that thou couldst hide the truth from the all-seeing Hesea of the Mountain? If so, spare thy breath, for I know all, and have known it from the first. I passed thy disobedience by; of thy false messages I took no heed. For my own purposes I, to whom time is naught, suffered even that thou shouldst hold these, my guests, thy prisoners whilst thou didst strive by threats and force to win a love denied."

She paused, then went on coldly: "Woman, I tell thee that, to complete thy sin, thou hast even dared to lie to me here, in my very Sanctuary."

"If so, what of it?" was the bold answer. "Dost thou love the man thyself? Nay, it is monstrous. Nature would cry aloud at such a shame. Oh! tremble not with rage. Hes, I know thy evil powers, but I know also that I am thy guest, and that in this hallowed place, beneath yonder symbol of eternal Love, thou may'st shed no blood. More, thou canst not harm me, Hes, who am thy equal."

"Atene," replied the measured Voice, "did I desire it, I could destroy thee where thou art. Yet thou art right, I shall not harm thee, thou faithless servant. Did not my writ bid thee through yonder searcher of the stars, thy uncle, to meet these guests of mine and bring them straight to my shrine? Tell me, for I seek to know, how comes it that thou didst disobey me?"

"Have then thy desire," answered Atene in a new and earnest voice, devoid now of bitterness and falsehood. "I disobeyed because that man is not thine, but mine, and no other woman's; because I love him and have loved him from of old. Aye, since first our souls sprang into life I have loved him, as he has loved me. My own heart tells me so; the magic of my uncle here tells me so, though how and where and when these things have been I know not. Therefore I come to thee, Mother of Mysteries, Guardian of the secrets of the past, to learn the truth. At least thou canst not lie at thine own altar, and I charge thee, by the dread name of that Power to which thou also must render thy account, that thou answer now and here.

"Who is this man to whom my being yearns? What has he been to me? What has he to do with thee? Speak, O Oracle and make the secret clear. Speak, I command, even though afterwards thou dost slay me—if thou canst."

"Aye, speak! speak!" said Leo, "for know I am in sore suspense. I also am bewildered by memories and rent with hopes and fears."

And I too echoed, "Speak!"

"Leo Vincey," asked the Hesea, after she had thought awhile, "whom dost thou believe me to be?"

"I believe," he answered solemnly, "that thou art that Ayesha at whose hands I died of old in the Caves of Kor in Africa. I believe thou art that Ayesha whom not twenty years ago I found and loved in those same Caves of Kor, and there saw perish miserably, swearing that thou wouldst return again."

"See now, how madness can mislead a man," broke in Atene triumphantly. "'Not twenty years ago,' he said, whereas I know well that more than eighty summers have gone by since my grandsire in his youth saw this same priestess sitting on the Mother's throne."

"And whom dost thou believe me to be, O Holly?" the Priestess asked, taking no note of the Khania's words.

"What he believes I believe," I answered. "The dead come back to life—sometimes. Yet alone thou knowest the truth, and by thee only it can be revealed."

"Aye," she said, as though musing, "the dead come back to life—sometimes—and in strange shape, and, mayhap, I know the truth. To-morrow when yonder body is borne on high for burial we will speak of it again. Till then rest you all, and prepare to face that fearful thing—the Truth."

While the Hesea still spoke the silvery curtains swung to their place as mysteriously as they had opened. Then, as though at some signal, the black-robed priests advanced. Surrounding Atene, they led her from the Sanctuary, accompanied by her uncle the Shaman, who, as it seemed to me, either through fatigue or fear, could scarcely stand upon his feet, but stood blinking his dim eyes as though the light dazed him. When these were gone, the priests and priestesses, who all this time had been ranged round the walls, far out of hearing of our talk, gathered themselves into their separate companies, and still chanting, departed also, leaving us alone with Oros and the corpse of the Khan, which remained where it had been set down.

Now the head-priest Oros beckoned to us to follow him, and we went also. Nor was I sorry to leave the place, for its death-like loneliness—enhanced, strangely enough, as it was, by the flood of light that filled it; a loneliness which was concentrated and expressed in the awful figure stretched upon the bier, oppressed and overcame us, whose nerves were broken by all that we had undergone. Thankful enough was I when, having passed the transepts and down the length of the vast nave, we came to the iron doors, the rock passage, and the outer gates, which, as before, opened to let us through, and so at last into the sweet, cold air of the night at that hour which precedes the dawn.

Oros led us to a house well-built and furnished, where at his bidding, like men in a dream, we drank of some liquor which he gave us. I think that drink was drugged, at least after swallowing it I remembered no more till I awoke to find myself lying on a bed and feeling wonderfully strong and well. This I thought strange, for a lamp burning in the room showed me that it was still dark, and therefore that I could have rested but a little time.

I tried to sleep again, but was not able, so fell to thinking till I grew weary of the task. For here thoughts would not help me; nothing could help, except the truth, "that fearful thing," as the veiled Priestess had called it.

Oh! what if she should prove not the Ayesha whom we desired, but some "fearful thing"? What were the meaning of the Khania's hints and of her boldness, that surely had been inspired by the strength of a hidden knowledge? What if—nay, it could not be—I would rise and dress my arm. Or I would wake Leo and make him dress it—anything to occupy my mind until the appointed hour, when we must learn—the best—or the worst.

I sat up in the bed and saw a figure advancing towards me. It was Oros, who bore a lamp in his hand.

"You have slept long, friend Holly," he said, "and now it is time to be up and doing."

"Long?" I answered testily. "How can that be, when it is still dark?"

"Because, friend, the dark is that of a new night. Many hours have gone by since you lay down upon this bed. Well, you were wise to rest you while you may, for who knows when you will sleep again! Come, let me bathe your arm."

"Tell me," I broke in——"Nay, friend," he interrupted firmly, "I will tell you nothing, except that soon you must start to be present at the funeral of the Khan, and, perchance, to learn the answer to your questions."

Ten minutes later he led me to the eating-chamber of the house, where I found Leo already dressed, for Oros had awakened him before he came to me and bidden him to prepare himself. Oros told us here that the Hesea had not suffered us to be disturbed until the night came again since we had much to undergo that day. So presently we started.

Once more we were led through the flame-lit hall till we came to the loop-shaped apse. The place was empty now, even the corpse of the Khan had gone, and no draped Oracle sat in the altar shrine, for its silver curtains were drawn, and we saw that it was untenanted.

"The Mother has departed to do honour to the dead, according to the ancient custom," Oros explained to us.

Then we passed the altar, and behind the statue found a door in the rock wall of the apse, and beyond the door a passage, and a hall as of a house, for out of it opened other doors leading to chambers. These, our guide told us, were the dwelling-places of the Hesea and her maidens. He added that they ran to the side of the Mountain and had windows that opened on to gardens and let in the light and air. In this hall six priests were waiting, each of whom carried a bundle of torches beneath his arm and held in his hand a lighted lamp.

"Our road runs through the dark," said Oros, "though were it day we might climb the outer snows, but this at night it is dangerous to do."

Then taking torches, he lit them at a lamp and gave one to each of us.

Now our climb began. Up endless sloping galleries we went, hewn with inconceivable labour by the primeval fire-worshippers from the living rock of the Mountain. It seemed to me that they stretched for miles, and indeed this was so, since, although the slope was always gentle, it took us more than an hour to climb them. At length we came to the foot of a great stair.

"Rest awhile here, my lord," Oros said, bowing to Leo with the reverence that he had shown him from the first, "for this stair is steep and long. Now we stand upon the Mountain's topmost lip, and are about to climb that tall looped column which soars above."

So we sat down in the vault-like place and let the sharp draught of air rushing to and from the passages play upon us, for we were heated with journeying up those close galleries. As we sat thus I heard a roaring sound and asked Oros what it might be. He answered that we were very near to the crater of the volcano, and that what we heard through the thickness of the rock was the rushing of its everlasting fires. Then the ascent commenced.

It was not dangerous though very wearisome, for there were nearly six hundred of those steps. The climb of the passages had reminded me of that of the gallery of the Great Pyramid drawn out for whole furlongs; that of the pillar was like the ascent of a cathedral spire, or rather of several spires piled one upon another.

Resting from time to time, we dragged ourselves up the steep steps, each of them quite a foot in height, till the pillar was climbed and only the loop remained. Up it we went also, Oros leading us, and glad was I that the stairway still ran within the substance of the rock, for I could feel the needle's mighty eye quiver in the rush of the winds which swept about its sides.

At length we saw light before us, and in another twenty steps emerged upon a platform. As Leo, who went in front of me, walked from the stairway I saw Oros and another priest seize him by the arms, and called to him to ask what they were doing.

"Nothing," he cried back, "except that this is a dizzy place and they feared lest I should fall. Mind how you come, Horace," and he stretched out his hand to me.

Now I was clear of the tunnel, and I believe that had it not been for that hand I should have sunk to the rocky floor, for the sight before me seemed to paralyse my brain. Nor was this to be wondered at, for I doubt whether the world can show such another.

We stood upon the very apex of the loop, a flat space of rock about eighty yards in length by some thirty in breadth, with the star-strewn sky above us. To the south, twenty thousand feet or more below, stretched the dim Plain of Kaloon, and to the east and west the snow-clad shoulders of the peak and the broad brown slopes beneath. To the north was a different sight, and one more awesome. There, right under us as it seemed, for the pillar bent inwards, lay the vast crater of the volcano, and in the centre of it a wide lake of fire that broke into bubbles and flowers of sudden flame or spouted, writhed and twisted like an angry sea.

From the surface of this lake rose smoke and gases that took fire as they floated upwards, and, mingling together, formed a gigantic sheet of living light. Right opposite to us burned this sheet and, the flare of it passing through the needle-eye of the pillar under us, sped away in one dazzling beam across the country of Kaloon, across the mountains beyond, till it was lost on the horizon.

The wind blew from south to north, being sucked in towards the hot crater of the volcano, and its fierce breath, that screamed through the eye of the pillar and against its rugged surface, bent the long crest of the sheet of flame, as an ocean roller is bent over by the gale, and tore from it fragments of fire, that floated away to leeward like the blown-out sails of a burning ship.

Had it not been for this strong and steady wind indeed, no creature could have lived upon the pillar, for the vapours would have poisoned him; but its unceasing blast drove these all away towards the north. For the same reason, in the thin air of that icy place the heat was not too great to be endured.

Appalled by that terrific spectacle, which seemed more appropriate to the terrors of the Pit than to this earth of ours, and fearful lest the blast should whirl me like a dead leaf into the glowing gulf beneath, I fell on to my sound hand and my knees, shouting to Leo to do likewise, and looked about me. Now I observed lines of priests wrapped in great capes, kneeling upon the face of the rock and engaged apparently in prayer, but of Hes the Mother, or of Atene, or of the corpse of the dead Khan I could see nothing.

Whilst I wondered where they might be, Oros, upon whose nerves this dread scene appeared to have no effect, and some of our attendant priests surrounded us and led us onwards by a path that ran perilously near to the rounded edge of the rock. A few downward steps and we found that we were under shelter, for the gale was roaring over us. Twenty more paces and we came to a recess cut, I suppose, by man in the face of the loop, in such fashion that a lava roof was left projecting half across its width.

This recess, or rock chamber, which was large enough to shelter a great number of people, we reached safely, to discover that it was already tenanted. Seated in a chair hewn from the rock was the Hesea, wearing a broidered, purple mantle above her gauzy wrappings that enveloped her from head to foot. There, too, standing near to her were the Khania Atene and her uncle the old Shaman, who looked but ill at ease, and lastly, stretched upon his funeral couch, the fiery light beating upon his stark form and face, lay the dead Khan, Rassen.

We advanced to the throne and bowed to her who sat thereon. The Hesea lifted her hooded head, which seemed to have been sunk upon her breast as though she were overcome by thought or care, and addressed Oros the priest. For in the shelter of those massive walls by comparison there was silence and folk could hear each other speak.

"So thou hast brought them safely, my servant," she said, "and I am glad, for to those that know it not this road is fearful. My guests, what say you of the burying-pit of the Children of Hes?"

"Our faith tells us of a hell, lady," answered Leo, "and I think that yonder cauldron looks like its mouth."

"Nay," she answered, "there is no hell, save that which from life to life we fashion for ourselves within the circle of this little star. Leo Vincey, I tell thee that hell is here, aye, here," and she struck her hand upon her breast, while once more her head drooped forward as though bowed down beneath some load of secret misery.

Thus she stayed awhile, then lifted it and spoke again, saying— "Midnight is past, and much must be done and suffered before the dawn. Aye, the darkness must be turned to light, or perchance the light to eternal darkness."

"Royal woman," she went on, addressing Atene, "as is his right, thou hast brought thy dead lord hither for burial in this consecrated place, where the ashes of all who went before him have become fuel for the holy fires. Oros, my priest, summon thou the Accuser and him who makes defence, and let the books be opened that I may pass my judgment on the dead, and call his soul to live again, or pray that from it the breath of life may be withheld.

"Priest, I say the Court of Death is open."

Oros bowed and left the place, whereon the Hesea signed to us to stand upon her right and to Atene to stand upon her left. Presently from either side the hooded priests and priestesses stole into the chamber, and to the number of fifty or more ranged themselves along its walls. Then came two figures draped in black and masked, who bore parchment books in their hands, and placed themselves on either side of the corpse, while Oros stood at its feet, facing the Hesea.

Now she lifted the sistrum that she held, and in obedience to the signal Oros said—"Let the books be opened."

Thereon the masked Accuser to the right broke the seal of his book and began to read its pages. It was a tale of the sins of this dead man entered as fully as though that officer were his own conscience given life and voice. In cold and horrible detail it told of the evil doings of his childhood, of his youth, and of his riper years, and thus massed together the record was black indeed.

I listened amazed, wondering what spy had been set upon the deeds of yonder man throughout his days; thinking also with a shudder of how heavy would be the tale against any one of us, if such a spy should companion him from the cradle to the grave; remembering too that full surely this count is kept by scribes even more watchful than the ministers of Hes.

At length the long story drew to its close. Lastly it told of the murder of that noble upon the banks of the river; it told of the plot against our lives for no just cause; it told of our cruel hunting with the death-hounds, and of its end. Then the Accuser shut his book and cast it on the ground, saying—"Such is the record, O Mother. Sum it up as thou hast been given wisdom."

Without speaking, the Hesea pointed with her sistrum to the Defender, who thereon broke the seal of his book and began to read.

Its tale spoke of all the good that the dead man had done; of every noble word that he had said, of every kind action; of plans which he had made for the welfare of his vassals; of temptations to ill that he had resisted;

of the true love that he had borne to the woman who became his wife; of the prayers which he had made and of the offerings which he had sent to the temple of Hes.

Making no mention of her name, it told of how that wife of his had hated him, of how she and the magician, who had fostered and educated her, and was her relative and guide, had set other women to lead him astray that she might be free of him. Of how too they had driven him mad with a poisonous drink which took away his judgment, unchained all the evil in his heart, and caused him by its baneful influence to shrink unnaturally from her whose love he still desired.

Also it set out that the heaviest of his crimes were inspired by this wife of his, who sought to befoul his name in the ears of the people whom she led him to oppress, and how bitter jealousy drove him to cruel acts, the last and worst of which caused him foully to violate the law of hospitality, and in attempting to bring about the death of blameless guests at their hands to find his own.

Thus the Defender read, and having read, closed the book and threw it on the ground, saying—"Such is the record, O Mother, sum it up as thou hast been given wisdom."

Then the Khania, who all this time had stood cold and impassive, stepped forward to speak, and with her her uncle, the Shaman Simbri. But before a word passed Atene's lips the Hesea raised her sceptre and forbade them, saying—"Thy day of trial is not yet, nor have we aught to do with thee. When thou liest where he lies and the books of thy deeds are read aloud to her who sits in judgment, then let thine advocate make answer for these things."

"So be it," answered Atene haughtily and fell back.

Now it was the turn of the high-priest Oros. "Mother," he said, "thou hast heard. Balance the writings, assess the truth, and according to thy wisdom, issue thy commands. Shall we hurl him who was Rassen feet first into the fiery gulf, that he may walk again in the paths of life, or head first, in token that he is dead indeed?"

Then while all waited in a hushed expectancy, the great Priestess delivered her verdict.

"I hear, I balance, I assess, but judge I do not, who claim no such power. Let the Spirit who sent him forth, to whom he is returned again, pass judgment on his spirit. This dead one has sinned deeply, yet has he been more deeply sinned against. Nor against that man can be reckoned the account of his deeds of madness. Cast him then to his grave feet first that his name may be whitened in the ears of those unborn, and that thence he may return again at the time appointed. It is spoken."

Now the Accuser lifted the book of his accusations from the ground and, advancing, hurled it into the gulf in token that it was blotted out. Then he turned and vanished from the chamber; while the Advocate, taking up his book, gave it into the keeping of the priest Oros, that it might be preserved in the archives of the temple for ever. This done, the priests began a funeral chant and a solemn invocation to the great Lord of the Under-world that he would receive this spirit and acquit it there as here it had been acquitted by the Hesea, his minister.

Ere their dirge ended certain of the priests, advancing with slow steps, lifted the bier and carried it to the edge of the gulf; then at a sign from the Mother, hurled it feet foremost into the fiery lake below, whilst all watched to see how it struck the flame. For this they held to be an omen, since should the body turn over in its descent it was taken as a sign that the judgment of mortal men had been refused in the Place of the Immortals. It did not turn; it rushed downwards straight as a plummet and plunged into the fire hundreds of feet below, and there for ever vanished. This indeed was not strange since, as we discovered afterwards, the feet were weighted.

In fact this solemn rite was but a formula that, down to the exact words of judgment and committal, had been practised here from unknown antiquity over the bodies of the priests and priestesses of the Mountain, and of certain of the great ones of the Plain. So it was in ancient Egypt, whence without doubt this ceremony of the trial of the dead was derived, and so it continued to be in the land of Hes, for no priestess ever ventured to condemn the soul of one departed.

The real interest of the custom, apart from its solemnity and awful surroundings, centred in the accurate knowledge displayed by the masked Accuser and Advocate of the life-deeds of the deceased. It showed that although the College of Hes affected to be indifferent to the doings and politics of the people of the Plain that they once ruled and over which, whilst secretly awaiting an opportunity of re-conquest, they still claimed a spiritual authority, the attitude was assumed rather than real. Moreover it suggested a system of espionage so piercing and extraordinary that it was difficult to believe it unaided by the habitual exercise of some gift of clairvoyance.

The service, if I may call it so, was finished; the dead man had followed the record of his sins into that lurid sea of fire, and by now was but a handful of charred dust. But if his book had closed, ours remained open and at its strangest chapter. We knew it, all of us, and waited, our nerves thrilled, with expectancy.

The Hesea sat brooding on her rocky throne. She also knew that the hour had come. Presently she sighed, then motioned with her sceptre and spoke a word or two, dismissing the priests and priestesses, who departed and were seen no more. Two of them remained however, Oros and the head priestess who was called Papave, a young woman of a noble countenance.

"Listen, my servants," she said. "Great things are about to happen, which have to do with the coming of yonder strangers, for whom I have waited these many years as is well known to you. Nor can I tell the issue since to me, to whom power is given so freely, foresight of the future is denied. It well may happen, therefore, that this seat will soon be empty and this frame but food for the eternal fires. Nay, grieve not, grieve not, for I do not die and if so, the spirit shall return again.

"Hearken, Papave. Thou art of the blood, and to thee alone have I opened all the doors of wisdom. If I pass now or at any time, take thou the ancient power, fill thou my place, and in all things do as I have instructed thee, that from this Mountain light may shine upon the world. Further I command thee, and thee also, Oros my priest, that if I be summoned hence you entertain these strangers hospitably until it is possible to escort them from the land, whether by the road they came or across the northern hills and deserts. Should the Khania Atene attempt to detain them against their will, then raise the Tribes upon her in the name of the Hesea; depose her from her seat, conquer her land and hold it. Hear and obey."

"Mother, we hear and we will obey," answered Oros and Papave as with a single voice.

She waved her hand to show that this matter was finished; then after long thought spoke again, addressing herself to the Khania.

"Atene, last night thou didst ask me a question—why thou dost love this man," and she pointed to Leo. "To that the answer would be easy, for is he not one who might well stir passion in the breast of a woman such as thou art? But thou didst say also that thine own heart and the wisdom of yonder magician, thy uncle, told thee that since thy soul first sprang to life thou hadst loved him, and didst adjure me by the Power to whom I must give my account to draw the curtain from the past and let the truth be known.

"Woman, the hour has come, and I obey thy summons—not because thou dost command but because it is my will. Of the beginning I can tell thee nothing, who am still human and no goddess. I know not why we three are wrapped in this coil of fate; I know not the destinies to which we journey up the ladder of a thousand lives, with grief and pain climbing the endless stair of circumstance, or, if I know, I may not say. Therefore I take up the tale where my own memory gives me light."

The Hesea paused, and we saw her frame shake as though beneath some fearful inward effort of the will. "Look now behind you," she cried, throwing her arms wide.

We turned, and at first saw nothing save the great curtain of fire that rose from the abyss of the volcano, whereof, as I have told, the crest was bent over by the wind like the crest of a breaking billow. But presently, as we watched, in the depths of this red veil, Nature's awful lamp-flame, a picture began to form as it forms in the seer's magic crystal.

Behold! a temple set amid sands and washed by a wide, palm-bordered river, and across its pyloned court processions of priests, who pass to and fro with flaunting banners. The court empties; I could see the shadow of a falcon's wings that fled across its sunlit floor. A man clad in a priest's white robe, shaven-headed, and barefooted, enters through the southern pylon gate and walks slowly towards a painted granite shrine, in which sits the image of a woman crowned with the double crown of Egypt, surmounted by a lotus bloom, and holding in her hand the sacred sistrum. Now, as though he heard some sound, he halts and looks towards us, and by the heaven above me, his face is the face of Leo Vincey in his youth, the face too of that Kallikrates whose corpse we had seen in the Caves of Kor!

"Look, look!" gasped Leo, catching me by the arm; but I only nodded my head in answer.

The man walks on again, and kneeling before the goddess in the shrine, embraces her feet and makes his prayer to her. Now the gates roll open, and a procession enters, headed by a veiled, noble-looking woman, who bears offerings, which she sets on the table before the shrine, bending her knee to the effigy of the goddess. Her oblations made, she turns to depart, and as she goes brushes her hand against the hand of the watching priest, who hesitates, then follows her.

When all her company have passed the gate she lingers alone in the shadow of the pylon, whispering to the priest and pointing to the river and the southern land beyond. He is disturbed; he reasons with her, till, after one swift glance round, she lets drop her veil, bending towards him and—their lips meet.

As time flies her face is turned towards us, and lo! it is the face of Atene, and amid her dusky hair the aura is reflected in jewelled gold, the symbol of her royal rank. She looks at the shaven priest; she laughs as though in triumph; she points to the westering sun and to the river, and is gone.

Aye, and that laugh of long ago is echoed by Atene at our side, for she also laughs in triumph and cries aloud to the old Shaman—"True diviners were my heart and thou! Behold how I won him in the past."

Then, like ice on fire fell the cold voice of the Hesea.

"Be silent, woman, and see how thou didst lose him in the past."

Lo! the scene changes, and on a couch a lovely shape lies sleeping. She dreams; she is afraid; and over her bends and whispers in her ear a shadowy form clad with the emblems of the goddess in the shrine, but now wearing upon her head the vulture cap. The woman wakes from her dream and looks round, and oh! the face is the face of Ayesha as it was seen of us when first she loosed her veil in the Caves of Kor.

A sigh went up from us; we could not speak who thus fearfully once more beheld her loveliness.

Again she sleeps, again the awful form bends over her and whispers. It points, the distance opens. Lo! on a stormy sea a boat, and in the boat two wrapped in each other's arms, the priest and the royal woman, while over them like a Vengeance, raw-necked and ragged-pinioned, hovers a following vulture, such a vulture as the goddess wore for headdress.

That picture fades from its burning frame, leaving the vast sheet of fire empty as the noonday sky. Then another forms. First a great, smooth-walled cave carpeted with sand, a cave that we remembered well. Then lying on the sand, now no longer shaven, but golden-haired, the corpse of the priest staring upwards with his glazed eyes, his white skin streaked with blood, and standing over him two women. One holds a javelin in her hand and is naked except for her flowing hair, and beautiful, beautiful beyond imagining. The other, wrapped in a dark cloak, beats the air with her hands, casting up her eyes as though to call the curse of Heaven upon her rival's head. And those women are she into whose sleeping ear the shadow had whispered, and the royal Egyptian who had kissed her lover beneath the pylon gate.

Slowly all the figures faded; it was as though the fire ate them up, for first they became thin and white as ashes; then vanished. The Hesea, who had been leaning forward, sank backwards in her chair, as if weary with the toil of her own magic.

For a while confused pictures flitted rapidly to and fro across the vast mirror of the flame, such as might be reflected from an intelligence crowded with the memories of over two thousand years which it was too exhausted to separate and define.

Wild scenes, multitudes of people, great caves, and in them faces, amongst others our own, starting up distorted and enormous, to grow tiny in an instant and depart; stark imaginations of Forms towering and divine; of Things monstrous and inhuman; armies marching, illimitable battle-fields, and corpses rolled in blood, and hovering over them the spirits of the slain.

These pictures died as the others had died, and the fire was blank again.

Then the Hesea spoke in a voice very faint at first, that by slow degrees grew stronger.

"Is thy question answered, O Atene?"

"I have seen strange sights, Mother, mighty limnings worthy of thy magic, but how know I that they are more than vapours of thine own brain cast upon yonder fire to deceive and mock us?"*

"Listen then," said the Hesea, in her weary voice, "to the interpretation of the writing, and cease to trouble me with thy doubts. Many an age ago, but shortly after I began to live this last, long life of mine, Isis, the great goddess of Egypt, had her Holy House at Behbit, near the Nile. It is a ruin now, and Isis has departed from Egypt, though still under the Power that fashioned it and her: she rules the world, for she is Nature's self. Of that shrine a certain man, a Greek, Kallikrates by name, was chief priest, chosen for her service by the favour of the goddess, vowed to her eternally and to her alone, by the dreadful oath that might not be broken without punishment as eternal.

* Considered in the light of subsequent revelations, vouchsafed to us by Ayesha herself, I am inclined to believe that Atene's shrewd surmise was accurate, and that these fearful pictures, although founded on events that had happened in the past, were in the main "vapours" cast upon the crater fire; visions raised in our minds to "deceive and mock us."

—L. H. H.

"In the flame thou sawest that priest, and here at thy side he stands, re-born, to fulfil his destiny and ours.

"There lived also a daughter of Pharaoh's house, one Amenartas, who cast eyes of love upon this Kallikrates, and, wrapping him in her spells—for then as now she practised witcheries—caused him to break his oaths and fly with her, as thou sawest written in the flame. Thou, Atene, wast that Amenartas.

"Lastly there lived a certain Arabian, named Ayesha, a wise and lovely woman, who, in the emptiness of her heart, and the sorrow of much knowledge, had sought refuge in the service of the universal Mother, thinking there to win the true wisdom which ever fled from her. That Ayesha, as thou sawest also, the goddess visited in a dream, bidding her to follow those faithless ones, and work Heaven's vengeance on them, and promising her in reward victory over death upon the earth and beauty such as had not been known in woman.

"She followed far; she awaited them where they wandered. Guided by a sage named Noot, one who from the beginning had been appointed to her service and that of another—thou, O Holly, wast that man—she found the essence in which to bathe is to outlive Generations, Faiths, and Empires, saying—"'I will slay these guilty ones. I will slay them presently, as I am commanded.'

"Yet Ayesha slew not, for now their sin was her sin, since she who had never loved came to desire this man. She led them to the Place of Life, purposing there to clothe him and herself with immortality, and let the woman die. But it was not so fated, for then the goddess smote. The life was Ayesha's as had been sworn, but in its first hour, blinded with jealous rage because he shrank from her unveiled glory to the mortal woman at his side, this Ayesha brought him to his death, and alas! alas! left herself undying.

"Thus did the angry goddess work woe upon her faithless ministers, giving to the priest swift doom, to the priestess Ayesha, long remorse and misery, and to the royal Amenartas jealousy more bitter than life or death, and the fate of unending effort to win back that love which, defying Heaven, she had dared to steal, but to be bereft thereof again.

"Lo! now the ages pass, and, at the time appointed, to that undying Ayesha who, whilst awaiting his re-birth, from century to century mourned his loss, and did bitter penance for her sins, came back the man, her heart's desire. Then, whilst all went well for her and him, again the goddess smote and robbed her of her reward. Before her lover's living eyes, sunk in utter shame and misery, the beautiful became hideous, the undying seemed to die.

"Yet, O Kallikrates, I tell thee that she died not. Did not Ayesha swear to thee yonder in the Caves of Kor that she would come again? for even in that awful hour this comfort kissed her soul. Thereafter, Leo Vincey, who art Killikrates, did not her spirit lead thee in thy sleep and stand with thee upon this very pinnacle which should be thy beacon light to guide thee back to her? And didst thou not search these many years, not knowing that she companioned thy every step and strove to guard thee in every danger, till at length in the permitted hour thou camest back to her?"

She paused, and looked towards Leo, as though awaiting his reply.

"Of the first part of the tale, except from the writing on the Sherd, I know nothing, Lady," he said; "of the rest I, or rather we, know that it is true. Yet I would ask a question, and I pray thee of thy charity let thy answer be swift and short. Thou sayest that in the permitted hour I came back to Ayesha. Where then is Ayesha? Art thou Ayesha? And if so why is thy voice changed? Why art thou less in stature? Oh! in the name of whatever god thou dost worship, tell me art thou Ayesha?"

"I am Ayesha" she answered solemnly, "that very Ayesha to whom thou didst pledge thyself eternally."

"She lies, she lies," broke in Atene. "I tell thee, husband—for such with her own lips she declares thou art to me—that yonder woman who says that she parted from thee young and beautiful, less than twenty years ago, is none other than the aged priestess who for a century at least has borne rule in these halls of Hes. Let her deny it if she can."

"Oros," said the Mother, "tell thou the tale of the death of that priestess of whom the Khania speaks."

The priest bowed, and in his usual calm voice, as though he were narrating some event of every day, said mechanically, and in a fashion that carried no conviction to my mind—"Eighteen years ago, on the fourth night of the first month of the winter in the year 2333 of the founding of the worship of Hes on this Mountain, the priestess of whom the Khania Atene speaks, died of old age in my presence in the hundred and eighth year of her rule. Three hours later we went to lift her from the throne on which she died, to prepare her corpse for burial in this fire, according to the ancient custom. Lo! a miracle, for she lived again, the same, yet very changed.

"Thinking this a work of evil magic, the Priests and Priestesses of the College rejected her, and would have driven her from the throne. Thereon the Mountain blazed and thundered, the light from the fiery pillars died, and great terror fell upon the souls of men. Then from the deep darkness above the altar where stands the statue of the Mother of Men, the voice of the living goddess spoke, saying—"'Accept ye her whom I have set to rule over you, that my judgments and my purposes may be fulfilled.'

"The Voice ceased, the fiery torches burnt again, and we bowed the knee to the new Hesea, and named her Mother in the ears of all. That is the tale to which hundreds can bear witness."

"Thou hearest, Atene," said the Hesea. "Dost thou still doubt?"

"Aye," answered the Khania, "for I hold that Oros also lies, or if he lies not, then he dreams, or perchance that voice he heard was thine own. Now if thou art this undying woman, this Ayesha, let proof be made of it to these two men who knew thee in the past. Tear away those wrappings that guard thy loveliness thus jealously. Let thy shape divine, thy beauty incomparable, shine out upon our dazzled sight. Surely thy lover will not forget such charms; surely he will know thee, and bow the knee, saying, 'This is my Immortal, and no other woman.'

"Then, and not till then, will I believe that thou art even what thou declarest thyself to be, an evil spirit, who bought undying life with murder and used thy demon loveliness to bewitch the souls of men."

Now the Hesea on the throne seemed to be much troubled, for she rocked herself to and fro, and wrung her white-draped hands.

"Kallikrates," she said in a voice that sounded like a moan, "is this thy will? For if it be, know that I must obey. Yet I pray thee command it not, for the time is not yet come; the promise unbreakable is not yet fulfilled. I am somewhat changed, Kallikrates, since I kissed thee on the brow and named thee mine, yonder in the Caves of Kor."

Leo looked about him desperately, till his eyes fell upon the mocking face of Atene, who cried—"Bid her unveil, my lord. I swear to thee I'll not be jealous."

At that taunt he took fire.

"Aye," he said, "I bid her unveil, that I may learn the best or worst, who otherwise must die of this suspense. Howsoever changed, if she be Ayesha I shall know her, and if she be Ayesha, I shall love her."

"Bold words, Kallikrates," answered the Hesea; "yet from my very heart I thank thee for them: those sweet words of trust and faithfulness to thou knowest not what. Learn now the truth, for I may keep naught back from thee. When I unveil it is decreed that thou must make thy choice for the last time on this earth between yonder woman, my rival from the beginning, and that Ayesha to whom thou art sworn. Thou canst reject me if thou wilt, and no ill shall come to thee, but many a blessing, as men reckon them—power and wealth and love. Only then thou must tear my memory from thy heart, for then I leave thee to follow thy fate alone, till at the last the purpose of these deeds and sufferings is made clear.

"Be warned. No light ordeal lies before thee. Be warned. I can promise thee naught save such love as woman never gave to man, love that perchance—I know not—must yet remain unsatisfied upon the earth."

Then she turned to me and said:

"Oh! thou, Holly, thou true friend, thou guardian from of old, thou, next to him most beloved by me, to thy clear and innocent spirit perchance wisdom may be given that is denied to us, the little children whom thine arms protect. Counsel thou him, my Holly, with the counsel that is given thee, and I will obey thy words and his, and, whatever befalls, will bless thee from my soul. Aye, and should he cast me off, then in the Land beyond the lands, in the Star appointed, where all earthly passions fade, together will we dwell eternally in a friendship glorious, thou and I alone.

"For thou wilt not reject; thy steel, forged in the furnace of pure truth and power, shall not lose its temper in these small fires of temptation and become a rusted chain to bind thee to another woman's breast—until it canker to her heart and thine."

"Ayesha, I thank thee for thy words," I answered simply, "and by them and that promise of thine, I, thy poor friend—for more I never thought to be—am a thousandfold repaid for many sufferings. This I will add, that for my part I know that thou art She whom we have lost, since, whatever the lips that speak them, those thoughts and words are Ayesha's and hers alone."

Thus I spoke, not knowing what else to say, for I was filled with a great joy, a calm and ineffable satisfaction, which broke thus feebly from my heart. For now I knew that I was dear to Ayesha as I had always been dear to Leo; the closest of friends, from whom she never would be parted. What more could I desire?

We fell back; we spoke together, whilst they watched us silently. What we said I do not quite remember, but the end of it was that, as the Hesea had done, Leo bade me judge and choose. Then into my mind there came a clear command, from my own conscience or otherwhere, who can say? This was the command, that I should bid her to unveil, and let fate declare its purposes.

"Decide," said Leo, "I cannot bear much more. Like that woman, whoever she may be, whatever happens, I will not blame you, Horace."

"Good," I answered, "I have decided," and, stepping forward, I said: "We have taken counsel, Hes, and it is our will, who would learn the truth and be at rest, that thou shouldst unveil before us, here and now."

"I hear and obey," the Priestess answered, in a voice like to that of a dying woman, "only, I beseech you both, be pitiful to me, spare me your mockeries; add not the coals of your hate and scorn to the fires of a soul in hell, for whate'er I am, I became it for thy sake, Kallikrates. Yet, yet I also am athirst for knowledge; for though I know all wisdom, although I wield much power, one thing remains to me to learn—what is the worth of the love of man, and if, indeed, it can live beyond the horrors of the grave?"

Then, rising slowly, the Hesea walked, or rather tottered to the unroofed open space in front of the rock chamber, and stood there quite near to the brink of the flaming gulf beneath.

"Come hither, Papave, and loose these veils," she cried in a shrill, thin voice.

Papave advanced, and with a look of awe upon her handsome face began the task. She was not a tall woman, yet as she bent over her I noted that she seemed to tower above her mistress, the Hesea.

The outer veils fell revealing more within. These fell also, and now before us stood the mummy-like shape, although it seemed to be of less stature, of that strange being who had met us in the Place of Bones. So it would seem that our mysterious guide and the high priestess Hes were the same.

Look! Length by length the wrappings sank from her. Would they never end? How small grew the frame within? She was very short now, unnaturally short for a full-grown woman, and oh! I grew sick at heart. The last bandages uncoiled themselves like shavings from a stick; two wrinkled hands appeared, if hands they could be called. Then the feet—once I had seen such on the mummy of a princess of Egypt, and even now by some fantastic play of the mind, I remembered that on her coffin this princess was named "The Beautiful."

Everything was gone now, except a shift and a last inner veil about the head. Hes waved back the priestess Papave, who fell half fainting to the ground and lay there covering her eyes with her hand. Then uttering something like a scream she gripped this veil in her thin talons, tore it away, and with a gesture of uttermost despair, turned and faced us.

Oh! she was—nay, I will not describe her. I knew her at once, for thus had I seen her last before the Fire of Life, and, strangely enough, through the mask of unutterable age, through that cloak of humanity's last decay, still shone some resemblance to the glorious and superhuman Ayesha: the shape of the face, the air of defiant pride that for an instant bore her up—I know not what.

Yes, there she stood, and the fierce light of the heartless fires beat upon her, revealing every shame.

There was a dreadful silence. I saw Leo's lips turn white and his knees begin to give; but by some effort he recovered himself, and stayed still and upright like a dead man held by a wire. Also I saw Atene—and this is to her credit—turn her head away. She had desired to see her rival humiliated, but that horrible sight shocked her; some sense of their common womanhood for the moment touched her pity. Only Simbri, who, I think, knew what to expect, and Oros remained quite unmoved; indeed, in that ghastly silence the latter spoke, and ever afterwards I loved him for his words.

"What of the vile vessel, rotted in the grave of time? What of the flesh that perishes?" he said. "Look through the ruined lamp to the eternal light which burns within. Look through its covering carrion to the inextinguishable soul."

My heart applauded these noble sentiments. I was of one mind with Oros, but oh, Heaven! I felt that my brain was going, and I wished that it would go, so that I might hear and see no more.

That look which gathered on Ayesha's mummy face? At first there had been a little hope, but the hope died, and anguish, anguish, anguish took its place.

Something must be done, this could not endure. My lips clave together, no word would come; my feet refused to move.

I began to contemplate the scenery. How wonderful were that sheet of flame, and the ripples which ran up and down its height. How awesome its billowy crest. It would be warm lying in yonder red gulf below with the dead Rassen, but oh! I wished that I shared his bed and had finished with these agonies.

Thank Heaven, Atene was speaking. She had stepped to the side of the naked-headed Thing, and stood by it in all the pride of her rich beauty and perfect womanhood.

"Leo Vincey, or Kallikrates," said Atene, "take which name thou wilt; thou thinkest ill of me perhaps, but know that at least I scorn to mock a rival in her mortal shame. She told us a wild tale but now, a tale true or false, but more false than true, I think, of how I robbed a goddess of a votary, and of how that goddess—Ayesha's self perchance—was avenged upon me for the crime of yielding to the man I loved. Well, let goddesses—if such indeed there be—take their way and work their will upon the helpless, and I, a mortal, will take mine until the clutch of doom closes round my throat and chokes out life and memory, and I too am a goddess—or a clod.

"Meanwhile, thou man, I shame not to say it before all these witnesses, I love thee, and it seems that this—this woman or goddess—loves thee also, and she has told us that now, now thou must choose between us once and for ever. She has told us too that if I sinned against Isis, whose minister be it remembered she declares herself, herself she sinned yet more. For she would have taken thee both from a heavenly mistress and from an earthly bride, and yet snatch that guerdon of immortality which is hers to-day. Therefore if I am evil, she is worse, nor does the flame that burns within the casket whereof Oros spoke shine so very pure and bright.

"Choose thou then Leo Vincey, and let there be an end. I vaunt not myself; thou knowest what I have been and seest what I am. Yet I can give thee love and happiness and, mayhap, children to follow after thee, and with them some place and power. What yonder witch can give thee thou canst guess. Tales of the past, pictures on the flame, wise maxims and honeyed words, and after thou art dead once more, promises perhaps, of joy to come when that terrible goddess whom she serves so closely shall be appeased. I have spoken. Yet I will add a word:

"O thou for whom, if the Hesea's tale be true, I did once lay down my royal rank and dare the dangers of an unsailed sea; O thou whom in ages gone I would have sheltered with my frail body from the sorceries of this cold, self-seeking witch; O thou whom but a little while ago at my own life's risk I drew from death in yonder river, choose, choose!"

To all this speech, so moderate yet so cruel, so well-reasoned and yet so false, because of its glosses and omissions, the huddled Ayesha seemed to listen with a fierce intentness. Yet she made no answer, not a single word, not a sign even; she who had said her say and scorned to plead her part.

I looked at Leo's ashen face. He leaned towards Atene, drawn perhaps by the passion shining in her beauteous eyes, then of a sudden straightened himself, shook his head and sighed. The colour flamed to his brow, and his eyes grew almost happy.

"After all," he said, thinking aloud rather than speaking, "I have to do not with unknowable pasts or with mystic futures, but with the things of my own life. Ayesha waited for me through two thousand years; Atene could marry a man she hated for power's sake, and then could poison him, as perhaps she would poison me when I wearied her. I know not what oaths I swore to Amenartas, if such a woman lived. I remember the oaths I swore to Ayesha. If I shrink from her now, why then my life is a lie and my belief a fraud; then love will not endure the touch of age and never can survive the grave.

"Nay, remembering what Ayesha was I take her as she is, in faith and hope of what she shall be. At least love is immortal and if it must, why let it feed on memory alone till death sets free the soul."

Then stepping to where stood the dreadful, shrivelled form, Leo knelt down before it and kissed her on the brow.

Yes, he kissed the trembling horror of that wrinkled head, and I think it was one of the greatest, bravest acts ever done by man.

"Thou hast chosen," said Atene in a cold voice, "and I tell thee, Leo Vincey, that the manner of thy choice makes me mourn my loss the more. Take now thy—thy bride and let me hence."

But Ayesha still said no word and made no sign, till presently she sank upon her bony knees and began to pray aloud. These were the words of her prayer, as I heard them, though the exact Power to which it was addressed is not very easy to determine, as I never discovered who or what it was that she worshipped in her heart—"O Thou minister of the almighty Will, thou sharp sword in the hand of Doom, thou inevitable Law that art named Nature; thou who wast crowned as Isis of the Egyptians, but art the goddess of all climes and ages; thou that leadest the man to the maid, and layest the infant on his mother's breast, that bringest our dust to its kindred dust, that givest life to death, and into the dark of death breathest the light of life again; thou who causest the abundant earth to bear, whose smile is Spring, whose laugh is the ripple of the sea, whose noontide rest is drowsy Summer, and whose sleep is Winter's night, hear thou the supplication of thy chosen child and minister:

"Of old thou gavest me thine own strength with deathless days, and beauty above every daughter of this Star. But I sinned against thee sore, and for my sin I paid in endless centuries of solitude, in the vileness that makes me loathsome to my lover's eyes, and for its diadem of perfect power sets upon my brow this crown of naked mockery. Yet in thy breath, the swift essence that brought me light, that brought me gloom, thou didst vow to me that I who cannot die should once more pluck the lost flower of my immortal loveliness from this foul slime of shame.

"Therefore, merciful Mother that bore me, to thee I make my prayer. Oh, let his true love atone my sin; or, if it may not be, then give me death, the last and most blessed of thy boons!"

XVI. THE CHANGE

She ceased, and there was a long, long silence. Leo and I looked at each other in dismay. We had hoped against hope that this beautiful and piteous prayer, addressed apparently to the great, dumb spirit of Nature, would be answered. That meant a miracle, but what of it? The prolongation of the life of Ayesha was a miracle, though it is true that some humble reptiles are said to live as long as she had done.

The transference of her spirit from the Caves of Kor to this temple was a miracle, that is, to our western minds, though the dwellers in these parts of Central Asia would not hold it so. That she should re-appear with the same hideous body was a miracle. But was it the same body? Was it not the body of the last Hesea? One very ancient woman is much like another, and eighteen years of the working of the soul or identity within might well wear away their trivial differences and give to the borrowed form some resemblance to that which it had left.

At least the figures on that mirror of the flame were a miracle. Nay, why so? A hundred clairvoyants in a hundred cities can produce or see their like in water and in crystal, the difference being only one of size. They were but reflections of scenes familiar to the mind of Ayesha, or perhaps not so much as that. Perhaps they were only phantasms called up in our minds by her mesmeric force.

Nay, none of these things were true miracles, since all, however strange, might be capable of explanation. What right then had we to expect a marvel now?

Such thoughts as these rose in our minds as the endless minutes were born and died and—nothing happened.

Yes, at last one thing did happen. The light from the sheet of flame died gradually away as the flame itself sank downwards into the abysses of the pit. But about this in itself there was nothing wonderful, for as we had seen with our own eyes from afar this fire varied much, and indeed it was customary for it to die down at the approach of dawn, which now drew very near.

Still that onward-creeping darkness added to the terrors of the scene.

By the last rays of the lurid light we saw Ayesha rise and advance some few paces to that little tongue of rock at the edge of the pit off which the body of Rassen had been hurled; saw her standing on it, also, looking like some black, misshapen imp against the smoky glow which still rose from the depths beneath.

Leo would have gone forward to her, for he believed that she was about to hurl herself to doom, which indeed I thought was her design. But the priest Oros, and the priestess Papave, obeying, I suppose, some secret command that reached them I know not how, sprang to him and seizing his arms, held him back. Then it became quite dark, and through the darkness we could hear Ayesha chanting a dirge-like hymn in some secret, holy tongue which was unknown to us.

A great flake of fire floated through the gloom, rocking to and fro like some vast bird upon its pinions. We had seen many such that night, torn by the gale from the crest of the blazing curtain as I have described. But—but—"Horace," whispered Leo through his chattering teeth, "that flame is coming up against the wind!"

"Perhaps the wind has changed," I answered, though I knew well that it had not; that it blew stronger than ever from the south.

Nearer and nearer sailed the rocking flame, two enormous wings was the shape of it, with something dark between them. It reached the little promontory. The wings appeared to fold themselves about the dwarfed figure that stood thereon—illuminating it for a moment. Then the light went out of them and they vanished—everything vanished.

A while passed, it may have been one minute or ten, when suddenly the priestess Papave, in obedience to some summons which we could not hear, crept by me. I knew that it was she because her woman's garments touched me as she went. Another space of silence and of deep darkness, during which I heard Papave return, breathing in short, sobbing gasps like one who is very frightened.

Ah! I thought, Ayesha has cast herself into the pit. The tragedy is finished!

Then it was that the wondrous music came. Of course it may have been only the sound of priests chanting beyond us, but I do not think so, since its quality was quite different to any that I heard in the temple before or afterwards: to any indeed that ever I heard upon the earth.

I cannot describe it, but it was awful to listen to, yet most entrancing. From the black, smoke-veiled pit where the fire had burned it welled and echoed—now a single heavenly voice, now a sweet chorus, and now an air-shaking thunder as of a hundred organs played to time.

That diverse and majestic harmony seemed to include, to express every human emotion, and I have often thought since then that in its all-embracing scope and range, this, the song or paean of her re-birth was symbolical of the infinite variety of Ayesha's spirit. Yet like that spirit it had its master notes; power, passion, suffering, mystery and loveliness. Also there could be no doubt as to the general significance of the chant by whomsoever it was sung. It was the changeful story of a mighty soul; it was worship, worship, worship of a queen divine!

Like slow clouds of incense fading to the bannered roof of some high choir, the bursts of unearthly melodies grew faint; in the far distance of the hollow pit they wailed themselves away.

Look! from the east a single ray of upward-springing light.

"Behold the dawn," said the quiet voice of Oros.

That ray pierced the heavens above our heads, a very sword of flame. It sank downwards, swiftly. Suddenly it fell, not upon us, for as yet the rocky walls of our chamber warded it away, but on to the little promontory at its edge.

Oh! and there—a Glory covered with a single garment—stood a shape celestial. It seemed to be asleep, since the eyes were shut. Or was it dead, for at first that face was a face of death? Look, the sunlight played upon her, shining through the thin veil, the dark eyes opened like the eyes of a wondering child; the blood of life flowed up the ivory bosom into the pallid cheeks; the raiment of black and curling tresses wavered in the wind; the head of the jewelled snake that held them sparkled beneath her breast.

Was it an illusion, or was this Ayesha as she had been when she entered the rolling flame in the caverns of Kor? Our knees gave way beneath us, and down, our arms about each other's necks, Leo and I sank till we lay upon the ground. Then a voice sweeter than honey, softer than the whisper of a twilight breeze among the reeds, spoke near to us, and these were the words it said—"Come hither to me, Kallikrates, who would pay thee back that redeeming kiss of faith and love thou gavest me but now!"

Leo struggled to his feet. Like a drunken man he staggered to where Ayesha stood, then overcome, sank before her on his knees.

"Arise," she said, "it is I who should kneel to thee," and she stretched out her hand to raise him, whispering in his ear the while.

Still he would not, or could not rise, so very slowly she bent over him and touched him with her lips upon the brow. Next she beckoned to me. I came and would have knelt also, but she suffered it not.

"Nay," she said, in her rich, remembered voice, "thou art no suitor; it shall not be. Of lovers and worshippers henceforth as before, I can find a plenty if I will, or even if I will it not. But where shall I find another friend like to thee, O Holly, whom thus I greet?" and leaning towards me, with her lips she touched me also on the brow—just touched me, and no more.

Fragrant was Ayesha's breath as roses, the odour of roses clung to her lovely hair; her sweet body gleamed like some white sea-pearl; a faint but palpable radiance crowned her head; no sculptor ever fashioned such a marvel as the arm with which she held her veil about her; no stars in heaven ever shone more purely bright than did her calm, entranced eyes.

Yet it is true, even with her lips upon me, all I felt for her was a love divine into which no human passion entered. Once, I acknowledge to my shame, it was otherwise, but I am an old man now and have done with such frailties. Moreover, had not Ayesha named me Guardian, Protector, Friend, and sworn to me that with her and Leo I should ever dwell where all earthly passions fail. I repeat: what more could I desire?

Taking Leo by the hand Ayesha returned with him into the shelter of the rock-hewn chamber and when she entered its shadows, shivered a little as though with cold. I rejoiced at this I remember, for it seemed to show me that she still was human, divine as she might appear. Here her priest and priestess prostrated themselves before her new-born splendour, but she motioned to them to rise, laying a hand upon the head of each as though in blessing. "I am cold," she said, "give me my mantle," and Papave threw the purple-broidered garment upon her shoulders, whence now it hung royally, like a coronation robe.

"Nay," she went on, "it is not this long-lost shape of mine, which in his kiss my lord gave back to me, that shivers in the icy wind, it is my spirit's self bared to the bitter breath of Destiny. O my love, my love, offended Powers are not easily appeased, even when they appear to pardon, and though I shall no more be made a mockery in thy sight, how long is given us together upon the world I know not; but a little hour perchance. Well, ere we pass otherwhere, we will make it glorious, drinking as deeply of the cup of joy as we have drunk of those of sorrows and of shame. This place is hateful to me, for here I have suffered more than ever woman did on earth or phantom in the deepest hell. It is hateful, it is ill-omened. I pray that never again may I behold it.

"Say, what is it passes in thy mind, magician?" and of a sudden she turned fiercely upon the Shaman Simbri who stood near, his arms crossed upon his breast.

"Only, thou Beautiful," he answered, "a dim shadow of things to come. I have what thou dost lack with all thy wisdom, the gift of foresight, and here I see a dead man lying——"

"Another word," she broke in with fury born of some dark fear, "and thou shalt be that man. Fool, put me not in mind that now I have strength again to rid me of the ancient foes I hate, lest I should use a sword thou thrustest to my hand," and her eyes that had been so calm and happy, blazed upon him like fire.

The old wizard felt their fearsome might and shrank from it till the wall stayed him.

"Great One! now as ever I salute thee. Yes, now as at the first beginning whereof we know alone," he stammered. "I had no more to say; the face of that dead man was not revealed to me. I saw only that some crowned Khan of Kaloon to be shall lie here, as he whom the flame has taken lay an hour ago."

"Doubtless many a Khan of Kaloon will lie here," she answered coldly. "Fear not, Shaman, my wrath is past, yet be wise, mine enemy, and prophesy no more evil to the great. Come, let us hence."

So, still led by Leo, she passed from that chamber and stood presently upon the apex of the soaring pillar. The sun was up now, flooding the Mountain flanks, the plains of Kaloon far beneath and the distant, misty peaks with a sheen of gold. Ayesha stood considering the mighty prospect, then addressing Leo, she said—"The world is very fair; I give it all to thee."

Now Atene spoke for the first time.

"Dost thou mean Hes—if thou art still the Hesea and not a demon arisen from the Pit—that thou offerest my territories to this man as a love-gift? If so, I tell thee that first thou must conquer them."

"Ungentle are thy words and mien," answered Ayesha, "yet I forgive them both, for I also can scorn to mock a rival in my hour of victory. When thou wast the fairer, thou didst proffer him these very lands, but say, who is the fairer now? Look at us, all of you, and judge," and she stood by Atene and smiled.

The Khania was a lovely woman. Never to my knowledge have I seen one lovelier, but oh! how coarse and poor she showed beside the wild, ethereal beauty of Ayesha born again. For that beauty was not altogether human, far less so indeed than it had been in the Caves of Kor; now it was the beauty of a spirit.

The little light that always shone upon Ayesha's brow; the wide-set, maddening eyes which were filled sometimes with the fire of the stars and sometimes with the blue darkness of the heavens wherein they float; the curved lips, so wistful yet so proud; the tresses fine as glossy silk that still spread and rippled as though with a separate life; the general air, not so much of majesty as of some secret power hard to be restrained, which strove in that delicate body and proclaimed its presence to the most careless; that flame of the soul within whereof Oros had spoken, shining now through no "vile vessel," but in a vase of alabaster and of pearl—none of these things and qualities were altogether human. I felt it and was afraid, and Atene felt it also, for she answered—"I am but a woman. What thou art, thou knowest best. Still a taper cannot shine midst yonder fires or a glow-worm against a fallen star; nor can my mortal flesh compare with the glory thou hast earned from hell in payment for thy gifts and homage to the lord of ill. Yet as woman I am thy equal, and as spirit I shall be thy mistress, when robbed of these borrowed beauties thou, Ayesha, standest naked and ashamed before the Judge of all whom thou hast deserted and defied; yes, as thou stoodest but now upon yonder brink above the burning pit where thou yet shalt wander wailing thy lost love. For this I know, mine enemy, that man and spirit cannot mate," and Atene ceased, choking in her bitter rage and jealousy.

Now watching Ayesha, I saw her wince a little beneath these evil-omened words, saw also a tinge of grey touch the carmine of her lips and her deep eyes grow dark and troubled. But in a moment her fears had gone and she was asking in a voice that rang clear as silver bells—"Why ravest thou, Atene, like some short-lived summer torrent against the barrier of a seamless cliff? Dost think, poor creature of an hour, to sweep away the rock of my eternal strength with foam and bursting bubbles? Have done and listen. I do not seek thy petty rule, who, if I will it, can take the empire of the world. Yet learn, thou holdest it of my hand. More—I purpose soon to visit thee in thy city—choose thou if it shall be in peace or war! Therefore, Khania, purge thy court and amend thy laws, that when I come I may find contentment in the land which now it lacks, and confirm thee in thy government. My counsel to thee also is that thou choose some worthy man to husband, let him be whom thou wilt, if only he is just and upright and one upon whom thou mayest rest, needing wise guidance as thou dost, Atene. Come, now, my guests, let us hence," and she walked past the Khania, stepping fearlessly upon the very edge of the wind-swept, rounded peak.

In a second the attempt had been made and failed, so quickly indeed that it was not until Leo and I compared our impressions afterwards that we could be sure of what had happened. As Ayesha passed her, the maddened Khania drew a hidden dagger and struck with all her force at her rival's back. I saw the knife vanish to the hilt in her body, as I thought, but this cannot have been so since it fell to the ground, and she who should have been dead, took no hurt at all.

Feeling that she had failed, with a movement like the sudden lurch of a ship, Atene thrust at Ayesha, proposing to hurl her to destruction in the depths beneath. Lo! her outstretched arms went past her although Ayesha never seemed to stir. Yes it was Atene who would have fallen, Atene who already fell, had not Ayesha put out her hand and caught her by the wrist, bearing all her backward-swaying weight as easily as though she were but an infant, and without effort drawing her to safety.

"Foolish woman!" she said in pitying tones. "Wast thou so vexed that thou wouldst strip thyself of the pleasant shape which heaven has given thee? Surely this is madness, Atene, for how knowest thou in what likeness thou mightest be sent to tread the earth again? As no queen perhaps, but as a peasant's child, deformed, unsightly; for such reward, it is said, is given to those that achieve self-murder. Or even, as many think, shaped like a beast—a snake, a cat, a tigress! Why, see," and she picked the dagger from the ground and cast it into the air, "that point was poisoned. Had it but pricked thee now!" and she smiled at her and shook her head.

But Atene could bear no more of this mockery, more venomed than her own steel.

"Thou art not mortal," she wailed. "How can I prevail against thee? To Heaven I leave thy punishment," and there upon the rocky peak Atene sank down and wept.

Leo stood nearest to her, and the sight of this royal woman in her misery proved too much for him to bear. Stepping to her side he stooped and lifted her to her feet, muttering some kind words. For a moment she rested on his arm, then shook herself free of him and took the proffered hand of her old uncle Simbri.

"I see," said Ayesha, "that as ever, thou art courteous, my lord Leo, but it is best that her own servant should take charge of her, for—she may hide more daggers. Come, the day grows, and surely we need rest."

XVII. THE BETROTHAL

Together we descended the multitudinous steps and passed the endless, rock-hewn passages till we came to the door of the dwelling of the high-priestess and were led through it into a hall beyond. Here Ayesha parted from us saying that she was outworn, as indeed she seemed to be with an utter weariness, not of the body, but of the spirit. For her delicate form drooped like a rain-laden lily, her eyes grew dim as those of a person in a trance, and her voice came in a soft, sweet whisper, the voice of one speaking in her sleep.

"Good-bye," she said to us. "Oros will guard you both, and lead you to me at the appointed time. Rest you well."

So she went and the priest led us into a beautiful apartment that opened on to a sheltered garden. So overcome were we also by all that we had endured and seen, that we could scarcely speak, much less discuss these marvellous events.

"My brain swims," said Leo to Oros, "I desire to sleep."

He bowed and conducted us to a chamber where were beds, and on these we flung ourselves down and slept, dreamlessly, like little children.

When we awoke it was afternoon. We rose and bathed, then saying that we wished to be alone, went together into the garden where even at this altitude, now, at the end of August, the air was still mild and pleasant. Behind a rock by a bed of campanulas and other mountain flowers and ferns, was a bench near to the banks of a little stream, on which we seated ourselves.

"What have you to say, Horace?" asked Leo laying his hand upon my arm.

"Say?" I answered. "That things have come about most marvellously; that we have dreamed aright and laboured not in vain; that you are the most fortunate of men and should be the most happy."

He looked at me somewhat strangely, and answered—"Yes, of course; she is lovely, is she not—but," and his voice dropped to its lowest whisper, "I wish, Horace, that Ayesha were a little more human, even as human as she was in the Caves of Kor. I don't think she is quite flesh and blood, I felt it when she kissed me—if you can call it a kiss—for she barely touched my hair. Indeed how can she be who changed thus in an hour? Flesh and blood are not born of flame, Horace."

"Are you sure that she was so born?" I asked. "Like the visions on the fire, may not that hideous shape have been but an illusion of our minds? May she not be still the same Ayesha whom we knew in Kor, not re-born, but wafted hither by some mysterious agency?"

"Perhaps. Horace, we do not know—I think that we shall never know. But I admit that to me the thing is terrifying. I am drawn to her by an infinite attraction, her eyes set my blood on fire, the touch of her hand is as that of a wand of madness laid upon my brain. And yet between us there is some wall, invisible, still present. Or perhaps it is only fancy. But, Horace, I think that she is afraid of Atene. Why, in the old days the Khania would have been dead and forgotten in an hour—you remember Ustane?"

"Perhaps she may have grown more gentle, Leo, who, like ourselves, has learned hard lessons."

"Yes," he answered, "I hope that is so. At any rate she has grown more divine—only, Horace, what kind of a husband shall I be for that bright being, if ever I get so far?"

"Why should you not get so far?" I asked angrily, for his words jarred upon my tense nerves.

"I don't know," he answered, "but on general principles do you think that such fortune will be allowed to a man? Also, what did Atene mean when she said that man and spirit cannot mate—and—other things?"

"She meant that she hoped they could not, I imagine, and, Leo, it is useless to trouble yourself with forebodings that are more fitted to my years than yours, and probably are based on nothing. Be a philosopher, Leo. You have striven by wonderful ways such as are unknown in the history of the world; you have attained. Take the goods the gods provide you—the glory, the love and the power—and let the future look to itself."

Before he could answer Oros appeared from round the rock, and, bowing with more than his usual humility to Leo, said that the Hesea desired our presence at a service in the Sanctuary. Rejoiced at the prospect of seeing her again before he had hoped to do so, Leo sprang up and we accompanied him back to our apartment.

Here priests were waiting, who, somewhat against his will, trimmed his hair and beard, and would have done the same for me had I not refused their offices. Then they placed gold-embroidered sandals on our feet and wrapped Leo in a magnificent, white robe, also richly worked with gold and purple; a somewhat similar robe but of less ornate design being given to me. Lastly, a silver sceptre was thrust into his hand and into mine a plain wand. This sceptre was shaped like a crook, and the sight of it gave me some clue to the nature of the forthcoming ceremony.

"The crook of Osiris!" I whispered to Leo.

"Look here," he answered, "I don't want to impersonate any Egyptian god, or to be mixed up in their heathen idolatries; in fact, I won't."

"Better go through with it," I suggested, "probably it is only something symbolical."

But Leo, who, notwithstanding the strange circumstances connected with his life, retained the religious principles in which I had educated him, very strongly indeed, refused to move an inch until the nature of this service was made clear to him. Indeed he expressed himself upon the subject with vigour to Oros. At first the priest seemed puzzled what to do, then explained that the forthcoming ceremony was one of betrothal.

On learning this Leo raised no further objections, asking only with some nervousness whether the Khania would be present. Oros answered "No," as she had already departed to Kaloon, vowing war and vengeance.

Then we were led through long passages, till finally we emerged into the gallery immediately in front of the great wooden doors of the apse. At our approach these swung open and we entered it, Oros going first, then Leo, then myself, and following us, the procession of attendant priests.

As soon as our eyes became accustomed to the dazzling glare of the flaming pillars, we saw that some great rite was in progress in the temple, for in front of the divine statue of Motherhood, white-robed and arranged in serried ranks, stood the company of the priests to the number of over two hundred, and behind these the company of the priestesses. Facing this congregation and a little in advance of the two pillars of fire that flared on either side of the shrine, Ayesha herself was seated in a raised chair so that she could be seen of all, while to her right stood a similar chair of which I could guess the purpose.

She was unveiled and gorgeously apparelled, though save for the white beneath, her robes were those of a queen rather than of a priestess. About her radiant brow ran a narrow band of gold, whence rose the head of a hooded asp cut out of a single, crimson jewel, beneath which in endless profusion the glorious waving hair flowed down and around, hiding even the folds of her purple cloak.

This cloak, opening in front, revealed an undertunic of white silk cut low upon her bosom and kept in place by a golden girdle, a double-headed snake, so like to that which She had worn in Kor that it might have been the same. Her naked arms were bare of ornament, and in her right hand she held the jewelled sistrum set with its gems and bells.

No empress could have looked more royal and no woman was ever half so lovely, for to Ayesha's human beauty was added a spiritual glory, her heritage alone. Seeing her we could see naught else. The rhythmic movement of the bodies of the worshippers, the rolling grandeur of their chant of welcome echoed from the mighty roof, the fearful torches of living flame; all these things were lost on us. For there re-born, enthroned, her arms stretched out in gracious welcome, sat that perfect and immortal woman, the appointed bride of one of us, the friend and lady of the other, her divine presence breathing power, mystery and love.

On we marched between the ranks of hierophants, till Oros and the priests left us and we stood alone face to face with Ayesha. Now she lifted her sceptre and the chant ceased. In the midst of the following silence, she rose from her seat and gliding down its steps, came to where Leo stood and touched him on the forehead with her sistrum, crying in a loud, sweet voice—"Behold the Chosen of the Hesea!" whereon all that audience echoed in a shout of thunder—"Welcome to the Chosen of the Hesea!"

Then while the echoes of that glad cry yet rang round the rocky walls, Ayesha motioned to me to stand at her side, and taking Leo by the hand drew him towards her, so that now he faced the white-robed company. Holding him thus she began to speak in clear and silvery tones.

"Priests and priestesses of Hes, servants with her of the Mother of the world, hear me. Now for the first time I appear among you as I am, you who heretofore have looked but on a hooded shape, not knowing its form or fashion. Learn now the reason that I draw my veil. Ye see this man, whom ye believed a stranger that with his companion had wandered to our shrine. I tell you that he is no stranger; that of old, in lives forgotten, he was my lord who now comes to seek his love again. Say, is it not so, Kallikrates?"

"It is so," answered Leo.

"Priests and priestesses of Hes, as ye know, from the beginning it has been the right and custom of her who holds my place to choose one to be her lord. Is it not so?"

"It is so, O Hes," they answered.

She paused a while, then with a gesture of infinite sweetness turned to Leo, bent towards him thrice and slowly sank upon her knee.

"Say thou," Ayesha said, looking up at him with her wondrous eyes, "say before these here gathered, and all those witnesses whom thou canst not see, dost thou again accept me as thy affianced bride?"

"Aye, Lady," he answered, in a deep but shaken voice, "now and for ever."

Then while all watched, in the midst of a great silence, Ayesha rose, cast down her sistrum sceptre that rang upon the rocky floor, and stretched out her arms towards him.

Leo also bent towards her, and would have kissed her upon the lips. But I who watched, saw his face grow white as it drew near to hers. While the radiance crept from her brow to his, turning his bright hair to gold, I saw also that this strong man trembled like a reed and seemed as though he were about to fall.

I think that Ayesha noted it too, for ere ever their lips met, she thrust him from her and again that grey mist of fear gathered on her face.

In an instant it passed. She had slipped from him and with her hand held his hand as though to support him. Thus they stood till his feet grew firm and his strength returned.

Oros restored the sceptre to her, and lifting it she said—"O love and lord, take thou the place prepared for thee, where thou shalt sit for ever at my side, for with myself I give thee more than thou canst know or than I will tell thee now. Mount thy throne, O Affianced of Hes, and receive the worship of thy priests."

"Nay," he answered with a start as that word fell upon his ears. "Here and now I say it once and for all. I am but a man who know nothing of strange gods, their attributes and ceremonials. None shall bow the knee to me and on earth, Ayesha, I bow mine to thee alone."

Now at this bold speech some of those who heard it looked astonished and whispered to each other, while a voice called—"Beware, thou Chosen, of the anger of the Mother!"

Again for a moment Ayesha looked afraid, then with a little laugh, swept the thing aside, saying—"Surely with that I should be content. For me, O Love, thy adoration for thee the betrothal song, no more."

So having no choice Leo mounted the throne, where notwithstanding his splendid presence, enhanced as it was by those glittering robes, he looked ill enough at ease, as indeed must any man of his faith and race. Happily however, if some act of semi-idolatrous homage had been proposed, Ayesha found a means to prevent its celebration, and soon all such matters were forgotten both by the singers who sang, and us who listened to the majestic chant that followed.

Of its words unfortunately we were able to understand but little, both because of the volume of sound and of the secret, priestly language in which it was given, though its general purport could not be mistaken.

The female voices began it, singing very low, and conveying a strange impression of time and distance. Now followed bursts of gladness alternating with melancholy chords suggesting sighs and tears and sorrows long endured, and at the end a joyous, triumphant paean thrown to and fro between the men and women singers, terminating in one united chorus repeated again and again, louder and yet louder, till it culminated in a veritable crash of melody, then of a sudden ceased.

Ayesha rose and waved her sceptre, whereon all the company bowed thrice, then turned and breaking into some sweet, low chant that sounded like a lullaby, marched, rank after rank, across the width of the Sanctuary and through the carven doors which closed behind the last of them.

When all had gone, leaving us alone, save for the priest Oros and the priestess Papave, who remained in attendance on their mistress, Ayesha, who sat gazing before her with dreaming, empty eyes, seemed to awake, for she rose and said—"A noble chant, is it not, and an ancient? It was the wedding song of the feast of Isis and Osiris at Behbit in Egypt, and there I heard it before ever I saw the darksome Caves of Kor. Often have I observed, my Holly, that music lingers longer than aught else in this changeful world, though it is rare that the very words should remain unvaried. Come, beloved—tell me, by what name shall I call thee? Thou art Kallikrates and yet——"

"Call me Leo, Ayesha," he answered, "as I was christened in the only life of which I have any knowledge. This Kallikrates seems to have been an unlucky man, and the deeds he did, if in truth he was aught other than a tool in the hand of destiny, have bred no good to the inheritors of his body—or his spirit, whichever it may be—or to those women with whom his life was intertwined. Call me Leo, then, for of Kallikrates I have had enough since that night when I looked upon the last of him in Kor."

"Ah! I remember," she answered, "when thou sawest thyself lying in that narrow bed, and I sang thee a song, did I not, of the past and of the future? I can recall two lines of it; the rest I have forgotten—

"'Onward, never weary, clad with splendour for a robe!

Till accomplished be our fate, and the night is rushing down.'

"Yes, my Leo, now indeed we are 'clad with splendour for a robe,' and now our fate draws near to its accomplishment. Then perchance will come the down-rushing of the night;" and she sighed, looked up tenderly and said, "See, I am talking to thee in Arabic. Hast thou forgotten it?"

"No."

"Then let it be our tongue, for I love it best of all, who lisped it at my mother's knee. Now leave me here alone awhile; I would think. Also," she added thoughtfully, and speaking with a strange and impressive inflexion of the voice, "there are some to whom I must give audience."

So we went, all of us, supposing that Ayesha was about to receive a deputation of the Chiefs of the Mountain Tribes who came to felicitate her upon her betrothal.

XVIII. THE THIRD ORDEAL

An hour, two hours passed, while we strove to rest in our sleeping place, but could not, for some influence disturbed us.

"Why does not Ayesha come?" asked Leo at length, pausing in his walk up and down the room. "I want to see her again; I cannot bear to be apart from her. I feel as though she were drawing me to her."

"How can I tell you? Ask Oros; he is outside the door."

So he went and asked him, but Oros only smiled, and answered that the Hesea had not entered her chamber, so doubtless she must still remain in the Sanctuary.

"Then I am going to look for her. Come, Oros, and you too, Horace."

Oros bowed, but declined, saying that he was bidden to bide at our door, adding that we, "to whom all the paths were open," could return to the Sanctuary if we thought well.

"I do think well," replied Leo sharply. "Will you come, Horace, or shall I go without you?"

I hesitated. The Sanctuary was a public place, it is true, but Ayesha had said that she desired to be alone there for awhile. Without more words, however, Leo shrugged his shoulders and started.

"You will never find your way," I said, and followed him.

We went down the long passages that were dimly lighted with lamps and came to the gallery. Here we found no lamps; still we groped our way to the great wooden doors. They were shut, but Leo pushed upon them impatiently, and one of them swung open a little, so that we could squeeze ourselves between them. As we passed it closed noiselessly behind us.

Now we should have been in the Sanctuary, and in the full blaze of those awful columns of living fire. But they were out, or we had strayed elsewhere; at least the darkness was intense. We tried to work our way back to the doors again, but could not. We were lost.

More, something oppressed us; we did not dare to speak. We went on a few paces and stopped, for we became aware that we were not alone. Indeed, it seemed to me that we stood in the midst of a thronging multitude, but not of men and women. Beings pressed about us; we could feel their robes, yet could not touch them; we could feel their breath, but it was cold. The air stirred all round us as they passed to and fro, passed in endless numbers. It was as though we had entered a cathedral filled with the vast congregation of all the dead who once had worshipped there. We grew afraid—my face was damp with fear, the hair stood up upon my head. We seemed to have wandered into a hall of the Shades.

At length light appeared far away, and we saw that it emanated from the two pillars of fire which had burned on either side of the Shrine, that of a sudden became luminous. So we were in the Sanctuary, and still near to the doors. Now those pillars were not bright; they were low and lurid; the rays from them scarcely reached us standing in the dense shadow.

But if we could not be seen in them we still could see. Look! Yonder sat Ayesha on a throne, and oh! she was awful in her death-like majesty. The blue light of the sunken columns played upon her, and in it she sat erect, with such a face and mien of pride as no human creature ever wore. Power seemed to flow from her; yes, it flowed from those wide-set, glittering eyes like light from jewels.

She seemed a Queen of Death receiving homage from the dead. More, she was receiving homage from dead or living—I know not which—for, as I thought it, a shadowy Shape arose before the throne and bent the knee to her, then another, and another, and another.

As each vague Being appeared and bowed its starry head she raised her sceptre in answering salutation. We could hear the distant tinkle of the sistrum bells, the only sound in all that place, yes, and see her lips move, though no whisper reached us from them. Surely spirits were worshipping her!

We gripped each other. We shrank back and found the door. It gave to our push. Now we were in the passages again, and now we had reached our room.

At its entrance Oros was standing as we had left him. He greeted us with his fixed smile, taking no note of the terror written on our faces. We passed him, and entering the room stared at each other.

"What is she?" gasped Leo. "An angel?"

"Yes," I answered, "something of that sort." But to myself I thought that there are doubtless many kinds of angels.

"And what were those—those shadows—doing?" he asked again.

"Welcoming her after her transformation, I suppose. But perhaps they were not shadows—only priests disguised and conducting some secret ceremonial!"

Leo shrugged his shoulders but made no other answer.

At length the door opened, and Oros, entering, said that the Hesea commanded our presence in her chamber.

So, still oppressed with fear and wonder—for what we had seen was perhaps more dreadful than anything that had gone before—we went, to find Ayesha seated and looking somewhat weary, but otherwise unchanged. With her was the priestess Papave, who had just unrobed her of the royal mantle which she wore in the Sanctuary.

Ayesha beckoned Leo to her, taking his hand and searching his face with her eyes, not without anxiety as I thought.

Now I turned, purposing to leave them alone, but she saw, and said to me, smiling—"Why wouldst thou forsake us, Holly? To go back to the Sanctuary once more?" and she looked at me with meaning in her glance. "Hast thou questions to ask of the statue of the Mother yonder that thou lovest the place so much? They say it speaks, telling of the future to those who dare to kneel beside it uncompanioned from night till dawn. Yet I have often done so, but to me it has never spoken, though none long to learn the future more."

I made no answer, nor did she seem to expect any, for she went on at once—"Nay, bide here and let us have done with all sad and solemn thoughts. We three will sup together as of old, and for awhile forget our fears and cares, and be happy as children who know not sin and death, or that change which is death indeed. Oros, await my lord without. Papave, I will call thee later to disrobe me. Till then let none disturb us."

The room that Ayesha inhabited was not very large, as we saw by the hanging lamps with which it was lighted. It was plainly though richly furnished, the rock walls being covered with tapestries, and the tables and chairs inlaid with silver, but the only token that here a woman had her home was that about it stood several bowls of flowers. One of these, I remember, was filled with the delicate harebells I had admired, dug up roots and all, and set in moss.

"A poor place," said Ayesha, "yet better than that in which I dwelt those two thousand years awaiting thy coming, Leo, for, see, beyond it is a garden, wherein I sit," and she sank down upon a couch by the table, motioning to us to take our places opposite to her.

The meal was simple; for us, eggs boiled hard and cold venison; for her, milk, some little cakes of flour, and mountain berries.

Presently Leo rose and threw off his gorgeous, purple-broidered robe, which he still wore, and cast upon a chair the crook-headed sceptre that Oros had again thrust into his hand. Ayesha smiled as he did so, saying—"It would seem that thou holdest these sacred emblems in but small respect."

"Very small," he answered. "Thou heardest my words in the Sanctuary, Ayesha, so let us make a pact. Thy religion I do not understand, but I understand my own, and not even for thy sake will I take part in what I hold to be idolatry."

Now I thought that she would be angered by this plain speaking, but she only bowed her head and answered meekly—"Thy will is mine, Leo, though it will not be easy always to explain thy absence from the ceremonies in the temple. Yet thou hast a right to thine own faith, which doubtless is mine also."

"How can that be?" he asked, looking up.

"Because all great Faiths are the same, changed a little to suit the needs of passing times and peoples. What taught that of Egypt, which, in a fashion, we still follow here? That hidden in a multitude of manifestations, one Power great and good, rules all the universes: that the holy shall inherit a life eternal and the vile, eternal death: that men shall be shaped and judged by their own hearts and deeds, and here and hereafter drink of the cup which they have brewed: that their real home is not on earth, but beyond the earth, where all riddles shall be answered and all sorrows cease. Say, dost thou believe these things, as I do?"

"Aye, Ayesha, but Hes or Isis is thy goddess, for hast thou not told us tales of thy dealings with her in the past, and did we not hear thee make thy prayer to her? Who, then, is this goddess Hes?"

"Know, Leo, that she is what I named her—Nature's soul, no divinity, but the secret spirit of the world; that universal Motherhood, whose symbol thou hast seen yonder, and in whose mysteries lie hid all earthly life and knowledge."

"Does, then, this merciful Motherhood follow her votaries with death and evil, as thou sayest she has followed thee for thy disobedience, and me—and another—because of some unnatural vows broken long ago?" Leo asked quietly.

Resting her arm upon the table, Ayesha looked at him with sombre eyes and answered—"In that Faith of thine of which thou speakest are there perchance two gods, each having many ministers: a god of good and a god of evil, an Osiris and a Set?"

He nodded.

"I thought it. And the god of ill is strong, is he not, and can put on the shape of good? Tell me, then, Leo, in the world that is to-day, whereof I know so little, hast thou ever heard of frail souls who for some earthly bribe have sold themselves to that evil one, or to his minister, and been paid their price in bitterness and anguish?"

"All wicked folk do as much in this form or in that," he answered.

"And if once there lived a woman who was mad with the thirst for beauty, for life, for wisdom, and for love, might she not—oh! might she not perchance——"

"Sell herself to the god called Set, or one of his angels? Ayesha, dost thou mean"—and Leo rose, speaking in a voice that was full of fear—"that thou art such a woman?"

"And if so?" she asked, also rising and drawing slowly near to him.

"If so," he answered hoarsely, "if so, I think that perhaps we had best fulfil our fates apart——"

"Ah!" she said, with a little scream of pain as though a knife had stabbed her, "wouldst thou away to Atene? I tell thee that thou canst not leave me. I have power—above all men thou shouldst know it, whom once I slew. Nay, thou hast no memory, poor creature of a breath, and I—I remember too well. I will not hold thee dead again—I'll hold thee living. Look now on my beauty, Leo"—and she bent her swaying form towards him, compelling him with her glorious, alluring eyes—"and begone if thou canst. Why, thou drawest nearer to me. Man, that is not the path of flight.

"Nay, I will not tempt thee with these common lures. Go, Leo, if thou wilt. Go, my love, and leave me to my loneliness and my sin. Now—at once. Atene will shelter thee till spring, when thou canst cross the mountains and return to thine own world again, and to those things of common life which are thy joy. See, Leo, I veil myself that thou mayest not be tempted," and she flung the corner of her cloak about her head, then asked a sudden question through it—"Didst thou not but now return to the Sanctuary with Holly after I bade thee leave me there alone? Methought I saw the two of you standing by its doors."

"Yes, we came to seek thee," he answered.

"And found more than ye sought, as often chances to the bold—is it not so? Well, I willed that ye should come and see, and protected you where others might have died."

"What didst thou there upon the throne, and whose were those forms which we saw bending before thee?" he asked coldly.

"I have ruled in many shapes and lands, Leo. Perchance they were ancient companions and servitors of mine come to greet me once again and to hear my tidings. Or perchance they were but shadows of thy brain, pictures like those upon the fire, that it pleased me to summon to thy sight, to try thy strength and constancy.

"Leo Vincey, know now the truth; that all things are illusions, even that there exists no future and no past, that what has been and what shall be already is eternally. Know that I, Ayesha, am but a magic wraith, foul when thou seest me foul, fair when thou seest me fair; a spirit-bubble reflecting a thousand lights in the sunshine of thy smile, grey as dust and gone in the shadow of thy frown. Think of the throned Queen before whom the shadowy Powers bowed and worship, for that is I. Think of the hideous, withered Thing thou sawest naked on the rock, and flee away, for that is I. Or keep me lovely, and adore, knowing all evil centred in my spirit, for that is I. Now, Leo, thou hast the truth. Put me from thee for ever and for ever if thou wilt, and be safe; or clasp me, clasp me to thy heart, and in payment for my lips and love take my sin upon thy head! Nay, Holly, be thou silent, for now he must judge alone."

Leo turned, as I thought, at first, to find the door. But it was not so, for he did but walk up and down the room awhile. Then he came back to where Ayesha stood, and spoke quite simply and in a very quiet voice, such as men of his nature often assume in moments of great emotion.

"Ayesha," he said, "when I saw thee as thou wast, aged and—thou knowest how—I clung to thee. Now, when thou hast told me the secret of this unholy pact of thine, when with my eyes, at least, I have seen thee reigning a mistress of spirits good or ill, yet I cling to thee. Let thy sin, great or little—whate'er it is—be my sin also. In truth, I feel its weight sink to my soul and become a part of me, and although I have no vision or power of prophecy, I am sure that I shall not escape its punishment. Well, though I be innocent, let me bear it for thy sake. I am content."

Ayesha heard, the cloak slipped from her head, and for a moment she stood silent like one amazed, then burst into a passion of sudden tears. Down she went before him, and clinging to his garments, she bowed her stately shape until her forehead touched the ground. Yes, that proud being, who was more than mortal, whose nostrils but now had drunk the incense of the homage of ghosts or spirits, humbled herself at this man's feet.

With an exclamation of horror, half-maddened at the piteous sight, Leo sprang to one side, then stooping, lifted and led her still weeping to the couch.

"Thou knowest not what thou hast done," Ayesha said at last. "Let all thou sawest on the Mountain's crest or in the Sanctuary be but visions of the night; let that tale of an offended goddess be a parable, a fable, if thou wilt. This at least is true, that ages since I sinned for thee and against thee and another; that ages since I bought beauty and life indefinite wherewith I might win thee and endow thee at a cost which few would dare; that I have paid interest on the debt, in mockery, utter loneliness, and daily pain which scarce could be endured, until the bond fell due at last and must be satisfied.

"Yes, how I may not tell thee, thou and thou alone stoodst between me and the full discharge of this most dreadful debt—for know that in mercy it is given to us to redeem one another."

Now he would have spoken, but with a motion of her hand she bade him be silent, and continued—"See now, Leo, three great dangers has thy body passed of late upon its journey to my side; the Death-hounds, the Mountains, and the Precipice. Know that these were but types and ordained foreshadowings of the last threefold trial of thy soul. From the pursuing passions of Atene which must have undone us both, thou hast escaped victorious. Thou hast endured the desert loneliness of the sands and snows starving for a comfort that never came. Even when the avalanche thundered round thee thy faith stood fast as it stood above the Pit of flame, while after bitter years of doubt a rushing flood of horror swallowed up thy hopes. As thou didst descend the glacier's steep, not knowing what lay beneath that fearful path, so but now and of thine own choice, for very love of me, thou hast plunged headlong into an abyss that is deeper far, to share its terrors with my spirit. Dost thou understand at last?"

"Something, not all, I think," he answered slowly.

"Surely thou art wrapped in a double veil of blindness," she cried impatiently. "Listen again:

"Hadst thou yielded to Nature's crying and rejected me but yesterday, in that foul shape I must perchance have lingered for uncounted time, playing the poor part of priestess of a forgotten faith. This was the first temptation, the ordeal of thy flesh—nay, not the first—the second, for Atene and her lurings were the first. But thou wast loyal, and in the magic of thy conquering love my beauty and my womanhood were re-born.

"Hadst thou rejected me to-night, when, as I was bidden to do, I showed thee that vision in the Sanctuary and confessed to thee my soul's black crime, then hopeless and helpless, unshielded by my earthly power, I must have wandered on into the deep and endless night of solitude. This was the third appointed test, the trial of thy spirit, and by thy steadfastness, Leo, thou hast loosed the hand of Destiny from about my throat. Now I am regenerate in thee—through thee may hope again for some true life beyond, which thou shalt share. And yet, and yet, if thou shouldst suffer, as well may chance——"

"Then I suffer, and there's an end," broke in Leo serenely. "Save for a few things my mind is clear, and there must be justice for us all at last. If I have broken the bond that bound thee, if I have freed thee from some threatening, spiritual ill by taking a risk upon my head, well, I have not lived, and if need be, shall not die in vain. So let us have done with all these problems, or rather first answer thou me one. Ayesha, how wast thou changed upon that peak?"

"In flame I left thee, Leo, and in flame I did return, as in flame, mayhap, we shall both depart. Or perhaps the change was in the eyes of all of you who watched, and not in this shape of mine. I have answered. Seek to learn no more."

"One thing I do still seek to learn. Ayesha, we were betrothed to-night. When wilt thou marry me?"

"Not yet, not yet," she answered hurriedly, her voice quivering as she spoke. "Leo, thou must put that hope from thy thoughts awhile, and for some few months, a year perchance, be content to play the part of friend and lover."

"Why so?" he asked, with bitter disappointment. "Ayesha, those parts have been mine for many a day; more, I grow no younger, and, unlike thee, shall soon be old. Also, life is fleeting, and sometimes I think that I near its end."

"Speak no such evil-omened words," she said, springing from the couch and stamping her sandalled foot upon the ground in anger born of fear. "Yet thou sayest truth; thou art unfortified against the accidents of time and chance. Oh! horrible, horrible; thou mightest die again, and leave me living."

"Then give me of thy life, Ayesha."

"That would I gladly, all of it, couldst thou but repay me with the boon of death to come.

"Oh! ye poor mortals," she went on, with a sudden burst of passion; "ye beseech your gods for the gift of many years, being ignorant that ye would sow a seed within your breasts whence ye must garner ten thousand miseries. Know ye not that this world is indeed the wide house of hell, in whose chambers from time to time the spirit tarries a little while, then, weary and aghast, speeds wailing to the peace that it has won.

"Think then what it is to live on here eternally and yet be human; to age in soul and see our beloved die and pass to lands whither we may not hope to follow; to wait while drop by drop the curse of the long centuries falls upon our imperishable being, like water slow dripping on a diamond that it cannot wear, till they be born anew forgetful of us, and again sink from our helpless arms into the void unknowable.

"Think what it is to see the sins we sin, the tempting look, the word idle or unkind—aye, even the selfish thought or struggle, multiplied ten thousandfold and more eternal than ourselves, spring up upon the universal bosom of the earth to be the bane of a million destinies, whilst the everlasting Finger writes its endless count, and a cold voice of Justice cries in our conscience-haunted solitude, 'Oh! soul unshriven, behold the ripening harvest thy wanton hand did scatter, and long in vain for the waters of forgetfulness.'

"Think what it is to have every earthly wisdom, yet to burn unsatisfied for the deeper and forbidden draught; to gather up all wealth and power and let them slip again, like children weary of a painted toy; to sweep the harp of fame, and, maddened by its jangling music, to stamp it small beneath our feet; to snatch at pleasure's goblet and find its wine is sand, and at length, outworn, to cast us down and pray the pitiless gods with whose stolen garment we have wrapped ourselves, to take it back again, and suffer us to slink naked to the grave.

"Such is the life thou askest, Leo. Say, wilt thou have it now?"

"If it may be shared with thee," he answered. "These woes are born of loneliness, but then our perfect fellowship would turn them into joy."

"Aye," she said, "while it was permitted to endure. So be it, Leo. In the spring, when the snows melt, we will journey together to Libya, and there thou shalt be bathed in the Fount of Life, that forbidden Essence of which once thou didst fear to drink. Afterwards I will wed thee."

"That place is closed for ever, Ayesha."

"Not to my feet and thine," she answered. "Fear not, my love, were this mountain heaped thereon, I would blast a path through it with mine eyes and lay its secret bare. Oh! would that thou wast as I am, for then before tomorrow's sun we'd watch the rolling pillar thunder by, and thou shouldst taste its glory.

"But it may not be. Hunger or cold can starve thee, and waters drown; swords can slay thee, or sickness sap away thy strength. Had it not been for the false Atene, who disobeyed my words, as it was foredoomed that she should do, by this day we were across the mountains, or had travelled northward through the frozen desert and the rivers. Now we must await the melting of the snows, for winter is at hand, and in it, as thou knowest, no man can live upon their heights."

"Eight months till April before we can start, and how long to cross the mountains and all the vast distances beyond, and the seas, and the swamps of Kor? Why, at the best, Ayesha, two years must go by before we can even find the place;" and he fell to entreating her to let them be wed at once and journey afterwards.

But she said, Nay, and nay, and nay, it should not be, till at length, as though fearing his pleading, or that of her own heart, she rose and dismissed us.

"Ah! my Holly," she said to me as we three parted, "I promised thee and myself some few hours of rest and of the happiness of quiet, and thou seest how my desire has been fulfilled. Those old Egyptians were wont to share their feasts with one grizzly skeleton, but here I counted four to-night that you both could see, and they are named Fear, Suspense, Foreboding, and Love-denied. Doubtless also, when these are buried others will come to haunt us, and snatch the poor morsel from our lips.

"So hath it ever been with me, whose feet misfortune dogs. Yet I hope on, and now many a barrier lies behind us; and Leo, thou hast been tried in the appointed, triple fires and yet proved true. Sweet be thy slumbers, O my love, and sweeter still thy dreams, for know, my soul shall share them. I vow to thee that to-morrow we'll be happy, aye, to-morrow without fail."

"Why will she not marry me at once?" asked Leo, when we were alone in our chamber. "Because she is afraid," I answered.

XIX. LEO AND THE LEOPARD

During the weeks that followed these momentous days often and often I wondered to myself whether a more truly wretched being had ever lived than the woman, or the spirit, whom we knew as She, Hes, and Ayesha. Whether in fact also, or in our imagination only, she had arisen from the ashes of her hideous age into the full bloom of perpetual life and beauty inconceivable.

These things at least were certain: Ayesha had achieved the secret of an existence so enduring that for all human purposes it might be called unending. Within certain limitations—such as her utter inability to foresee the future—undoubtedly also, she was endued with powers that can only be described as supernatural.

Her rule over the strange community amongst whom she lived was absolute; indeed, its members regarded her as a goddess, and as such she was worshipped. After marvellous adventures, the man who was her very life, I might almost say her soul, whose being was so mysteriously intertwined with hers, whom she loved also with the intensest human passion of which woman can be capable, had sought her out in this hidden corner of the world.

More, thrice he had proved his unalterable fidelity to her. First, by his rejection of the royal and beautiful, if undisciplined, Atene. Secondly, by clinging to Ayesha when she seemed to be repulsive to every natural sense. Thirdly, after that homage scene in the Sanctuary—though with her unutterable perfections before his eyes this did not appear to be so wonderful—by steadfastness in the face of her terrible avowal, true or false, that she had won her gifts and him through some dim, unholy pact with the powers of evil, in the unknown fruits and consequences of which he must be involved as the price of her possession.

Yet Ayesha was miserable. Even in her lightest moods it was clear to me that those skeletons at the feast of which she had spoken were her continual companions. Indeed, when we were alone she would acknowledge it in dark hints and veiled allegories or allusions. Crushed though her rival the Khania Atene might be, also she was still jealous of her.

Perhaps "afraid" would be a better word, for some instinct seemed to warn Ayesha that soon or late her hour would come to Atene again, and that then it would be her own turn to drink of the bitter waters of despair.

What troubled her more a thousandfold, however, were her fears for Leo. As may well be understood, to stand in his intimate relationship to this half divine and marvellous being, and yet not to be allowed so much as to touch her lips, did not conduce to his physical or mental well-being, especially as he knew that the wall of separation must not be climbed for at least two years. Little wonder that Leo lost appetite, grew thin and pale, and could not sleep, or that he implored her continually to rescind her decree and marry him.

But on this point Ayesha was immovable. Instigated thereto by Leo, and I may add my own curiosity, when we were alone I questioned her again as to the reasons of this self-denying ordinance. All she would tell me, however, was that between them rose the barrier of Leo's mortality, and that until his physical being had been impregnated with the mysterious virtue of the Vapour of Life, it was not wise that she should take him as a husband.

I asked her why, seeing that though a long-lived one, she was still a woman, whereon her face assumed a calm but terrifying smile, and she answered—"Art so sure, my Holly? Tell me, do your women wear such jewels as that set upon my brow?" and she pointed to the faint but lambent light which glowed about her forehead.

More, she began slowly to stroke her abundant hair, then her breast and body. Wherever her fingers passed the mystic light was born, until in that darkened room—for the dusk was gathering—she shimmered from head to foot like the water of a phosphorescent sea, a being glorious yet fearful to behold. Then she waved her hand, and, save for the gentle radiance on her brow, became as she had been.

"Art so sure, my Holly?" Ayesha repeated. "Nay, shrink not; that flame will not burn thee. Mayhap thou didst but imagine it, as I have noted thou dost imagine many things; for surely no woman could clothe herself in light and live, nor has so much as the smell of fire passed upon my garments."

Then at length my patience was outworn, and I grew angry.

"I am sure of nothing, Ayesha," I answered, "except that thou wilt make us mad with all these tricks and changes. Say, art thou a spirit then?"

"We are all spirits," she said reflectively, "and I, perhaps, more than some. Who can be certain?"

"Not I," I answered. "Yet I implore, woman or spirit, tell me one thing. Tell me the truth. In the beginning what wast thou to Leo, and what was he to thee?"

She looked at me very solemnly and answered—"Does my memory deceive me, Holly, or is it written in the first book of the Law of the Hebrews, which once I used to study, that the sons of Heaven came down to the daughters of men, and found that they were fair?"

"It is so written," I answered.

"Then, Holly, might it not have chanced that once a daughter of Heaven came down to a man of Earth and loved him well? Might it not chance that for her great sin, she, this high, fallen star, who had befouled her immortal state for him, was doomed to suffer till at length his love, made divine by pain and faithful even to a memory, was permitted to redeem her?"

Now at length I saw light and sprang up eagerly, but in a cold voice she added:

"Nay, Holly, cease to question me, for there are things of which I can but speak to thee in figures and in parables, not to mock and bewilder thee, but because I must. Interpret them as thou wilt. Still, Atene thought me no mortal, since she told us that man and spirit may not mate; and there are matters in which I let her judgment weigh with me, as without doubt now, as in other lives, she and that old Shaman, her uncle, have wisdom, aye, and foresight. So bid my lord press me no more to wed him, for it gives me pain to say him nay—ah! thou knowest not how much.

"Moreover, I will declare myself to thee, old friend; whatever else I be, at least I am too womanly to listen to the pleadings of my best beloved and not myself be moved. See, I have set a curb upon desire and drawn it until my heart bleeds; but if he pursues me with continual words and looks of burning love, who knoweth but that I shall kindle in his flame and throw the reins of reason to the winds?

"Oh, then together we might race adown our passions' steep; together dare the torrent that rages at its foot, and there perchance be whelmed or torn asunder. Nay, nay, another space of journeying, but a little space, and we reach the bridge my wisdom found, and cross it safely, and beyond for ever ride on at ease through the happy meadows of our love."

Then she was silent, nor would she speak more upon the matter. Also—and this was the worst of it—even now I was not sure that she told me the truth, or, at any rate, all of it, for to Ayesha's mind truth seemed many coloured as are the rays of light thrown from the different faces of a cut jewel. We never could be certain which shade of it she was pleased to present, who, whether by preference or of necessity, as she herself had said, spoke of such secrets in figures of speech and parables.

It is a fact that to this hour I do not know whether Ayesha is spirit or woman, or, as I suspect, a blend of both. I do not know the limits of her powers, or if that elaborate story of the beginning of her love for Leo was true—which personally I doubt—or but a fable, invented by her mind, and through it, as she had hinted, pictured on the flame for her own hidden purposes.

I do not know whether when first we saw her on the Mountain she was really old and hideous, or did but put on that shape in our eyes in order to test her lover. I do not know whether, as the priest Oros bore witness—which he may well have been bidden to do—her spirit passed into the body of the dead priestess of Hes, or whether when she seemed to perish there so miserably, her body and her soul were wafted straightway from the Caves of Kor to this Central Asian peak.

I do not know why, as she was so powerful, she did not come to seek us, instead of leaving us to seek her through so many weary years, though I suggest that some superior force forbade her to do more than companion us unseen, watching our every act, reading our every thought, until at length we reached the predestined place and hour. Also, as will appear, there were other things of which this is not the time to speak, whereby I am still more tortured and perplexed.

In short, I know nothing, except that my existence has been intertangled with one of the great mysteries of the world; that the glorious being called Ayesha won the secret of life from whatever power holds it in its keeping; that she alleged—although of this, remember, we have no actual proof—such life was to be attained by bathing in a certain emanation, vapour or essence; that she was possessed by a passion not easy to understand, but terrific in its force and immortal in its nature, concentrated upon one other being and one alone. That through this passion also some angry fate smote her again, again, and yet again, making of her countless days a burden, and leading the power and the wisdom which knew all but could foreknow nothing, into abysses of anguish, suspense, and disappointment such as—Heaven be thanked!—we common men and women are not called upon to plumb.

For the rest, should human eyes ever fall upon it, each reader must form his own opinion of this history, its true interpretation and significance.

These and the exact parts played by Atene and myself in its development I hope to solve shortly, though not here.

Well, as I have said, the upshot of it all was that Ayesha was devoured with anxiety about Leo. Except in this matter of marriage, his every wish was satisfied, and indeed forestalled. Thus he was never again asked to share in any of the ceremonies of the Sanctuary, though, indeed, stripped of its rites and spiritual symbols, the religion of the College of Hes proved pure and harmless enough. It was but a diluted version of the Osiris and Isis worship of old Egypt, from which it had been inherited, mixed with the Central Asian belief in the transmigration or reincarnation of souls and the possibility of drawing near to the ultimate Godhead by holiness of thought and life.

In fact, the head priestess and Oracle was only worshipped as a representative of the Divinity, while the temporal aims of the College in practice were confined to good works, although it is true that they still sighed for their lost authority over the country of Kaloon. Thus they had hospitals, and during the long and severe winters, when the Tribes of the Mountain slopes were often driven to the verge of starvation, gave liberally to the destitute from their stores of food.

Leo liked to be with Ayesha continually, so we spent each evening in her company, and much of the day also, until she found that this inactivity told upon him who for years had been accustomed to endure every rigour of climate in the open air. After this came home to her—although she was always haunted by terror lest any accident should befall him—Ayesha insisted upon his going out to kill the wild sheep and the ibex, which lived in numbers on the mountain ridges, placing him in the charge of the chiefs and huntsmen of the Tribes, with whom thus he became well acquainted. In this exercise, however, I accompanied him but rarely, as, if used too much, my arm still gave me pain.

Once indeed such an accident did happen. I was seated in the garden with Ayesha and watching her. Her head rested on her hand, and she was looking with her wide eyes, across which the swift thoughts passed like clouds over a windy sky, or dreams through the mind of a sleeper—looking out vacantly towards the mountain snows. Seen thus her loveliness was inexpressible, amazing; merely to gaze upon it was an intoxication. Contemplating it, I understood indeed that, like to that of the fabled Helen, this gift of hers alone—and it was but one of many—must have caused infinite sorrows, had she ever been permitted to display it to the world. It would have driven humanity to madness: the men with longings and the women with jealousy and hate.

And yet in what did her surpassing beauty lie? Ayesha's face and form were perfect, it is true; but so are those of some other women. Not in these then did it live alone, but rather, I think, especially while what I may call her human moods were on her, in the soft mystery that dwelt upon her features and gathered and changed in her splendid eyes. Some such mystery may be seen, however faintly, on the faces of certain of the masterpieces of the Greek sculptors, but Ayesha it clothed like an ever-present atmosphere, suggesting a glory that was not of earth, making her divine.

As I gazed at her and wondered thus, of a sudden she became terribly agitated, and, pointing to a shoulder of the Mountain miles and miles away, said—"Look!"

I looked, but saw nothing except a sheet of distant snow.

"Blind fool, canst thou not see that my lord is in danger of his life?" she cried. "Nay, I forgot, thou hast no vision. Take it now from me and look again;" and laying her hand, from which a strange, numbing current seemed to flow, upon my head, she muttered some swift words.

Instantly my eyes were opened, and, not upon the distant Mountain, but in the air before me as it were, I saw Leo rolling over and over at grips with a great snow-leopard, whilst the chief and huntsmen with him ran round and round, seeking an opportunity to pierce the savage brute with their spears and yet leave him unharmed.

Ayesha, rigid with terror, swayed to and fro at my side, till presently the end came, for I could see Leo drive his long knife into the bowels of the leopard, which at once grew limp, separated from him, and after a struggle or two in the bloodstained snow, lay still. Then he rose, laughing and pointing to his rent garments, whilst one of the huntsmen came forward and began to bandage some wounds in his hands and thigh with strips of linen torn from his under-robe.

The vision vanished suddenly as it had come, and I felt Ayesha leaning heavily upon my shoulder like any other frightened woman, and heard her gasp—"That danger also has passed by, but how many are there to follow? Oh! tormented heart, how long canst thou endure!"

Then her wrath flamed up against the chief and his huntsmen, and she summoned messengers and sent them out at speed with a litter and ointments, bidding them to bear back the lord Leo and to bring his companions to her very presence.

"Thou seest what days are mine, my Holly, aye, and have been these many years," she said; "but those hounds shall pay me for this agony."

Nor would she suffer me to reason with her.

Four hours later Leo returned, limping after the litter in which, instead of himself, for whom it was sent, lay a mountain sheep and the skin of the snow-leopard that he had placed there to save the huntsmen the labour of carrying them. Ayesha was waiting for him in the hall of her dwelling, and gliding to him—I cannot say she walked—overwhelmed him with mingled solicitude and reproaches. He listened awhile, then asked—"How dost thou know anything of this matter? The leopard skin has not yet been brought to thee."

"I know because I saw," she answered. "The worst hurt was above thy knee; hast thou dressed it with the salve I sent?"

"Not I," he said. "But thou hast not left this Sanctuary; how didst thou see? By thy magic?"

"If thou wilt, at least I saw, and Holly also saw thee rolling in the snow with that fierce brute, while those curs ran round like scared children."

"I am weary of this magic," interrupted Leo crossly. "Cannot a man be left alone for an hour even with a leopard of the mountain? As for those brave men——"

At this moment Oros entered and whispered something, bowing low.

"As for those 'brave men,' I will deal with them," said Ayesha with bitter emphasis, and covering herself—for she never appeared unveiled to the people of the Mountain—she swept from the place.

"Where has she gone, Horace?" asked Leo. "To one of her services in the Sanctuary?"

"I don't know," I answered; "but if so, I think it will be that chief's burial service."

"Will it?" he exclaimed, and instantly limped after her.

A minute or two later I thought it wise to follow. In the Sanctuary a curious scene was in progress. Ayesha was seated in front of the statue. Before her, very much frightened, knelt a brawny, red-haired chieftain and five of his followers, who still carried their hunting spears, while with folded arms and an exceedingly grim look upon his face, Leo, who, as I learned afterwards, had already interfered and been silenced, stood upon one side listening to what passed. At a little distance behind were a dozen or more of the temple guards, men armed with swords and picked for their strength and stature.

Ayesha, in her sweetest voice, was questioning the men as to how the leopard, of which the skin lay before her, had come to attack Leo. The chief answered that they had tracked the brute to its lair between two rocks; that one of them had gone in and wounded it, whereon it sprang upon him and struck him down; that then the lord Leo had engaged it while the man escaped, and was also struck down, after which, rolling with it on the ground, he stabbed and slew the animal. That was all.

"No, not all," said Ayesha; "for you forget, cowards that you are, that, keeping yourselves in safety, you left my lord to the fury of this beast. Good. Drive them out on to the Mountain, there to perish also at the fangs of beasts, and make it known that he who gives them food or shelter dies."

Offering no prayer for pity or excuse, the chief and his followers rose, bowed, and turned to go.

"Stay a moment, comrades," said Leo, "and, chief, give me your arm; my scratch grows stiff; I cannot walk fast. We will finish this hunt together."

"What doest thou? Art mad?" asked Ayesha.

"I know not whether I am mad," he answered, "but I know that thou art wicked and unjust. Look now, than these hunters none braver ever breathed. That man"—and he pointed to the one whom the leopard had struck down—"took my place and went in before me because I ordered that we should attack the creature, and thus was felled. As thou seest all, thou mightest have seen this also. Then it sprang on me, and the rest of these, my friends, ran round waiting a chance to strike, which at first they could not do unless they would have killed me with it, since I and the brute rolled over and over in the snow. As it was, one of them seized it with his bare hands: look at the teeth marks on his arm. So if they are to perish on the Mountain, I, who am the man to blame, perish with them."

Now, while the hunters looked at him with fervent gratitude in their eyes, Ayesha thought a little, then said cleverly enough—"In truth, my lord Leo, had I known all the tale, well mightest thou have named me wicked and unjust; but I knew only what I saw, and out of their own mouths did I condemn them. My servants, my lord here has pleaded for you, and you are forgiven; more, he who rushed in upon the leopard and he who seized it with his hands shall be rewarded and advanced. Go; but I warn you if you suffer my lord to come into more danger, you shall not escape so easily again."

So they bowed and went, still blessing Leo with their eyes, since death by exposure on the Mountain snows was the most terrible form of punishment known to these people, and one only inflicted by the direct order of Hes upon murderers or other great criminals.

When we had left the Sanctuary and were alone again in the hall, the storm that I had seen gathering upon Leo's face broke in earnest. Ayesha renewed her inquiries about his wounds, and wished to call Oros, the physician, to dress them, and as he refused this, offered to do so herself. He begged that she would leave his wounds alone, and then, his great beard bristling with wrath, asked her solmenly if he was a child in arms, a query so absurd that I could not help laughing.

Then he scolded her—yes, he scolded Ayesha! Wishing to know what she meant (1) by spying upon him with her magic, an evil gift that he had always disliked and mistrusted; (2) by condemning brave and excellent men, his good friends, to a death of fiendish cruelty upon such evidence, or rather out of temper, on no evidence at all; and (3) by giving him into charge of them, as though he were a little boy, and telling them that they would have to answer for it if he were hurt: he who, in his time, had killed every sort of big game known and passed through some perils and encounters?

Thus he beat her with his words, and, wonderful to say, Ayesha, this being more than woman, submitted to the chastisement meekly. Yet had any other man dared to address her with roughness even, I doubt not that his speech and his life would have come to a swift and simultaneous end, for I knew that now, as of old, she could slay by the mere effort of her will. But she did not slay; she did not even threaten, only, as any other loving woman might have done, she began to cry. Yes, great tears gathered in those lovely eyes of hers and, rolling one by one down her face, fell—for her head was bent humbly forward—like heavy raindrops on the marble floor.

At the sight of this touching evidence of her human, loving heart all Leo's anger melted. Now it was he who grew penitent and prayed her pardon humbly. She gave him her hand in token of forgiveness, saying—

"Let others speak to me as they will" (sorry should I have been to try it!) "but from thee, Leo, I cannot bear harsh words. Oh, thou art cruel, cruel. In what have I offended? Can I help it if my spirit keeps its watch upon thee, as indeed, though thou knewest it not, it has done ever since we parted yonder in the Place of Life? Can I help it if, like some mother who sees her little child at play upon a mountain's edge, my soul is torn with agony when I know thee in dangers that I am powerless to prevent or share? What are the lives of a few half-wild huntsmen that I should let them weigh for a single breath against thy safety, seeing that if I slew these, others would be more careful of thee? Whereas if I slay them not, they or their fellows may even lead thee into perils that would bring about—thy death," and she gasped with horror at the word.

"Listen, beloved," said Leo. "The life of the humblest of those men is of as much value to him as mine is to me, and thou hast no more right to kill him than thou hast to kill me. It is evil that because thou carest for me thou shouldst suffer thy love to draw thee into cruelty and crime. If thou art afraid for me, then clothe me with that immortality of thine, which, although I dread it somewhat, holding it a thing unholy, and, on this earth, not permitted by my Faith, I should still rejoice to inherit for thy dear sake, knowing that then we could never more be parted. Or, if as thou sayest, this as yet thou canst not do, then let us be wed and take what fortune gives us. All men must die; but at least before I die I shall have been happy with thee for a while—yes, if only for a single hour."

"Would that I dared," Ayesha answered with a little piteous motion of her hand. "Oh! urge me no more, Leo, lest that at last I should take the risk and lead thee down a dreadful road. Leo, hast thou never heard of the love which slays, or of the poison that may lurk in a cup of joy too perfect?"

Then, as though she feared herself, Ayesha turned from him and fled.

Thus this matter ended. In itself it was not a great one, for Leo's hurts were mere scratches, and the hunters, instead of being killed, were promoted to be members of his body-guard. Yet it told us many things. For instance, that whenever she chose to do so, Ayesha had the power of perceiving all Leo's movements from afar, and even of communicating her strength of mental vision to others, although to help him in any predicament she appeared to have no power, which, of course, accounted for the hideous and ever-present might of her anxiety.

Think what it would be to any one of us were we mysteriously acquainted with every open danger, every risk of sickness, every secret peril through which our best-beloved must pass. To see the rock trembling to its fall and they loitering beneath it; to see them drink of water and know it full of foulest poison; to see them embark upon a ship and be aware that it was doomed to sink, but not to be able to warn them or to prevent them.

Surely no mortal brain could endure such constant terrors, since hour by hour the arrows of death flit unseen and unheard past the breasts of each of us, till at length one finds its home there.

What then must Ayesha have suffered, watching with her spirit's eyes all the hair-breadth escapes of our journeyings? When, for instance, in the beginning she saw Leo at my house in Cumberland about to kill himself in his madness and despair, and by some mighty effort of her superhuman will, wrung from whatever Power it was that held her in its fearful thraldom, the strength to hurl her soul across the world and thereby in his sleep reveal to him the secret of the hiding-place where he would find her.

Or to take one more example out of many—when she saw him hanging by that slender thread of yak's hide from the face of the waterfall of ice and herself remained unable to save him, or even to look forward for a single moment and learn whether or no he was about to meet a hideous death, in which event she must live on alone until in some dim age he was born again.

Nor can her sorrows have ended with these more material fears, since others as piercing must have haunted her. Imagine, for instance, the agonies of her jealous heart when she knew her lover to be exposed to the temptations incident to his solitary existence, and more especially to those of her ancient rival Atene, who, by Ayesha's own account, had once been his wife. Imagine also her fears lest time and human change should do their natural work on him, so that by degrees the memory of her wisdom and her strength, and the image of her loveliness faded from his thought, and with them his desire for her company; thus leaving her who had endured so long, forgotten and alone at last.

Truly, the Power that limited our perceptions did so in purest mercy, for were it otherwise with us, our race would go mad and perish raving in its terrors.

Thus it would seem that Ayesha, great tormented soul, thinking to win life and love eternal and most glorious, was in truth but another blind Pandora. From her stolen casket of beauty and super-human power had leapt into her bosom, there to dwell unceasingly, a hundred torturing demons, of whose wings mere mortal kind do but feel the far-off, icy shadowing.

Yes; and that the parallel might be complete, Hope alone still lingered in that rifled chest.

XX. AYESHA'S ALCHEMY

It was shortly after this incident of the snow-leopard that one of these demon familiars of Ayesha's, her infinite ambition, made its formidable appearance. When we had dined with her in the evening, Ayesha's habit was to discuss plans for our mighty and unending future, that awful inheritance which she had promised to us.

Here I must explain, if I have not done so already, that she had graciously informed me that notwithstanding my refusal in past years of such a priceless opportunity, I also was to be allowed to bathe my superannuated self in the vital fires, though in what guise I should emerge from them, like Herodotus when he treats of the mysteries of old Egypt, if she knew, she did not think it lawful to reveal.

Secretly I hoped that my outward man might change for the better, as the prospect of being fixed for ever in the shape of my present and somewhat unpleasing personality, did not appeal to me as attractive. In truth, so far as I was concerned, the matter had an academic rather than an actual interest, such as we take in a fairy tale, since I did not believe that I should ever put on this kind of immortality. Nor, I may add, now as before, was I at all certain that I wished to do so.

These plans of Ayesha's were far reaching and indeed terrific. Her acquaintance with the modern world, its political and social developments, was still strictly limited; for if she had the power to follow its growth and activities, certainly it was one of which she made no use.

In practice her knowledge seemed to be confined to what she had gathered during the few brief talks which took place between us upon this subject in past time at Kor. Now her thirst for information proved insatiable, although it is true that ours was scarcely up to date, seeing that ever since we lost touch with the civilized peoples, namely, for the last fifteen years or so, we had been as much buried as she was herself.

Still we were able to describe to her the condition of the nations and their affairs as they were at the period when we bade them farewell, and, more or less incorrectly, to draw maps of the various countries and their boundaries, over which she pondered long.

The Chinese were the people in whom she proved to be most interested, perhaps because she was acquainted with the Mongolian type, and like ourselves, understood a good many of their dialects. Also she had a motive for her studies, which one night she revealed to us in the most matter-of-fact fashion.

Those who have read the first part of her history, which I left in England to be published, may remember that when we found her at Kor, She horrified us by expressing a determination to possess herself of Great Britain, for the simple reason that we belonged to that country. Now, however, like her powers, her ideas had grown, for she purposed to make Leo the absolute monarch of the world. In vain did he assure her most earnestly that he desired no such empire. She merely laughed at him and said—"If I arise amidst the Peoples, I must rule the Peoples, for how can Ayesha take a second place among mortal men? And thou, my Leo, rulest me, yes, mark the truth, thou art my master! Therefore it is plain that thou wilt be the master of this earth, aye, and perchance of others which do not yet appear, for of these also I know something, and, I think, can reach them if I will, though hitherto I have had no mind that way. My true life has not yet begun. Its little space within this world has been filled with thought and care for thee; in waiting till thou wast born again, and during these last years of separation, until thou didst return.

"But now a few more months, and the days of preparation past, endowed with energy eternal, with all the wisdom of the ages, and with a strength that can bend the mountains or turn the ocean from its bed, and we begin to be. Oh! how I sicken for that hour when first, like twin stars new to the firmament of heaven, we break in our immortal splendour upon the astonished sight of men. It will please me, I tell thee, Leo, it will please me, to see Powers, Principalities and Dominions, marshalled by their kings and governors, bow themselves before our thrones and humbly crave the liberty to do our will. At least," she added, "it will please me for a little time, until we seek higher things."

So she spoke, while the radiance upon her brow increased and spread itself, gleaming above her like a golden fan, and her slumbrous eyes took fire from it till, to my thought, they became glowing mirrors in which I saw pomp enthroned and suppliant peoples pass.

"And how," asked Leo, with something like a groan—for this vision of universal rule viewed from afar did not seem to charm him—"how, Ayesha, wilt thou bring these things about?"

"How, my Leo? Why, easily enough. For many nights I have listened to the wise discourses of our Holly here, at least he thinks them wise who still has so much to learn, and pored over his crooked maps, comparing them with those that are written in my memory, who of late have had no time for the study of such little matters. Also I have weighed and pondered your reports of the races of this world; their various follies, their futile struggling for wealth and small supremacies, and I have determined that it would be wise and kind to weld them to one whole, setting ourselves at the head of them to direct their destinies, and cause wars, sickness, and poverty to cease, so that these creatures of a little day (ephemeridae was the word she used) may live happy from the cradle to the grave.

"Now, were it not because of thy strange shrinking from bloodshed, however politic and needful—for my Leo, as yet thou art no true philosopher—this were quickly done, since I can command a weapon which would crush their armouries and whelm their navies in the deep; yes, I, whom even the lightnings and Nature's elemental powers must obey. But thou shrinkest from the sight of death, and thou believest that Heaven would be displeased because I make myself—or am chosen—the instrument of Heaven. Well, so let it be, for thy will is mine, and therefore we will tread a gentler path."

"And how wilt thou persuade the kings of the earth to place their crowns upon thy head?" I asked, astonished.

"By causing their peoples to offer them to us," she answered suavely. "Oh! Holly, Holly, how narrow is thy mind, how strained the quality of thine imagination! Set its poor gates ajar, I pray, and bethink thee. When we appear among men, scattering gold to satisfy their want, clad in terrifying power, in dazzling beauty and in immortality of days, will they not cry, 'Be ye our monarchs and rule over us!'"

"Perhaps," I answered dubiously, "but where wilt thou appear?"

She took a map of the eastern hemisphere which I had drawn and, placing her finger upon Pekin, said—"There is the place that shall be our home for some few centuries, say three, or five, or seven, should it take so long to shape this people to my liking and our purposes. I have chosen these Chinese because thou tellest me that their numbers are uncountable, that they are brave, subtle, and patient, and though now powerless because ill-ruled and untaught, able with their multitudes to flood the little western nations. Therefore among them we will begin our reign and for some few ages be at rest while they learn wisdom from us, and thou, my Holly, makest their armies unconquerable and givest their land good government, wealth, peace, and a new religion."

What the new religion was to be I did not ask. It seemed unnecessary, since I was convinced that in practice it would prove a form of Ayesha-worship, Indeed, my mind was so occupied with conjectures, some of them quaint and absurd enough, as to what would happen at the first appearance of Ayesha in China that I forgot this subsidiary development of our future rule.

"And if the 'little western nations' will not wait to be flooded?" suggested Leo with irritation, for her contemptuous tone angered him, one of a prominent western nation. "If they combine, for instance, and attack thee first?"

"Ah!" she said, with a flash of her eyes. "I have thought of it, and for my part hope that it will chance, since then thou canst not blame me if I put out my strength. Oh! then the East, that has slept so long, shall awake—shall awake, and upon battlefield after battlefield such as history cannot tell of, thou shalt see my flaming standards sweep on to victory. One by one thou shalt watch the nations fall and perish, until at length I build thy throne upon the hecatombs of their countless dead and crown thee emperor of a world regenerate in blood and fire."

Leo, whom this new gospel of regeneration seemed to appall, who was, in fact, a hater of absolute monarchies and somewhat republican in his views and sympathies, continued the argument, but I took no further heed. The thing was grotesque in its tremendous and fantastic absurdity; Ayesha's ambitions were such as no imperial-minded madman could conceive.

Yet—here came the rub—I had not the slightest doubt but that she was well able to put them into practice and carry them to some marvellous and awful conclusion. Why not? Death could not touch her; she had triumphed over death. Her beauty—that "cup of madness" in her eyes, as she named it once to me—and her reckless will would compel the hosts of men to follow her. Her piercing intelligence would enable her to invent new weapons with which the most highly-trained army could not possibly compete. Indeed, it might be as she said, and as I for one believed, with good reason, it proved, that she held at her command the elemental forces of Nature, such as those that lie hid in electricity, which would give all living beings to her for a prey.

Ayesha was still woman enough to have worldly ambitions, and the most dread circumstance about her superhuman powers was that they appeared to be unrestrained by any responsibility to God or man. She was as we might well imagine a fallen angel to be, if indeed, as she herself once hinted and as Atene and the old Shaman believed, this were not her true place in creation. By only two things that I was able to discover could she be moved—her love for Leo and, in a very small degree, her friendship for myself.

Yet her devouring passion for this one man, inexplicable in its endurance and intensity, would, I felt sure even then, in the future as in the past, prove to be her heel of Achilles. When Ayesha was dipped in the waters of Dominion and Deathlessness, this human love left her heart mortal, that through it she might be rendered harmless as a child, who otherwise would have devastated the universe.

I was right.

Whilst I was still indulging myself in these reflections and hoping that Ayesha would not take the trouble to read them in my mind, I became aware that Oros was bowing to the earth before her.

"Thy business, priest?" she asked sharply; for when she was with Leo Ayesha did not like to be disturbed.

"Hes, the spies are returned."

"Why didst thou send them out?" she asked indifferently. "What need have I of thy spies?"

"Hes, thou didst command me."

"Well, their report?"

"Hes, it is most grave. The people of Kaloon are desperate because of the drought which has caused their crops to fail, so that starvation stares them in the eyes, and this they lay to the charge of the strangers who came into their land and fled to thee. The Khania Atene also is mad with rage against thee and our holy College. Labouring night and day, she has gathered two great armies, one of forty, and one of twenty thousand men, and the latter of these she sends against the Mountain under the command of her uncle, Simbri the Shaman. In case it should be defeated she purposes to remain with the second and greater army on the plains about Kaloon."

"Tidings indeed," said Ayesha with a scornful laugh. "Has her hate made this woman mad that she dares thus to match herself against me? My Holly, it crossed thy mind but now that it was I who am mad, boasting of what I have no power to perform. Well, within six days thou shalt learn—oh! verily thou shalt learn, and, though the issue be so very small, in such a fashion that thou wilt doubt no more for ever. Stay, I will look, though the effort of it wearies me, for those spies may be but victims to their own fears, or to the falsehoods of Atene."

Then suddenly, as was common with her when thus Ayesha threw her sight afar, which either from indolence, or because, as she said, it exhausted her, she did but rarely, her lovely face grew rigid like that of a person in a trance; the light faded from her brow, and the great pupils of her eyes contracted themselves and lost their colour.

In a little while, five minutes perhaps, she sighed like one awakening from a deep sleep, passed her hand across her forehead and was as she had been, though somewhat languid, as though strength had left her.

"It is true enough," she said, "and soon I must be stirring lest many of my people should be killed. My lord, wouldst thou see war? Nay, thou shalt bide here in safety whilst I go forward—to visit Atene as I promised."

"Where thou goest, I go," said Leo angrily, his face flushing to the roots of his hair with shame.

"I pray thee not, I pray thee not," she answered, yet without venturing to forbid him. "We will talk of it hereafter. Oros, away! Send round the Fire of Hes to every chief. Three nights hence at the moonrise bid the Tribes gather—nay, not all, twenty thousand of their best will be enough, the rest shall stay to guard the Mountain and this Sanctuary. Let them bring food with them for fifteen days. I join them at the following dawn. Go."

He bowed and went, whereon, dismissing the matter from her mind, Ayesha began to question me again about the Chinese and their customs.

It was in course of a somewhat similar conversation on the following night, of which, however, I forget the exact details, that a remark of Leo's led to another exhibition of Ayesha's marvellous powers.

Leo—who had been considering her plans for conquest, and again combating them as best he could, for they were entirely repugnant to his religious, social and political views—said suddenly that after all they must break down, since they would involve the expenditure of sums of money so vast that even Ayesha herself would be unable to provide them by any known methods of taxation. She looked at him and laughed a little.

"Verily, Leo," she said, "to thee, yes; and to Holly here I must seem as some madcap girl blown to and fro by every wind of fancy, and building me a palace wherein to dwell out of dew and vapours, or from the substance of the sunset fires. Thinkest thou then that I would enter on this war—one woman against all the world"—and as she spoke her shape grew royal and in her awful eyes there came a look that chilled my blood—"and make no preparation for its necessities? Why, since last we spoke upon this matter, foreseeing all, I have considered in my mind, and now thou shalt learn how, without cost to those we rule—and for that reason alone shall they love us dearly—I will glut the treasuries of the Empress of the Earth.

"Dost remember, Leo, how in Kor I found but a single pleasure during all those weary ages—that of forcing my mother Nature one by one to yield me up her choicest secrets; I, who am a student of all things which are and of the forces that cause them to be born. Now follow me, both of you, and ye shall look on what mortal eyes have not yet beheld."

"What are we to see?" I asked doubtfully, having a lively recollection of Ayesha's powers as a chemist.

"That thou shalt learn, or shalt not learn if it pleases thee to stay behind. Come, Leo, my love, my love, and leave this wise philosopher first to find his riddle and next to guess it."

Then turning her back to me she smiled on him so sweetly that although really he was more loth to go than I, Leo would have followed her through a furnace door, as indeed, had he but known it, he was about to do.

So they started, and I accompanied them since with Ayesha it was useless to indulge in any foolish pride, or to make oneself a victim to consistency. Also I was anxious to see her new marvel, and did not care to rely for an account of it upon Leo's descriptive skill, which at its best was never more than moderate.

She took us down passages that we had not passed before, to a door which she signed to Leo to open. He obeyed, and from the cave within issued a flood of light. As we guessed at once, the place was her laboratory, for about it stood metal flasks and various strange-shaped instruments. Moreover, there was a furnace in it, one of the best conceivable, for it needed neither fuel nor stoking, whose gaseous fires, like those of the twisted columns in the Sanctuary, sprang from the womb of the volcano beneath our feet.

When we entered two priests were at work there: one of them stirring a cauldron with an iron rod and the other receiving its molten contents into a mould of clay. They stopped to salute Ayesha, but she bade them to continue their task, asking them if all went well.

"Very well, O Hes," they answered; and we passed through that cave and sundry doors and passages to a little chamber cut in the rock. There was no lamp or flame of fire in it, and yet the place was filled with a gentle light which seemed to flow from the opposing wall.

"What were those priests doing?" I said, more to break the silence than for any other reason.

"Why waste breath upon foolish questions?" she replied. "Are no metals smelted in thy country, O Holly? Now hadst thou sought to know what I am doing—But that, without seeing, thou wouldst not believe, so, Doubter, thou shalt see."

Then she pointed to and bade us don, two strange garments that hung upon the wall, made of a material which seemed to be half cloth and half wood and having headpieces not unlike a diver's helmet.

So under her directions Leo helped me into mine, lacing it up behind, after which, or so I gathered from the sounds—for no light came through the helmet—she did the same service for him.

"I seem very much in the dark," I said presently; for now there was silence again, and beneath this extinguisher I felt alarmed and wished to be sure that I was not left alone.

"Aye Holly," I heard Ayesha's mocking voice make answer, "in the dark, as thou wast ever, the thick dark of ignorance and unbelief. Well, now, as ever also, I will give thee light." As she spoke I heard something roll back; I suppose that it must have been a stone door.

Then, indeed, there was light, yes, even through the thicknesses of that prepared garment, such light as seemed to blind me. By it I saw that the wall opposite to us had opened and that we were all three of us, on the threshold of another chamber. At the end of it stood something like a little altar of hard, black stone, and on this altar lay a mass of substance of the size of a child's head, but fashioned, I suppose from fantasy, to the oblong shape of a human eye.

Out of this eye there poured that blistering and intolerable light. It was shut round by thick, funnel-shaped screens of a material that looked like fire-brick, yet it pierced them as though they were but muslin. More, the rays thus directed upwards struck full upon a lump of metal held in place above them by a massive frame-work.

And what rays they were! If all the cut diamonds of the world were brought together and set beneath a mighty burning-glass, the light flashed from them would not have been a thousandth part so brilliant. They scorched my eyes and caused the skin of my face and limbs to smart, yet Ayesha stood there unshielded from them. Aye, she even went down the length of the room and, throwing back her veil, bent over them, as it seemed a woman of molten steel in whose body the bones were visible, and examined the mass that was supported by the hanging cradle.

"It is ready and somewhat sooner than I thought," she said. Then as though it were but a feather weight, she lifted the lump in her bare hands and glided back with it to where we stood, laughing and saying—"Tell me now, O thou well-read Holly, if thou hast ever heard of a better alchemist than this poor priestess of a forgotten faith?" And she thrust the glowing substance up almost to the mask that hid my face.

Then I turned and ran, or rather waddled, for in that gear I could not run, out of the chamber until the rock wall beyond stayed me, and there, with my back towards her, thrust my helmeted head against it, for I felt as though red-hot bradawls had been plunged into my eyes. So I stood while she laughed and mocked behind me until at length I heard the door close and the blessed darkness came like a gift from Heaven.

Then Ayesha began to loose Leo from his ray-proof armour, if so it can be called, and he in turn loosed me; and there in that gentle radiance we stood blinking at each other like owls in the sunlight, while the tears streamed down our faces.

"Well, art satisfied, my Holly?" she asked.

"Satisfied with what?" I answered angrily, for the smarting of my eyes was unbearable. "Yes, with burnings and bedevilments I am well satisfied."

"And I also," grumbled Leo, who was swearing softly but continuously to himself in the other corner of the place.

But Ayesha only laughed, oh! she laughed until she seemed the goddess of all merriment come to earth, laughed till she also wept, then said—"Why, what ingratitude is this? Thou, my Leo, didst wish to see the wonders that I work, and thou, O Holly, didst come unbidden after I bade thee stay behind, and now both of you are rude and angry, aye, and weeping like a child with a burnt finger. Here take this," and she gave us some salve that stood upon a shelf, "and rub it on your eyes and the smart will pass away."

So we did, and the pain went from them, though, for hours afterwards, mine remained red as blood.

"And what are these wonders?" I asked her presently. "If thou meanest that unbearable flame——"

"Nay, I mean what is born of the flame, as, in thine ignorance thou dost call that mighty agent. Look now;" and she pointed to the metallic lump she had brought with her, which, still gleaming faintly, lay upon the floor. "Nay, it has no heat. Thinkest thou that I would wish to burn my tender hands and so make them unsightly? Touch it, Holly."

But I would not, who thought to myself that Ayesha might be well accustomed to the hottest fires, and feared her impish mischief. I looked, however, long and earnestly.

"Well, what is it, Holly?"

"Gold," I said, then corrected myself and added, "Copper," for the dull, red glow might have been that of either metal.

"Nay, nay," she answered, "it is gold, pure gold."

"The ore in this place must be rich," said Leo, incredulously, for I would not speak any more.

"Yes, my Leo, the iron ore is rich."

"Iron ore?" and he looked at her.

"Surely," she answered, "for from what mine do men dig out gold in such great masses? Iron ore, beloved, that by my alchemy I change to gold, which soon shall serve us in our need."

Now Leo stared and I groaned, for I did not believe that it was gold, and still less that she could make that metal. Then, reading my thought, with one of those sudden changes of mood that were common to her, Ayesha grew very angry.

"By Nature's self!" she cried; "wert thou not my friend, Holly, the fool whom it pleases me to cherish, I would bind that right hand of thine in those secret rays till the very bones within it were turned to gold. Nay, why should I be vexed with thee, who art both blind and deaf? Yet thou shalt be persuaded," and leaving us, she passed down the passages, called something to the priests who were labouring in the workshop, then returned to us.

Presently they followed her, carrying on a kind of stretcher between them an ingot of iron ore that seemed to be as much as they could lift.

"Now," she said, "how wilt thou that I mark this mass which as thou must admit is only iron? With the sign of Life? Good," and at her bidding the priests took cold-chisels and hammers and roughly cut upon its surface the symbol of the looped cross—the crux ansata.

"It is not enough," she said when they had finished. "Holly, lend me that knife of thine, to-morrow I will return it to thee, and of more value."

So I drew my hunting knife, an Indian-made thing, that had a handle of plated iron, and gave it her.

"Thou knowest the marks on it," and she pointed to various dents and to the maker's name upon the blade; for though the hilt was Indian work the steel was of Sheffield manufacture.

I nodded. Then she bade the priests put on the ray-proof armour that we had discarded, and told us to go without the chamber and lie in the darkness of the passage with our faces against the floor.

This we did, and remained so until, a few minutes later, she called us again. We rose and returned into the chamber to find the priests, who had removed the protecting garments, gasping and rubbing the salve upon their eyes; to find also that the lump of iron ore and my knife were gone. Next she commanded them to place the block of gold-coloured metal upon their stretcher and to bring it with them. They obeyed, and we noted that, although those priests were both of them strong men they groaned beneath its weight.

"How came it," said Leo, "that thou, a woman, couldst carry what these men find so heavy?"

"It is one of the properties of that force which thou callest fire," she answered sweetly, "to make what has been exposed to it, if for a little while only, as light as thistle-down. Else, how could I, who am so frail, have borne yonder block of gold?"

"Quite so! I understand now," answered Leo.

Well, that was the end of it. The lump of metal was hid away in a kind of rock pit, with an iron cover, and we returned to Ayesha's apartments.

"So all wealth is thine, as well as all power," said Leo, presently, for remembering Ayesha's awful threat I scarcely dared to open my mouth.

"It seems so," she answered wearily, "since centuries ago I discovered that great secret, though until ye came I had put it to no use. Holly here, after his common fashion, believes that this is magic, but I tell thee again that there is no magic, only knowledge which I have chanced to win."

"Of course," said Leo, "looked at in the right way, that is in thy way, the thing is simple." I think he would have liked to add, "as lying," but as the phrase would have involved explanations, did not. "Yet, Ayesha," he went on, "hast thou thought that this discovery of thine will wreck the world?"

“Leo,” she answered, “is there then nothing that I can do which will not wreck this world, for which thou hast such tender care, who shouldst keep all thy care—for me?”

I smiled, but remembering in time, turned the smile into a frown at Leo, then fearing lest that also might anger her, made my countenance as blank as possible.

“If so,” she continued, “well, let the world be wrecked. But what meanest thou? Oh! my lord, Leo, forgive me if I am so dull that I cannot always follow thy quick thought—I who have lived these many years alone, without converse with nobler minds, or even those to which mine own is equal.”

“It pleases thee to mock me,” said Leo, in a vexed voice, “and that is not too brave.”

Now Ayesha turned on him fiercely, and I looked towards the door. But he did not shrink, only folded his arms and stared her straight in the face. She contemplated him a little, then said—“After that great ordained reason which thou dost not know, I think, Leo, that why I love thee so madly is that thou alone art not afraid of me. Not like Holly there, who, ever since I threatened to turn his bones to gold—which, indeed, I was minded to do,” and she laughed—“trembles at my footsteps and cowers beneath my softest glance.

“Oh! my lord, how good thou art to me, how patient with my moods and woman’s weaknesses,” and she made as though she were about to embrace him. Then suddenly remembering herself, with a little start that somehow conveyed more than the most tragic gesture, she pointed to the couch in token that he should seat himself. When he had done so she drew a footstool to his feet and sank upon it, looking up into his face with attentive eyes, like a child who listens for a story.

“Thy reasons, Leo, give me thy reasons. Doubtless they are good, and, oh! be sure I’ll weigh them well.”

“Here they are in brief,” he answered. “The world, as thou knewest in thy—” and he stopped.

“Thy earlier wanderings there,” she suggested.

“Yes—thy earlier wanderings there, has set up gold as the standard of its wealth. On it all civilizations are founded. Make it as common as it seems thou canst, and these must fall to pieces. Credit will fail and, like their savage forefathers, men must once more take to barter to supply their needs as they do in Kaloon to-day.”

"Why not?" she asked. "It would be more simple and bring them closer to the time when they were good and knew not luxury and greed."

"And smashed in each other's heads with stone axes," added Leo.

"Who now pierce each other's hearts with steel, or those leaden missiles of which thou hast told me. Oh! Leo, when the nations are beggared and their golden god is down; when the usurer and the fat merchant tremble and turn white as chalk because their hoards are but useless dross; when I have made the bankrupt Exchanges of the world my mock, and laugh across the ruin of its richest markets, why, then, will not true worth come to its heritage again?

"What of it if I do discomfort those who think more of pelf than of courage and of virtue; those who, as that Hebrew prophet wrote, lay field to field and house to house, until the wretched whom they have robbed find no place left whereon to dwell? What if I proved your sagest chapmen fools, and gorge your greedy moneychangers with the gold that they desire until they loathe its very sight and touch? What if I uphold the cause of the poor and the oppressed against the ravening lusts of Mammon? Why, will not this world of yours be happier then?"

"I do not know," answered Leo. "All that I know is that it would be a different world, one shaped upon a new plan, governed by untried laws and seeking other ends. In so strange a place who can say what might or might not chance?"

"That we shall learn in its season, Leo. Or, rather, if it be against thy wish, we will not turn this hidden page. Since thou dost desire it, that old evil, the love of lucre, shall still hold its mastery upon the earth. Let the peoples keep their yellow king, I'll not crown another in his place, as I was minded—such as that living Strength thou sawest burning eternally but now; that Power whereof I am the mistress, which can give health to men, or even change the character of metals, and in truth, if I so desire, obedient to my word, destroy a city or rend this Mountain from its roots.

"But see, Holly is wearied with much wondering and needs his rest. Oh, Holly! thou wast born a critic of things done, not a doer of them. I know thy tribe for even in my day the colleges of Alexandria echoed with their wranglings and already the winds blew thick with the dust of their forgotten bones. Holly, I tell thee that at times those who create and act are impatient of such petty doubts and cavillings. Yet fear not, old friend, nor take my anger ill. Already thy heart is gold without alloy, so what need have I to gild thy bones?"

I thanked Ayesha for her compliment, and went to my bed wondering which was real, her kindness or her wrath, or if both were but assumed. Also I wondered in what way she had fallen foul of the critics of Alexandria. Perhaps once she had published a poem or a system of philosophy and been roughly handled by them! It is quite possible, only if Ayesha had ever written poetry I think that it would have endured, like Sappho's.

In the morning I discovered that whatever else about her might be false, Ayesha was a true chemist, the very greatest, I suppose, who ever lived. For as I dressed myself, those priests whom we had seen in the laboratory, staggered into the room carrying between them a heavy burden, that was covered with a cloth, and, directed by Oros, placed it upon the floor.

"What is that?" I asked of Oros.

"A peace-offering sent by the Hesea," he said, "with whom, as I am told, you dared to quarrel yesterday."

Then he withdrew the cloth, and there beneath it shone that great lump of metal which, in the presence of myself and Leo, had been marked with the Symbol of Life, that still appeared upon its surface. Only now it was gold, not iron, gold so good and soft that I could write my name upon it with a nail. My knife lay with it also, and of that too the handle, though not the blade, had been changed from iron into gold.

Ayesha asked to see this afterwards and was but ill-pleased with the result of her experiment. She pointed out to me that lines and blotches of gold ran for an inch or more down the substance of the steel, which she feared that they might weaken or distemper, whereas it had been her purpose that the hilt only should be altered.*

* I proved in after days how real were Ayesha's alchemy, and the knowledge which enabled her to solve the secret that chemists have hunted for in vain, and, like Nature's self, to transmute the commonest into the most precious of the metals. At the first town that I reached on the frontiers of India, I took this knife to a jeweller, a native, who was as clever as he proved dishonest, and asked him to test the handle. He did so with acids and by other means, and told me that it was of very pure gold, twenty-four carats, I think he said. Also he pointed out that this gold became gradually merged into the steel of the blade in a way which was quite inexplicable to him, and asked me to clear up the matter. Of course I could not, but at his request I left the knife in his shop to give him an opportunity of examining it further. The next day I was taken ill with one of the heart-attacks to which I have been liable of late, and when I became able to move about again a while afterwards, I found that this jeweller had gone, none knew whither. So had my knife. —L. H. H.

Often since that time I have marvelled how Ayesha performed this miracle, and from what substances she gathered or compounded the lightning-like material, which was her servant in the work; also, whether or no it had been impregnated with the immortalizing fire of Life that burned in the caves of Kor.* Yet to this hour I have found no answer to the problem, for it is beyond my guessing.

I suppose that, in preparation for her conquest of the inhabitants of this globe—to which, indeed, it would have sufficed unaided by any other power—the manufacture of gold from iron went on in the cave unceasingly.

However this may be, during the few days that we remained together Ayesha never so much as spoke of it again. It seemed to have served her purpose for the while, or in the press of other and more urgent matters to have been forgotten or thrust from her mind. Still, amongst others, of which I have said nothing, since it is necessary to select, I record this strange incident, and our conversations concerning it at length, for the reason that it made a great impression upon me and furnishes a striking example of Ayesha's dominion over the hidden forces of Nature whereof we were soon to experience a more fearful instance.

---

* Recent discoveries would appear to suggest that this mysterious "Fire of Life," which, whatever else it may have been, was evidently a force and no true fire, since it did not burn, owed its origin to the emanations from radium, or some kindred substance. Although in the year 1885, Mr. Holly would have known nothing of the properties of these marvellous rays or emanations, doubtless Ayesha was familiar with them and their enormous possibilities, of which our chemists and scientific men have, at present, but explored the fringe.

—Editor.

XXI. THE PROPHECY OF ATENE

On the day following this strange experience of the iron that was turned to gold some great service was held in the Sanctuary, as we understood, "to consecrate the war." We did not attend it, but that night we ate together as usual. Ayesha was moody at the meal, that is, she varied from sullenness to laughter.

"Know you," she said, "that to-day I was an Oracle, and those fools of the Mountain sent their medicine-men to ask of the Hesea how the battle would go and which of them would be slain, and which gain honour. And I—I could not tell them, but juggled with my words, so that they might take them as they would. How the battle will go I know well, for I shall direct it, but the future—ah! that I cannot read better than thou canst, my Holly, and that is ill indeed. For me the past and all the present lie bathed in light reflected from that black wall—the future."

Then she fell to brooding, and looking up at length with an air of entreaty, said to Leo—"Wilt thou not hear my prayer and bide where thou art for some few days, or even go a-hunting? Do so, and I will stay with thee, and send Holly and Oros to command the Tribes in this petty fray."

"I will not," answered Leo, trembling with indignation, for this plan of hers that I should be sent out to war, while he bided in safety in a temple, moved him, a man brave to rashness, who, although he disapproved of it in theory, loved fighting for its own sake also, to absolute rage.

"I say, Ayesha, that I will not," he repeated; "moreover, that if thou leavest me here I will find my way down the mountain alone, and join the battle."

"Then come," she answered, "and on thine own head be it. Nay, not on thine beloved, on mine, on mine."

After this, by some strange reaction, she became like a merry girl, laughing more than I have ever seen her do, and telling us many tales of the far, far past, but none that were sad or tragic. It was very strange to sit and listen to her while she spoke of people, one or two of them known as names in history and many others who never have been heard of, that had trod this earth and with whom she was familiar over two thousand years ago. Yet she told us anecdotes of their loves and hates, their strength or weaknesses, all of them touched with some tinge of humorous satire, or illustrating the comic vanity of human aims and aspirations.

At length her talk took a deeper and more personal note. She spoke of her searchings after truth; of how, aching for wisdom, she had explored the religions of her day and refused them one by one; of how she had preached in Jerusalem and been stoned by the Doctors of the Law. Of how also she had wandered back to Arabia and, being rejected by her own people as a reformer, had travelled on to Egypt, and at the court of the Pharaoh of that time met a famous magician, half charlatan and half seer who, because she was far-seeing, 'clairvoyante' we should call it, instructed her in his art so well that soon she became his master and forced him to obey her.

Then, as though she were unwilling to reveal too much, suddenly Ayesha's history passed from Egypt to Kor. She spoke to Leo of his arrival there, a wanderer who was named Kallikrates, hunted by savages and accompanied by the Egyptian Amenartas, whom she appeared to have known and hated in her own country, and of how she entertained them. Yes, she even told of a supper that the three of them had eaten together on the evening before they started to discover the Place of Life, and of an evil prophecy that this royal Amenartas had made as to the issue of their journey.

"Aye," Ayesha said, "it was such a silent night as this and such a meal as this we ate, and Leo, not so greatly changed, save that he was beardless then and younger, was at my side. Where thou sittest, Holly, sat the royal Amenartas, a very fair woman; yes, even more beautiful than I before I dipped me in the Essence, fore-sighted also, though not so learned as I had grown. From the first we hated each other, and more than ever now, when she guessed how I had learned to look upon thee, her lover, Leo; for her husband thou never wast, who didst flee too fast for marriage. She knew also that the struggle between us which had begun of old and afar was for centuries and generations, and that until the end should declare itself neither of us could harm the other, who both had sinned to win thee, that wast appointed by fate to be the lodestone of our souls. Then Amenartas spoke and said—"'Lo! to my sight, Kallikrates, the wine in thy cup is turned to blood, and that knife in thy hand, O daughter of Yarab'—for so she named me—'drips red blood. Aye, and this place is a sepulchre, and thou, O Kallikrates, sleepest here, nor can she, thy murderess, kiss back the breath of life into those cold lips of thine.'

"So indeed it came about as was ordained," added Ayesha reflectively, "for I slew thee in yonder Place of Life, yes, in my madness I slew thee because thou wouldst not or couldst not understand the change that had come over me, and shrankest from my loveliness like a blind bat from the splendour of flame, hiding thy face in the tresses of her dusky hair—Why, what is it now, thou Oros? Can I never be rid of thee for an hour?"

"O Hes, a writing from the Khania Atene," the priest said with his deprecating bow.

"Break the seal and read," she answered carelessly. "Perchance she has repented of her folly and makes submission."

So he read—

"To the Hesea of the College on the Mountain, known as Ayesha upon earth, and in the household of the Over-world whence she has been permitted to wander, as 'Star-that-hath-fallen—'"

"A pretty sounding name, forsooth," broke in Ayesha; "ah! but, Atene, set stars rise again—even from the Under-world. Read on, thou Oros."

"Greetings, O Ayesha. Thou who art very old, hast gathered much wisdom in the passing of the centuries, and with other powers, that of making thyself seem fair in the eyes of men blinded by thine arts. Yet one thing thou lackest that I have—vision of those happenings which are not yet. Know, O Ayesha, that I and my uncle, the great seer, have searched the heavenly books to learn what is written there of the issue of this war.

"This is written:—For me, death, whereat I rejoice. For thee a spear cast by thine own hand. For the land of Kaloon blood and ruin bred of thee!

"Atene,

"Khania of Kaloon."

Ayesha listened in silence, but her lips did not tremble, nor her cheek pale. To Oros she said proudly—"Say to the messenger of Atene that I have received her message, and ere long will answer it, face to face with her in her palace of Kaloon. Go, priest, and disturb me no more."

When Oros had departed she turned to us and said—"That tale of mine of long ago was well fitted to this hour, for as Amenartas prophesied of ill, so does Atene prophesy of ill, and Amenartas and Atene are one. Well, let the spear fall, if fall it must, and I will not flinch from it who know that I shall surely triumph at the last. Perhaps the Khania does but think to frighten me with a cunning lie, but if she has read aright, then be sure, beloved, that it is still well with us, since none can escape their destiny, nor can our bond of union which was fashioned with the universe that bears us, ever be undone."

She paused awhile then went on with a sudden outburst of poetic thought and imagery.

"I tell thee, Leo, that out of the confusions of our lives and deaths order shall yet be born. Behind the mask of cruelty shine Mercy's tender eyes; and the wrongs of this rough and twisted world are but hot, blinding sparks which stream from the all-righting sword of pure, eternal Justice. The heavy lives we see and know are only links in a golden chain that shall draw us safe to the haven of our rest; steep and painful steps are they whereby we climb to the alloted palace of our joy. Henceforth I fear no more, and fight no more against that which must befall. For I say we are but winged seeds blown down the gales of fate and change to the appointed garden where we shall grow, filling its blest air with the immortal fragrance of our bloom.

"Leave me now, Leo, and sleep awhile, for we ride at dawn."

It was midday on the morrow when we moved down the mountain-side with the army of the Tribes, fierce and savage-looking men. The scouts were out before us, then came the great body of their cavalry mounted on wiry horses, while to right and left and behind, the foot soldiers marched in regiments, each under the command of its own chief.

Ayesha, veiled now—for she would not show her beauty to these wild folk—rode in the midst of the horse-men on a white mare of matchless speed and shape. With her went Leo and myself, Leo on the Khan's black horse, and I on another not unlike it, though thicker built. About us were a bodyguard of armed priests and a regiment of chosen soldiers, among them those hunters that Leo had saved from Ayesha's wrath, and who were now attached to his person.

We were merry, all of us, for in the crisp air of late autumn flooded with sunlight, the fears and forebodings that had haunted us in those gloomy, firelit caves were forgotten. Moreover, the tramp of thousands of armed men and the excitement of coming battle thrilled our nerves.

Not for many a day had I seen Leo look so vigorous and happy. Of late he had grown somewhat thin and pale, probably from causes that I have suggested, but now his cheeks were red and his eyes shone bright again. Ayesha also seemed joyous, for the moods of this strange woman were as fickle as those of Nature's self, and varied as a landscape varies under the sunshine or the shadow. Now she was noon and now dark night; now dawn, now evening, and now thoughts came and went in the blue depths of her eyes like vapours wafted across the summer sky, and in the press of them her sweet face changed and shimmered as broken water shimmers beneath the beaming stars.

"Too long," she said, with a little thrilling laugh, "have I been shut in the bowels of sombre mountains, accompanied only by mutes and savages or by melancholy, chanting priests, and now I am glad to look upon the world again. How beautiful are the snows above, and the brown slopes below, and the broad plains beyond that roll away to those bordering hills! How glorious is the sun, eternal as myself; how sweet the keen air of heaven.

"Believe me, Leo, more than twenty centuries have gone by since I was seated on a steed, and yet thou seest I have not forgot my horsemanship, though this beast cannot match those Arabs that I rode in the wide deserts of Arabia. Oh! I remember how at my father's side I galloped down to war against the marauding Bedouins, and how with my own hand I speared their chieftain and made him cry for mercy. One day I will tell thee of that father of mine, for I was his darling, and though we have been long apart, I hold his memory dear and look forward to our meeting.

"See, yonder is the mouth of that gorge where lived the cat-worshipping sorcerer, who would have murdered both of you because thou, Leo, didst throw his familiar to the fire. It is strange, but several of the tribes of this Mountain and of the lands behind it make cats their gods or divine by means of them. I think that the first Rassen, the general of Alexander, must have brought the practice here from Egypt. Of this Macedonian Alexander I could tell thee much, for he was almost a contemporary of mine, and when I last was born the world still rang with the fame of his great deeds.

"It was Rassen who on the Mountain supplanted the primeval fire-worship whereof the flaming pillars which light its Sanctuary remain as monuments, by that of Hes, or Isis, or rather blended the two in one. Doubtless among the priests in his army were some of Pasht or Sekket the Cat-headed, and these brought with them their secret cult, that to-day has dwindled down to the vulgar divinations of savage sorcerers. Indeed I remember dimly that it was so, for I was the first Hesea of this Temple, and journeyed hither with that same general Rassen, a relative of mine."

Now both Leo and I looked at her wonderingly, and I could see that she was watching us through her veil. As usual, however, it was I whom she reproved, since Leo might think and do what he willed and still escape her anger.

"Thou, Holly," she said quickly, "who art ever of a cavilling and suspicious mind, remembering what I said but now, believest that I lie to thee."

I protested that I was only reflecting upon an apparent variation between two statements.

"Play not with words," she answered; "in thy heart thou didst write me down a liar, and I take that ill. Know, foolish man, that when I said that the Macedonian Alexander lived before me, I meant before this present life of mine. In the existence that preceded it, though I outlasted him by thirty years, we were born in the same summer, and I knew him well, for I was the Oracle whom he consulted most upon his wars, and to my wisdom he owed his victories. Afterwards we quarrelled, and I left him and pushed forward with Rassen. From that day the bright star of Alexander began to wane." At this Leo made a sound that resembled a whistle. In a very agony of apprehension, beating back the criticisms and certain recollections of the strange tale of the old abbot, Kou-en, which would rise within me, I asked quickly—"And dost thou, Ayesha, remember well all that befell thee in this former life?"

"Nay, not well," she answered, meditatively, "only the greater facts, and those I have for the most part recovered by that study of secret things which thou callest vision or magic. For instance, my Holly, I recall that thou wast living in that life. Indeed I seem to see an ugly philosopher clad in a dirty robe and filled both with wine and the learning of others, who disputed with Alexander till he grew wroth with him and caused him to be banished, or drowned: I forget which."

"I suppose that I was not called Diogenes?" I asked tartly, suspecting, perhaps not without cause, that Ayesha was amusing herself by fooling me.

"No," she replied gravely, "I do not think that was thy name. The Diogenes thou speakest of was a much more famous man, one of real if crabbed wisdom; moreover, he did not indulge in wine. I am mindful of very little of that life, however, not of more indeed than are many of the followers of the prophet Buddha, whose doctrines I have studied and of whom thou, Holly, hast spoken to me so much. Maybe we did not meet while it endured. Still I recollect that the Valley of Bones, where I found thee, my Leo, was the place where a great battle was fought between the

Fire-priests with their vassals, the Tribes of the Mountain and the army of Rassen aided by the people of Kaloon. For between these and the Mountain, in old days as now, there was enmity, since in this present war history does but rewrite itself."

"So thou thyself wast our guide," said Leo, looking at her sharply.

"Aye, Leo, who else? though it is not wonderful that thou didst not know me beneath those deathly wrappings. I was minded to wait and receive thee in the Sanctuary, yet when I learned that at length both of you had escaped Atene and drew near, I could restrain myself no more, but came forth thus hideously disguised. Yes, I was with you even at the river's bank, and though you saw me not, there sheltered you from harm.

"Leo, I yearned to look upon thee and to be certain that thy heart had not changed, although until the alloted time thou mightest not hear my voice or see my face who wert doomed to undergo that sore trial of thy faith. Of Holly also I desired to learn whether his wisdom could pierce through my disguise, and how near he stood to truth. It was for this reason that I suffered him to see me draw the lock from the satchel on thy breast and to hear me wail over thee yonder in the Rest-house. Well he did not guess so ill, but thou, thou knewest me—in thy sleep—knewest me as I am, and not as I seemed to be, yes," she added softly, "and didst say certain sweet words which I remember well."

"Then beneath that shroud was thine own face," asked Leo again, for he was very curious on this point, "the same lovely face I see to-day?"

"Mayhap—as thou wilt," she answered coldly; "also it is the spirit that matters, not the outward seeming, though men in their blindness think otherwise. Perchance my face is but as thy heart fashions it, or as my will presents it to the sight and fancy of its beholders. But hark! The scouts have touched."

As Ayesha spoke a sound of distant shouting was borne upon the wind, and presently we saw a fringe of horsemen falling back slowly upon our foremost line. It was only to report, however, that the skirmishers of Atene were in full retreat. Indeed, a prisoner whom they brought with them, on being questioned by the priests, confessed at once that the Khania had no mind to meet us upon the holy Mountain. She proposed to give battle on the river's farther bank, having for a defence its waters which we must ford, a decision that showed good military judgment.

So it happened that on this day there was no fighting.

All that afternoon we descended the slopes of the Mountain, more swiftly by far than we had climbed them after our long flight from the city of Kaloon. Before sunset we came to our prepared camping ground, a wide and sloping plain that ended at the crest of the Valley of Dead Bones, where in past days we had met our mysterious guide. This, however, we did not reach through the secret mountain tunnel along which she had led us, the shortest way by miles, as Ayesha told us now, since it was unsuited to the passage of an army.

Bending to the left, we circled round a number of unclimbable koppies, beneath which that tunnel passed, and so at length arrived upon the brow of the dark ravine where we could sleep safe from attack by night.

Here a tent was pitched for Ayesha, but as it was the only one, Leo and I with our guard bivouacked among some rocks at a distance of a few hundred yards. When she found that this must be so, Ayesha was very angry and spoke bitter words to the chief who had charge of the food and baggage, although, he, poor man, knew nothing of tents.

Also she blamed Oros, who replied meekly that he had thought us captains accustomed to war and its hardships. But most of all she was angry with herself, who had forgotten this detail, and until Leo stopped her with a laugh of vexation, went on to suggest that we should sleep in the tent, since she had no fear of the rigours of the mountain cold.

The end of it was that we supped together outside, or rather Leo and I supped, for as there were guards around us Ayesha did not even lift her veil.

That evening Ayesha was disturbed and ill at ease, as though new fears which she could not overcome assailed her. At length she seemed to conquer them by some effort of her will and announced that she was minded to sleep and thus refresh her soul; the only part of her, I think, which ever needed rest. Her last words to us were—"Sleep you also, sleep sound, but be not astonished, my Leo, if I send to summon both of you during the night, since in my slumbers I may find new counsels and need to speak of them to thee ere we break camp at dawn."

Thus we parted, but ah! little did we guess how and where the three of us would meet again.

We were weary and soon fell fast asleep beside our camp-fire, for, knowing that the whole army guarded us, we had no fear. I remember watching the bright stars which shone in the immense vault above me until they paled in the pure light of the risen moon, now somewhat past her full, and hearing Leo mutter drowsily from beneath his fur rug that

Ayesha was quite right, and that it was pleasant to be in the open air again, as he was tired of caves.

After that I knew no more until I was awakened by the challenge of a sentry in the distance; then after a pause, a second challenge from the officer of our own guard. Another pause, and a priest stood bowing before us, the flickering light from the fire playing upon his shaven head and face, which I seemed to recognize.

"I"—and he gave a name that was familiar to me, but which I forget—"am sent, my lords, by Oros, who commands me to say that the Hesea would speak with you both and at once."

Now Leo sat up yawning and asked what was the matter. I told him, whereon he said he wished that Ayesha could have waited till daylight, then added—"Well, there is no help for it. Come on, Horace," and he rose to follow the messenger.

The priest bowed again and said—"The commands of the Hesea are that my lords should bring their weapons and their guard."

"What," grumbled Leo, "to protect us for a walk of a hundred yards through the heart of an army?"

"The Hesea," explained the man, "has left her tent; she is in the gorge yonder, studying the line of advance."

"How do you know that?" I asked.

"I do not know it," he replied. "Oros told me so, that is all, and therefore the Hesea bade my lords bring their guard, for she is alone."

"Is she mad," ejaculated Leo, "to wander about in such a place at midnight? Well, it is like her."

I too thought it was like her, who did nothing that others would have done, and yet I hesitated. Then I remembered that Ayesha had said she might send for us; also I was sure that if any trick had been intended we should not have been warned to bring an escort. So we called the guard—there were twelve of them—took our spears and swords and started.

We were challenged by both the first and second lines of sentries, and I noticed that as we gave them the password the last picket, who of course recognized us, looked astonished. Still, if they had doubts they did not dare to express them. So we went on.

Now we began to descend the sides of the ravine by a very steep path, with which the priest, our guide, seemed to be curiously familiar, for he went down it as though it were the stairway of his own house.

"A strange place to take us to at night," said Leo doubtfully, when we were near the bottom and the chief of the bodyguard, that great red-bearded hunter who had been mixed up in the matter of the snow-leopard also muttered some words of remonstrance. Whilst I was trying to catch what he said, of a sudden something white walked into the patch of moonlight at the foot of the ravine, and we saw that it was the veiled figure of Ayesha herself. The chief saw her also and said contentedly—"Hes! Hes!"

"Look at her," grumbled Leo, "strolling about in that haunted hole as though it were Hyde Park;" and on he went at a run.

The figure turned and beckoned to us to follow her as she glided forward, picking her way through the skeletons which were scattered about upon the lava bed of the cleft. Thus she went on into the shadow of the opposing cliff that the moonlight did not reach. Here in the wet season a stream trickled down a path which it had cut through the rock in the course of centuries, and the grit that it had brought with it was spread about the lava floor of the ravine, so that many of the bones were almost completely buried in the sand.

These, I noticed, as we stepped into the shadow, were more numerous than usual just here, for on all sides I saw the white crowns of skulls, or the projecting ends of ribs and thigh bones. Doubtless, I thought to myself, that streamway made a road to the plain above, and in some past battle, the fighting around it was very fierce and the slaughter great.

Here Ayesha had halted and was engaged in the contemplation of this boulder-strewn path, as though she meditated making use of it that day. Now we drew near to her, and the priest who guided us fell back with our guard, leaving us to go forward alone, since they dared not approach the Hesea unbidden. Leo was somewhat in advance of me, seven or eight yards perhaps, and I heard him say—"Why dost thou venture into such places at night, Ayesha, unless indeed it is not possible for any harm to come to thee?"

She made no answer, only turned and opened her arms wide, then let them fall to her side again. Whilst I wondered what this signal of hers might mean, from the shadows about us came a strange, rustling sound.

I looked, and lo! everywhere the skeletons were rising from their sandy beds. I saw their white skulls, their gleaming arm and leg bones, their hollow ribs. The long-slain army had come to life again, and look! in their hands were the ghosts of spears.

Of course I knew at once that this was but another manifestation of

Ayesha's magic powers, which some whim of hers had drawn us from our beds to witness. Yet I confess that I felt frightened. Even the boldest of men, however free from superstition, might be excused should their nerve fail them if, when standing in a churchyard at midnight, suddenly on every side they saw the dead arising from their graves. Also our surroundings were wilder and more eerie than those of any civilized burying-place.

"What new devilment of thine is this?" cried Leo in a scared and angry voice. But Ayesha made no answer. I heard a noise behind me and looked round. The skeletons were springing upon our body-guard, who for their part, poor men, paralysed with terror, had thrown down their weapons and fallen, some of them, to their knees. Now the ghosts began to stab at them with their phantom spears, and I saw that beneath the blows they rolled over. The veiled figure above me pointed with her hand at Leo and said—"Seize him, but I charge you, harm him not."

I knew the voice; it was that of Atene!

Then too late I understood the trap into which we had fallen.

"Treachery!" I began to cry, and before the word was out of my lips, a particularly able-bodied skeleton silenced me with a violent blow upon the head. But though I could not speak, my senses still stayed with me for a little. I saw Leo fighting furiously with a number of men who strove to pull him down, so furiously, indeed that his frightful efforts caused the blood to gush out of his mouth from some burst vessel in the lungs.

Then sight and hearing failed me, and thinking that this was death, I fell and remembered no more.

Why I was not killed outright I do not know, unless in their hurry the disguised soldiers thought me already dead, or perhaps that my life was to be spared also. At least, beyond the knock upon the head I received no injury.

XXII. THE LOOSING OF THE POWERS

When I came to myself again, it was daylight. I saw the calm, gentle face of Oros bending over me as he poured some strong fluid down my throat that seemed to shoot through all my body, and melt a curtain in my mind. I saw also that beside him stood Ayesha.

"Speak, man, speak," she said in a terrible voice. "What hast chanced here? Thou livest, then where is my lord? Where hast thou hid my lord? Tell me—or die."

It was the vision that I saw when my senses left me in the snow of the avalanche, fulfilled to the last detail!

"Atene has taken him," I answered.

"Atene has taken him and thou art left alive?"

"Do not be wrath with me," I answered, "it is no fault of mine. Little wonder we were deceived after thou hadst said that thou mightest summon us ere dawn."

Then as briefly as I could I told the story.

She listened, went to where our murdered guards lay with unstained spears, and looked at them.

"Well for these that they are dead," she exclaimed. "Now, Holly, thou seest what is the fruit of mercy. The men whose lives I gave my lord have failed him at his need."

Then she passed forward to the spot where Leo was captured. Here lay a broken sword—Leo's—that had been the Khan Rassen's, and two dead men. Both of these were clothed in some tight-fitting black garments, having their heads and faces whitened with chalk and upon their vests a rude imitation of a human skeleton, also daubed in chalk.

"A trick fit to frighten fools with," she said contemptuously. "But oh! that Atene should have dared to play the part of Ayesha, that she should have dared!" and she clenched her little hand. "See, surprised and overwhelmed, yet he fought well. Say! was he hurt, Holly? It comes upon me—no, tell me that I see amiss."

"Not much, I think," I answered doubtfully, "a little blood was running from his mouth, no more. Look, there go the stains of it upon that rock."

"For every drop I'll take a hundred lives. By myself I swear it," Ayesha muttered with a groan. Then she cried in a ringing voice,

"Back and to horse, for I have deeds to do this day. Nay, bide thou here, Holly; we go a shorter path while the army skirts the gorge. Oros, give him food and drink and bathe that hurt upon his head. It is but a bruise, for his hood and hair are thick."

So while Oros rubbed some stinging lotion on my scalp, I ate and drank as best I could till my brain ceased to swim, for the blow, though heavy, had not fractured the bone. When I was ready they brought the horses to us, and mounting them, slowly we scrambled up the steep bed of the water-course.

"See," Ayesha said, pointing to tracks and hoof-prints on the plain at its head, "there was a chariot awaiting him, and harnessed to it were four swift horses. Atene's scheme was clever and well laid, and I, grown oversure and careless, slept through it all!"

On this plain the army of the Tribes that had broken camp before the dawn was already gathering fast; indeed, the cavalry, if I may call them so, were assembled there to the number of about five thousand men, each of whom had a led horse. Ayesha summoned the chiefs and captains, and addressed them. "Servants of Hes," she said, "the stranger lord, my betrothed and guest, has been tricked by a false priest and, falling into a cunning snare, captured as a hostage. It is necessary that I follow him fast, before harm comes—to him. We move down to attack the army of the Khania beyond the river. When its passage is forced I pass on with the horsemen, for I must sleep in the city of Kaloon to-night. What sayest thou, Oros? That a second and greater army defends its walls? Man, I know it, and if there is need, that army I will destroy. Nay, stare not at me. Already they are as dead. Horsemen, you accompany me.

"Captains of the Tribes, you follow, and woe be to that man who hangs back in the hour of battle, for death and eternal shame shall be his portion, but wealth and honour to those who bear them bravely. Yes, I tell you, theirs shall be the fair land of Kaloon. You have your orders for the passing of yonder river. I, with the horsemen, take the central ford. Let the wings advance."

The chiefs answered with a cheer, for they were fierce men whose ancestors had loved war for generations. Moreover, mad as seemed the enterprise, they trusted in their Oracle, the Hesea, and, like all hill peoples, were easily fired by the promise of rich plunder.

An hour's steady march down the slopes brought the army to the edge of the marsh lands. These, as it chanced, proved no obstacle to our progress, for in that season of great drought they were quite dry, and for the same reason the shrunken river was not so impassable a defence as I feared that it would be. Still, because of its rocky bottom and steep, opposing banks, it looked formidable enough, while on the crests of those banks, in squadrons and companies of horse and foot, were gathered the regiments of Atene.

While the wings of footmen deployed to right and left, the cavalry halted in the marshes and let their horses fill themselves with the long grass, now a little browned by frost, that grew on this boggy soil, and afterwards drink some water.

All this time Ayesha stood silent, for she also had dismounted, that the mare she rode and her two led horses might graze with the others. Indeed, she spoke but once, saying—"Thou thinkest this adventure mad, my Holly? Say, art afraid?"

"Not with thee for captain," I answered. "Still, that second army——"

"Shall melt before me like mist before the gale," she replied in a low and thrilling voice. "Holly, I tell thee thou shalt see things such as no man upon the earth has ever seen. Remember my words when I loose the Powers and thou followest the rent veil of Ayesha through the smitten squadrons of Kaloon. Only—what if Atene should dare to murder him? Oh, if she should dare!"

"Be comforted," I replied, wondering what she might mean by this loosing of the Powers. "I think that she loves him too well."

"I bless thee for the words, Holly, yet—I know he will refuse her, and then her hate for me and her jealous rage may overcome her love for him. Should this be so, what will avail my vengeance? Eat and drink again, Holly—nay, I touch no food until I sit in the palace of Kaloon—and look well to girth and bridle, for thou ridest far and on a wild errand. Mount thee on Leo's horse, which is swift and sure; if it dies the guards will bring thee others."

I obeyed her as best I could, and once more bathed my head in a pool, and with the help of Oros tied a rag soaked in the liniment on the bruise, after which I felt sound enough. Indeed, the mad excitement of those minutes of waiting, and some foreshadowing of the terrible wonders that were about to befall, made me forget my hurts.

Now, Ayesha was standing staring upwards, so that although I could not see her veiled face, I guessed that her eyes must be fixed on the sky above the mountain top. I was certain, also, that she was concentrating her fearful will upon an unknown object, for her whole frame quivered like a reed shaken in the wind.

It was a very strange morning—cold and clear, yet curiously still, and with a heaviness in the air such as precedes a great fall of snow, although for much snow the season was yet too early. Once or twice, too, in that utter calm, I thought that I felt everything shudder; not the ordinary trembling of earthquake, however, for the shuddering seemed to be of the atmosphere quite as much as of the land. It was as though all Nature around us were a living creature which is very much afraid.

Following Ayesha's earnest gaze, I perceived that thick, smoky clouds were gathering one by one in the clear sky above the peak, and that they were edged, each of them, with a fiery rim. Watching these fantastic and ominous clouds, I ventured to say to her that it looked as though the weather would change—not a very original remark, but one which the circumstances suggested.

"Aye," she answered, "ere night the weather will be wilder even than my heart. No longer shall they cry for water in Kaloon! Mount, Holly, mount! The advance begins!" and unaided she sprang to the saddle of the mare that Oros brought her.

Then, in the midst of the five thousand horsemen, we moved down upon the ford. As we reached its brink I noted that the two divisions of tribesmen were already entering the stream half a mile to the right and left of us. Of what befell them I can tell nothing from observation, although I learned later that they forced it after great slaughter on both sides.

In front of us was gathered the main body of the Khania's army, massed by regiments upon the further bank, while hundreds of picked men stood up to their middles in the water, waiting to spear or hamstring our horses as we advanced.

Now, uttering their wild, whistling cry, our leading companies dashed into the river, leaving us upon the bank, and soon were engaged hotly with the footmen in midstream. While this fray went on, Oros came to Ayesha, told her a spy had reported that Leo, bound in a two-wheeled carriage and accompanied by Atene, Simbri and a guard, had passed through the enemy's camp at night, galloping furiously towards Kaloon.

"Spare thy words, I know it," she answered, and he fell back behind her.

Our squadrons gained the bank, having destroyed most of the men in the water, but as they set foot upon it the enemy charged them and drove them back with loss. Thrice they returned to the attack, and thrice were repulsed in this fashion. At length Ayesha grew impatient.

"They need a leader, and I will give them one," she said. "Come with me, my Holly," and, followed by the main body of the horsemen, she rode a little way into the river, and there waited until the shattered troops had fallen back upon us. Oros whispered to me—"It is madness, the Hesea will be slain."

"Thinkest thou so?" I answered. "More like that we shall be slain," a saying at which he smiled a little more than usual and shrugged his shoulders, since for all his soft ways, Oros was a brave man. Also I believe that he spoke to try me, knowing that his mistress would take no harm.

Ayesha held up her hand, in which there was no weapon, and waved it forwards. A great cheer answered that signal to advance, and in the midst of it this frail, white-robed woman spoke to her horse, so that it plunged deep into the water.

Two minutes later, and spears and arrows were flying about us so thickly that they seemed to darken the sky. I saw men and horses fall to right and left, but nothing touched me or the white robes that floated a yard or two ahead. Five minutes and we were gaining the further bank, and there the worst fight began.

It was fierce indeed, yet never an inch did the white robes give back, and where they went men would follow them or fall. We were up the bank and the enemy was packed about us, but through them we passed slowly, like a boat through an adverse sea that buffets but cannot stay it. Yes, further and further, till at last the lines ahead grew thin as the living wedge of horsemen forced its path between them—grew thin, broke and vanished.

We had passed through the heart of the host, and leaving the tribesmen who followed to deal with its flying fragments, rode on half a mile or so and mustered. Many were dead and more were hurt, but the command was issued that all sore-wounded men should fall out and give their horses to replace those that had been killed.

This was done, and presently we moved on, three thousand of us now, not more, heading for Kaloon. The trot grew to a canter, and the canter to a gallop, as we rushed forward across that endless plain, till at midday, or a little after—for this route was far shorter than that taken by Leo and myself in our devious flight from Rassen and his death-hounds—we dimly saw the city of Kaloon set upon its hill.

Now a halt was ordered, for here was a reservoir in which was still some water, whereof the horses drank, while the men ate of the food they carried with them; dried meat and barley meal. Here, too, more spies met us, who said that the great army of Atene was posted guarding the city bridges, and that to attack it with our little force would mean destruction. But Ayesha took no heed of their words; indeed, she scarcely seemed to hear them. Only she ordered that all wearied horses should be abandoned and fresh ones mounted.

Forward again for hour after hour, in perfect silence save for the thunder of our horses' hoofs. No word spoke Ayesha, nor did her wild escort speak, only from time to time they looked over their shoulders and pointed with their red spears at the red sky behind.

I looked also, nor shall I forget its aspect. The dreadful, fire-edged clouds had grown and gathered so that beneath their shadows the plain lay almost black. They marched above us like an army in the heavens, while from time to time vaporous points shot forward, thin like swords, or massed like charging horse.

Under them a vast stillness reigned. It was as though the earth lay dead beneath their pall.

Kaloon, lit in a lurid light, grew nearer. The pickets of the foe flew homeward before us, shaking their javelins, and their mocking laughter reached us in hollow echoes. Now we saw the vast array, posted rank on rank with silken banners drooping in that stirless air, flanked and screened by glittering regiments of horse.

An embassy approached us, and at the signal of Ayesha's uplifted arm we halted. It was headed by a lord of the court whose face I knew. He pulled rein and spoke boldly.

"Listen, Hes, to the words of Atene. Ere now the stranger lord, thy darling, is prisoner in her palace. Advance, and we destroy thee and thy little band; but if by any miracle thou shouldst conquer, then he dies. Get thee gone to thy Mountain fastness and the Khania gives thee peace, and thy people their lives. What answer to the words of the Khania?"

Ayesha whispered to Oros, who called aloud—"There is no answer. Go, if ye love life, for death draws near to you."

So they went fast as their swift steeds would carry them, but for a little while Ayesha still sat lost in thought.

Presently she turned and through her thin veil I saw that her face was white and terrible and that the eyes in it glowed like those of a lioness at night. She said to, me—hissing the words between her clenched teeth—"Holly, prepare thyself to look into the mouth of hell. I desired to spare them if I could, I swear it, but my heart bids me be bold, to put off human pity, and use all my secret might if I would see Leo living. Holly, I tell thee they are about to murder him!"

Then she cried aloud, "Fear nothing, Captains. Ye are but few, yet with you goes the strength of ten thousand thousand. Now follow the Hesea, and whate'er ye meet, be not dismayed. Repeat it to the soldiers, that fearing nothing they follow the Hesea through yonder host and across the bridge and into the city of Kaloon."

So the chiefs rode hither and thither, crying out her words, and the savage tribesmen answered—"Aye, we who followed through the water, will follow across the plain. Onward, Hes, for darkness swallows us."

Now some orders were given, and the companies fell into a formation that resembled a great wedge, Ayesha herself being its very point and apex, for though Oros and I rode on either side of her, spur as we would, our horses' heads never passed her saddle bow. In front of that dark mass she shone a single spot of white—one snowy feather on a black torrent's breast.

A screaming bugle note—and, like giant arms, from the shelter of some groves of poplar trees, curved horns of cavalry shot out to surround us, while the broad bosom of the opposing army, shimmering with spears, rolled forward as a wave rolls crowned with sunlit foam, and behind it, line upon line, uncountable, lay a surging sea of men.

Our end was near. We were lost, or so it seemed.

Ayesha tore off her veil and held it on high, flowing from her like a pennon, and lo! upon her brow blazed that wide and mystic diadem of light which once only I had seen before.

Denser and denser grew the rushing clouds above; brighter and brighter gleamed the unearthly star of light beneath. Louder and louder beat the sound of the falling hoofs of ten thousand horses. From the Mountain peak behind us went up sudden sheets of flame; it spouted fire as a whale spouts foam.

The scene was dreadful. In front, the towers of Kaloon lurid in a monstrous sunset. Above, a gloom as of an eclipse. Around the darkling, sunburnt plain. On it Atene's advancing army, and our rushing wedge of horsemen destined, it would appear, to inevitable doom.

Ayesha let fall her rein. She tossed her arms, waving the torn, white veil as though it were a signal cast to heaven.

Instantly from the churning jaws of the unholy night above belched a blaze of answering flame, that also wavered like a rent and shaken veil in the grasp of a black hand of cloud.

Then did Ayesha roll the thunder of her might upon the Children of Kaloon. Then she called, and the Terror came, such as men had never seen and perchance never more will see. Awful bursts of wind tore past us, lifting the very stones and soil before them, and with the wind went hail and level, hissing rain, made visible by the arrows of perpetual lightnings that leapt downwards from the sky and upwards from the earth.

It was as she had warned me. It was as though hell had broken loose upon the world, yet through that hell we rushed on unharmed. For always these furies passed before us. No arrow flew, no javelin was stained. The jagged hail was a herald of our coming; the levens that smote and stabbed were our sword and spear, while ever the hurricane roared and screamed with a million separate voices which blended to one yell of sound, hideous and indescribable.

As for the hosts about us they melted and were gone.

Now the darkness was dense, like to that of thickest night; yet in the fierce flares of the lightnings I saw them run this way and that, and amidst the volleying, elemental voices I heard their shouts of horror and of agony. I saw horses and riders roll confused upon the ground; like storm-drifted leaves I saw their footmen piled in high and whirling heaps, while the brands of heaven struck and struck them till they sank together and grew still.

I saw the groves of trees bend, shrivel up and vanish. I saw the high walls of Kaloon blown in and flee away, while the houses within the walls took fire, to go out beneath the torrents of the driving rain, and again take fire. I saw blackness sweep over us with great wings, and when I looked, lo! those wide wings were flame, floods of pulsing flame that flew upon the tormented air.

Blackness, utter blackness; turmoil, doom, dismay! Beneath me the labouring horse; at my side the steady crest of light which sat on Ayesha's brow, and through the tumult a clear, exultant voice that sang—"I promised thee wild weather! Now, Holly, dost thou believe that I can loose the prisoned Powers of the world?"

Lo! all was past and gone, and above us shone the quiet evening sky, and before us lay the empty bridge, and beyond it the flaming city of Kaloon. But the armies of Atene, where were they? Go, ask of those great cairns that hide their bones. Go, ask it of her widowed land.

Yet of our wild company of horsemen not one was lost. After us they galloped trembling, white-lipped, like men who face to face had fought and conquered Death, but triumphant—ah, triumphant!

On the high head of the bridge Ayesha wheeled her horse, and so for one proud moment stood to welcome them. At the sight of her glorious, star-crowned countenance, which now her Tribes beheld for the first time and the last, there went up such a shout as men have seldom heard.

"The Goddess!" that shout thundered. "Worship the Goddess!"

Then she turned her horse's head again, and they followed on through the long straight street of the burning city, up to the palace on its crest.

As the sun set we sped beneath its gateway. Silence in the courtyard, silence everywhere, save for the distant roar of fire and the scared howlings of the death-hounds in their kennel.

Ayesha sprang from her horse, and waving back all save Oros and myself, swept through the open doors into the halls beyond.

They were empty, every one—all were fled or dead. Yet she never paused or doubted, but so swiftly that we scarce could follow her, flitted up the wide stone stair that led to the topmost tower. Up, still up, until we reached the chamber where had dwelt Simbri the Shaman, that same chamber whence he was wont to watch his stars, in which Atene had threatened us with death.

Its door was shut and barred; still, at Ayesha's coming, yes, before the mere breath of her presence, the iron bolts snapped like twigs, the locks flew back, and inward burst that massive portal.

Now we were within the lamp-lit chamber, and this is what we saw. Seated in a chair, pale-faced, bound, yet proud and defiant-looking, was Leo. Over him, a dagger in his withered hand—yes, about to strike, in the very act—stood the old Shaman, and on the floor hard by, gazing upward with wide-set eyes, dead and still majestic in her death, lay Atene, Khania of Kaloon.

Ayesha waved her arm and the knife fell from Simbri's hand, clattering on the marble, while in an instant he who had held it was smitten to stillness and became like a man turned to stone.

She stooped, lifted the dagger, and with a swift stroke severed Leo's bonds; then, as though overcome at last, sank on to a bench in silence.

Leo rose, looking about him bewildered, and said in the strained voice of one who is weak with much suffering—"But just in time, Ayesha. Another second, and that murderous dog"—and he pointed to the Shaman—"well, it was in time. But how went the battle, and how camest thou here through that awful hurricane? And, oh, Horace, thank heaven they did not kill you after all!"

"The battle went ill for some," Ayesha answered, "and I came not through the hurricane, but on its wings. Tell me now, what has befallen thee since we parted?"

"Trapped, overpowered, bound, brought here, told that I must write to thee and stop thy advance, or die—refused, of course, and then——" and he glanced at the dead body on the floor.

"And then?" repeated Ayesha.

"Then that fearful tempest, which seemed to drive me mad. Oh! if thou couldst have heard the wind howling round these battlements, tearing off their stones as though they were dry leaves; if thou hadst seen the lightnings falling thick and fast as rain——"

"They were my messengers. I sent them to save thee," said Ayesha simply.

Leo stared at her, making no comment, but after a pause, as though he were thinking the matter over, he went on—"Atene said as much, but I did not believe her. I thought the end of the world had come, that was all. Well, she returned just now more mad even than I was, and told me that her people were destroyed and that she could not fight against the strength of hell, but that she could send me thither, and took a knife to kill me.

"I said, 'Kill on,' for I knew that wherever I went thou wouldst follow, and I was sick with the loss of blood from some hurt I had in that struggle, and weary of it all. So I shut my eyes waiting for the stroke, but instead I felt her lips pressed upon my forehead, and heard her say—"'Nay, I will not do it. Fare thee well; fulfil thou thine own destiny, as I fulfil mine. For this cast the dice have fallen against me; elsewhere it may be otherwise. I go to load them if I may.'

"I opened my eyes and looked. There Atene stood, a glass in her hand—see, it lies beside her.

"'Defeated, yet I win,' she cried, 'for I do but pass before thee to prepare the path that thou shalt tread, and to make ready thy place in the Under-world. Till we meet again I pledge thee, for I am destroyed.

Ayesha's horsemen are in my streets, and, clothed in lightnings at their head, rides Ayesha's avenging self.'

"So she drank, and fell dead—but now. Look, her breast still quivers. Afterwards, that old man would have murdered me, for, being roped, I could not resist him, but the door burst in and thou camest. Spare him, he is of her blood, and he loved her."

Then Leo sank back into the chair where we had discovered him bound, and seemed to fall into a kind of torpor, for of a sudden he grew to look like an old man.

"Thou art sick," said Ayesha anxiously. "Oros, thy medicine, the draught I bade thee bring! Be swift, I say."

The priest bowed, and from some pocket in his ample robe produced a phial which he opened and gave to Leo, saying—"Drink, my lord; this stuff will give thee back thy health, for it is strong."

"The stronger the better," answered Leo, rousing himself, and with something like his old, cheerful laugh. "I am thirsty who have touched nothing since last night, and have fought hard and been carried far, yes—and lived through that hellish storm."

Then he took the draught and emptied it. There must have been virtue in that potion; at least, the change which it produced in him was wonderful. Within a minute his eyes grew bright again, and the colour returned into his cheeks.

"Thy medicines are very good, as I have learned of old," he said to Ayesha; "but the best of all of them is to see thee safe and victorious before me, and to know that I, who looked for death, yet live to greet thee, my beloved. There is food," and he pointed to a board upon which were meats, "say, may I eat of them, for I starve?"

"Aye," she answered softly, "eat, and, my Holly, eat thou also."

So we fell to, yes, we fell to and ate even in the presence of that dead woman who looked so royal in her death; of the old magician who stood there powerless, like a man petrified, and of Ayesha, the wondrous being that could destroy an army with the fearful weapons which were servant to her will.

Only Oros ate nothing, but remained where he was, smiling at us benignantly, nor did Ayesha touch any food.

XXIII. THE YIELDING OF AYESHA

When I had satisfied myself, Leo was still at his meal, for loss of blood or the effects of the tremendous nerve tonic which Ayesha ordered to be administered to him, had made him ravenous.

I watched his face and became aware of a curious change in it, no immediate change indeed, but one, I think, that had come upon him gradually, although I only fully appreciated it now, after our short separation. In addition to the thinness of which I have spoken, his handsome countenance had grown more ethereal; his eyes were full of the shadows of things that were to come.

His aspect pained me, I knew not why. It was no longer that of the Leo with whom I was familiar, the deep-chested, mighty-limbed, jovial, upright traveller, hunter and fighting-man who had chanced to love and be loved of a spiritual power incarnated in a mould of perfect womanhood and armed with all the might of Nature's self. These things were still present indeed, but the man was changed, and I felt sure that this change came from Ayesha, since the look upon his face had become exceeding like to that which often hovered upon hers at rest.

She also was watching him, with speculative, dreamy eyes, till presently, as some thought swept through her, I saw those eyes blaze up, and the red blood pour to cheek and brow. Yes, the mighty Ayesha whose dead, slain for him, lay strewn by the thousand on yonder plain, blushed and trembled like a maiden at her first lover's kiss.

Leo rose from the table. "I would that I had been with thee in the fray," he said.

"At the drift there was fighting," she answered, "afterwards none. My ministers of Fire, Earth and Air smote, no more; I waked them from their sleep and at my command they smote for thee and saved thee."

"Many lives to take for one man's safety," Leo said solemnly, as though the thought pained him.

"Had they been millions and not thousands, I would have spent them every one. On my head be their deaths, not on thine. Or rather on hers," and she pointed to the dead Atene. "Yes, on hers who made this war. At least she should thank me who have sent so royal a host to guard her through the darkness."

"Yet it is terrible," said Leo, "to think of thee, beloved, red to the hair with slaughter."

"What reck I?" she answered with a splendid pride. "Let their blood suffice to wash the stain of thy blood from off these cruel hands that once did murder thee."

"Who am I that I should blame thee?" Leo went on as though arguing with himself, "I who but yesterday killed two men—to save myself from treachery."

"Speak not of it," she exclaimed in cold rage. "I saw the place and, Holly, thou knowest how I swore that a hundred lives should pay for every drop of that dear blood of thine, and I, who lie not, have kept the oath. Look now on that man who stands yonder struck by my will to stone, dead yet living, and say again what was he about to do to thee when I entered here?"

"To take vengeance on me for the doom of his queen and of her armies," answered Leo, "and Ayesha, how knowest thou that a Power higher than thine own will not demand it yet?"

As he spoke a pale shadow flickered on Leo's face, such a shadow as might fall from Death's advancing wing, and in the fixed eyes of the Shaman there shone a stony smile.

For a moment terror seemed to take Ayesha, then it was gone as quickly as it came.

"Nay," she said. "I ordain that it shall not be, and save One who listeth not, what power reigns in this wide earth that dare defy my will?"

So she spoke, and as her words of awful pride—for they were very awful—rang round that stone-built chamber, a vision came to me—Holly.

I saw illimitable space peopled with shining suns, and sunk in the infinite void above them one vast Countenance clad in a calm so terrific that at its aspect my spirit sank to nothingness. Yes, and I knew that this was Destiny enthroned above the spheres. Those lips moved and obedient worlds rushed upon their course. They moved again and these rolling chariots of the heavens were turned or stayed, appeared or disappeared. I knew also that against this calm Majesty the being, woman or spirit, at my side had dared to hurl her passion and her strength. My soul reeled. I was afraid.

The dread phantasm passed, and when my mind cleared again Ayesha was speaking in new, triumphant tones.

"Nay, nay," she cried. "Past is the night of dread; dawns the day of victory! Look!" and she pointed through the window-places shattered by the hurricane, to the flaming town beneath, whence rose one continual wail of misery, the wail of women mourning their countless slain while the fire roared through their homes like some unchained and rejoicing demon. "Look Leo on the smoke of the first sacrifice that I offer to thy royal state and listen to its music. Perchance thou deemst it naught. Why then I'll give thee others. Thou lovest war. Good! we will go down to war and the rebellious cities of the earth shall be the torches of our march."

She paused a moment, her delicate nostrils quivering, and her face alight with the prescience of ungarnered splendours; then like a swooping swallow flitted to where, by dead Atene, the gold circlet fallen from the Khania's hair lay upon the floor.

She stooped, lifted it, and coming to Leo held it high above his head. Slowly she let her hand fall until the glittering coronet rested for an instant on his brow. Then she spoke, in her glorious voice that rolled out rich and low, a very paean of triumph and of power.

"By this poor, earthly symbol I create thee King of Earth; yea in its round for thee is gathered all her rule. Be thou its king, and mine!"

Again the coronet was held aloft, again it sank, and again she said or rather chanted—"With this unbroken ring, token of eternity, I swear to thee the boon of endless days. Endure thou while the world endures, and be its lord, and mine."

A third time the coronet touched his brow.

"By this golden round I do endow thee with Wisdom's perfect gold uncountable, that is the talisman whereat all nature's secret paths shall open to thy feet. Victorious, victorious, tread thou her wondrous ways with me, till from her topmost peak at last she wafts us to our immortal throne whereof the columns twain are Life and Death."

Then Ayesha cast away the crown and lo! it fell upon the breast of the lost Atene and rested there.

"Art content with these gifts of mine, my lord?" she cried.

Leo looked at her sadly and shook his head.

"What more wilt thou then? Ask and I swear it shall be thine."

"Thou swearest; but wilt thou keep the oath?"

"Aye, by myself I swear; by myself and by the Strength that bred me. If it be ought that I can grant—then if I refuse it to thee, may such destruction fall upon me as will satisfy even Atene's watching soul."

I heard and I think that another heard also, at least once more the stony smile shone in the eyes of the Shaman.

"I ask of thee nothing that thou canst not give. Ayesha, I ask of thee thyself—not at some distant time when I have been bathed in a mysterious fire, but now, now this night."

She shrank back from him a little, as though dismayed.

"Surely," she said slowly, "I am like that foolish philosopher who, walking abroad to read the destinies of nations in the stars, fell down a pitfall dug by idle children and broke his bones and perished there. Never did I guess that with all these glories stretched before thee like mountain top on glittering mountain top, making a stairway for thy mortal feet to the very dome of heaven, thou wouldst still clutch at thy native earth and seek of it—but the common boon of woman's love.

"Oh! Leo, I thought that thy soul was set upon nobler aims, that thou wouldst pray me for wider powers, for a more vast dominion; that as though they were but yonder fallen door of wood and iron, I should break for thee the bars of Hades, and like the Eurydice of old fable draw thee living down the steeps of Death, or throne thee midst the fires of the furthest sun to watch its subject worlds at play.

"Or I thought that thou wouldst bid me reveal what no woman ever told, the bitter, naked truth—all my sins and sorrows, all the wandering fancies of my fickle thought; even what thou knowest not and perchance ne'er shalt know, who I am and whence I came, and how to thy charmed eyes I seemed to change from foul to fair, and what is the purpose of my love for thee, and what the meaning of that tale of an angry goddess—who never was except in dreams.

"I thought—nay, no matter what I thought, save that thou wert far other than thou art, my Leo, and in so high a moment that thou wouldst seek to pass the mystic gates my glory can throw wide and with me tread an air supernal to the hidden heart of things. Yet thy prayer is but the same that the whole world whispers beneath the silent moon, in the palace and the cottage, among the snows and on the burning desert's waste. 'Oh! my love, thy lips, thy lips. Oh! my love, be mine, now, now, beneath the moon, beneath the moon!'

"Leo, I thought better, higher, of thee."

"Mayhap, Ayesha, thou wouldest have thought worse of me had I been content with thy suns and constellations and spiritual gifts and dominations that I neither desire nor understand.

"If I had said to thee: Be thou my angel, not my wife; divide the ocean that I may walk its bed; pierce the firmament and show me how grow the stars; tell me the origins of being and of death and instruct me in their issues; give up the races of mankind to my sword, and the wealth of all the earth to fill my treasuries. Teach me also how to drive the hurricane as thou canst do, and to bend the laws of nature to my purpose: on earth make me half a god—as thou art.

"But Ayesha, I am no god; I am a man, and as a man I seek the woman whom I love. Oh! divest thyself of all these wrappings of thy power—that power which strews thy path with dead and keeps me apart from thee. If only for one short night forget the ambition that gnaws unceasingly at thy soul; I say forget thy greatness and be a woman and—my wife."

She made no answer, only looked at him and shook her head, causing her glorious hair to ripple like water beneath a gentle breeze.

"Thou deniest me," he went on with gathering strength, "and that thou canst not do, that thou mayest not do, for Ayesha, thou hast sworn, and I demand the fulfilment of thine oath.

"Hark thou. I refuse thy gifts; I will have none of thy rule who ask no Pharaoh's throne and wish to do good to men and not to kill them—that the world may profit. I will not go with thee to Kor, nor be bathed in the breath of Life. I will leave thee and cross the mountains, or perish on them, nor with all thy strength canst thou hold me to thy side, who indeed needest me not. No longer will I endure this daily torment, the torment of thy presence and thy sweet words; thy loving looks, thy promises for next year, next year—next year. So keep thine oath or let me begone."

Still Ayesha stood silent, only now her head drooped and her breast began to heave. Then Leo stepped forward; he seized her in his arms and kissed her. She broke from his embrace, I know not how, for though she returned it was close enough, and again stood before him but at a little distance.

"Did I not warn Holly," she whispered with a sigh, "to bid thee beware lest I should catch thy human fire? Man, I say to thee, it begins to smoulder in my heart, and should it grow to flame——"

"Why then," he answered laughing, "we will be happy for a little while."

"Aye, Leo, but how long? Why wert thou sole lord of this loveliness of mine and not set above their harming, night and day a hundred jealous daggers would seek thy heart and—find it."

"How long, Ayesha? A lifetime, a year, a month, a minute—I neither know nor care, and while thou art true to me I fear no stabs of envy."

"Is it so? Wilt take the risk? I can promise thee nothing. Thou mightest—yes, in this way or in that, thou mightest—die."

"And if I die, what then? Shall we be separated?"

"Nay, nay, Leo, that is not possible. We never can be severed, of this I am sure; it is sworn to me. But then through other lives and other spheres, higher lives and higher spheres mayhap, our fates must force a painful path to their last goal of union."

"Why then I take the hazard, Ayesha. Shall the life that I can risk to slay a leopard or a lion in the sport of an idle hour, be too great a price to offer for the splendours of thy breast? Thine oath! Ayesha, I claim thine oath."

Then it was that in Ayesha there began the most mysterious and thrilling of her many changes. Yet how to describe it I know not unless it be by simile.

Once in Thibet we were imprisoned for months by snows that stretched down from the mountain slopes into the valleys and oh! how weary did we grow of those arid, aching fields of purest white. At length rain set in, and blinding mists in which it was not safe to wander, that made the dark nights darker yet.

So it was, until there came a morning when seeing the sun shine, we went to our door and looked out. Behold a miracle! Gone were the snows that choked the valley and in the place of them appeared vivid springing grass, starred everywhere with flowers, and murmuring brooks and birds that sang and nested in the willows. Gone was the frowning sky and all the blue firmament seemed one tender smile. Gone were the austerities of winter with his harsh winds, and in their place spring, companioned by her zephyrs, glided down the vale singing her song of love and life.

There in this high chamber, in the presence of the living and the dead, while the last act of the great tragedy unrolled itself before me, looking on Ayesha that forgotten scene sprang into my mind. For on her face just such a change had come. Hitherto, with all her loveliness, the heart of Ayesha had seemed like that winter mountain wrapped in its unapproachable snow and before her pure brow and icy self-command, aspirations sank abashed and desires died.

She swore she loved and her love fulfilled itself in death and many a mysterious way. Yet it was hard to believe that this passion of hers was more than a spoken part, for how can the star seek the moth although the moth may seek the star? Though the man may worship the goddess, for all her smiles divine, how can the goddess love the man?

But now everything was altered! Look! Ayesha grew human; I could see her heart beat beneath her robes and hear her breath come in soft, sweet sobs, while o'er her upturned face and in her alluring eyes there spread itself that look which is born of love alone. Radiant and more radiant did she seem to grow, sweeter and more sweet, no longer the veiled Hermit of the Caves, no longer the Oracle of the Sanctuary, no longer the Valkyrie of the battle-plain, but only the loveliest and most happy bride that ever gladdened a husband's eyes.

She spoke, and it was of little things, for thus Ayesha proclaimed the conquest of herself.

"Fie!" she said, showing her white robes torn with spears and stained by the dust and dew of war; "Fie, my lord, what marriage garments are these in which at last I come to thee, who would have been adorned in regal gems and raiment befitting to my state and thine?"

"I seek the woman not her garment," said Leo, his burning eyes fixed upon her face.

"Thou seekest the woman. Ah! there it lies. Tell me, Leo, am I woman or spirit? Say that I am woman, for now the prophecy of this dead Atene lies heavy on my soul, Atene who said that mortal and immortal may not mate."

"Thou must be woman, or thou wouldst not have tormented me as thou hast done these many weeks."

"I thank thee for the comfort of thy words. Yet, was it woman whose breath wrought destruction upon yonder plain? Was it to a woman that Blast and Lightning bowed and said, 'We are here: Command us, we obey'? Did that dead thing (and she pointed to the shattered door) break inward at a woman's will? Or could a woman charm this man to stone?

"Oh! Leo, would that I were woman! I tell thee that I'd lay all my grandeur down, a wedding offering at thy feet, could I be sure that for one short year I should be naught but woman and—thy happy wife.

"Thou sayest that I did torment thee, but it is I who have known torment, I who desired to yield and dared not. Aye, I tell thee, Leo, were I not sure that thy little stream of life is draining dry into the great ocean of my life, drawn thither as the sea draws its rivers, or as the sun draws mists, e'en now I would not yield. But I know, for my wisdom tells it me, ere ever we could reach the shores of Libya, the ill work would be done, and thou dead of thine own longing, thou dead and I widowed who never was a wife.

"Therefore see! like lost Atene I take the dice and cast them, not knowing how they shall fall. Not knowing how they shall fall, for good or ill I cast," and she made a wild motion as of some desperate gamester throwing his last throw.

"So," Ayesha went on, "the thing is done and the number summed for aye, though it be hidden from my sight. I have made an end of doubts and fears, and come death, come life, I'll meet it bravely.

"Say, how shall we be wed? I have it. Holly here must join our hands; who else? He that ever was our guide shall give me unto thee, and thee to me. This burning city is our altar, the dead and living are our witnesses on earth and heaven. In place of rites and ceremonials for this first time I lay my lips on thine, and when 'tis done, for music I'll sing thee a nuptial chant of love such as mortal poet has not written nor have mortal lovers heard.

"Come, Holly, do now thy part and give this maiden to this man."

Like one in a dream I obeyed her and took Ayesha's outstretched hand and Leo's. As I held them thus, I tell the truth:—it was as though some fire rushed through my veins from her to him, shaking and shattering me with swift waves of burning and unearthly Bliss. With the fire too came glorious visions and sounds of mighty music, and a sense as though my brain, filled with over-flowing life, must burst asunder beneath its weight.

I joined their hands; I know not how; I blessed them, I know not in what words. Then I reeled back against the wall and watched.

This is what I saw.

With an abandonment and a passion so splendid and intense that it seemed more than human, with a murmured cry of "Husband!" Ayesha cast her arms about her lover's neck and drawing down his head to hers so that the gold hair was mingled with her raven locks, she kissed him on the lips.

Thus they clung a little while, and as they clung the gentle diadem of light from her brow spread to his brow also, and through the white wrappings of her robe became visible her perfect shape shining with faint fire. With a little happy laugh she left him, saying,

"Thus, Leo Vincey, oh! thus for the second time do I give myself to thee, and with this flesh and spirit all I swore to thee, there in the dim Caves of Kor and here in the palace of Kaloon. Know thou this, come what may, never, never more shall we be separate who are ordained one. Whilst thou livest I live at thy side, and when thou diest, if die thy must, I'll follow thee through worlds and firmaments, nor shall all the doors of heaven or hell avail against my love. Where thou goest, thither I will go. When thou sleepest, with thee will I sleep and it is my voice that thou shalt hear murmuring through the dreams of life and death; my voice that shall summon thee to awaken in the last hour of everlasting dawn, when all this night of misery hath furled her wings for aye.

"Listen now while I sing to thee and hear that song aright, for in its melody at length thou shalt learn the truth, which unwed I might not tell to thee. Thou shalt learn who and what I am, and who and what thou art, and of the high purposes of our love, and this dead woman's hate, and of all that I have hid from thee in veiled, bewildering words and visions.

"Listen then, my love and lord, to the burden of the Song of Fate."

She ceased speaking and gazed heavenwards with a rapt look as though she waited for some inspiration to fall upon her, and never, never—not even in the fires of Kor had Ayesha seemed so divine as she did now in this moment of the ripe harvest of her love.

My eyes wandered from her to Leo, who stood before her pale and still, still as the death-like figure of the Shaman, still as the Khania's icy shape which stared upwards from the ground. What was passing in his mind, I wondered, that he could remain thus insensible while in all her might and awful beauty this proud being worshipped him.

Hark! she began to sing in a voice so rich and perfect that its honied notes seemed to cloy my blood and stop my breath.

"The world was not, was not, and in the womb of Silence
Slept the souls of men. Yet I was and thou——"

Suddenly Ayesha stopped, and I felt rather than saw the horror on her face.

Look! Leo swayed to and fro as though the stones beneath him were but a rocking boat. To and fro he swayed, stretched out his blind arms to clasp her—then suddenly fell backwards, and lay still.

Oh! what a shriek was that she gave! Surely it must have wakened the very corpses upon the plain. Surely it must have echoed in the stars. One shriek only—then throbbing silence.

I sprang to him, and there, withered in Ayesha's kiss, slain by the fire of her love, Leo lay dead—lay dead upon the breast of dead Atene!

I heard Ayesha say presently, and the words struck me as dreadful in their hopeless acceptance of a doom against which even she had no strength to struggle.

"It seems that my lord has left me for awhile; I must hasten to my lord afar."

After that I do not quite know what happened. I had lost the man who was all in all to me, friend and child in one, and I was crushed as I had never been before. It seemed so sad that I, old and outworn, should still live on whilst he in the flower of his age, snatched from joy and greatness such as no man hath known, lay thus asleep.

I think that by an afterthought, Ayesha and Oros tried to restore him, tried without result, for here her powers were of no avail. Indeed my conviction is that although some lingering life still kept him on his feet, Leo had really died at the moment of her embrace, since when I looked at him before he fell, his face was that of a dead man.

Yes, I believe that last speech of hers, although she knew it not, was addressed to his spirit, for in her burning kiss his flesh had perished.

When at length I recovered myself a little, it was to hear Ayesha in a cold, calm voice—her face I could not see for she had veiled herself—commanding certain priests who had been summoned to "bear away the body of that accursed woman and bury her as befits her rank." Even then I bethought me, I remember, of the tale of Jehu and Jezebel.

Leo, looking strangely calm and happy, lay now upon a couch, the arms folded on his breast. When the priests had tramped away carrying their royal burden, Ayesha, who sat by his body brooding, seemed to awake, for she rose and said—"I need a messenger, and for no common journey, since he must search out the habitations of the Shades," and she turned herself towards Oros and appeared to look at him.

Now for the first time I saw that priest change countenance a little, for the eternal smile, of which even this scene had not quite rid it, left his face and he grew pale and trembled.

"Thou art afraid," she said contemptuously. "Be at rest, Oros, I will not send one who is afraid. Holly, wilt thou go for me—and him?"

"Aye," I answered. "I am weary of life and desire no other end. Only let it be swift and painless."

She mused a while, then said—"Nay, thy time is not yet, thou still hast work to do. Endure, my Holly, 'tis only for a breath."

Then she looked at the Shaman, the man turned to stone who all this while had stood there as a statue stands, and cried—"Awake!"

Instantly he seemed to thaw into life, his limbs relaxed, his breast heaved, he was as he had always been: ancient, gnarled, malevolent.

"I hear thee, mistress," he said, bowing as a man bows to the power that he hates.

"Thou seest, Simbri," and she waved her hand.

"I see. Things have befallen as Atene and I foretold, have they not? 'Ere long the corpse of a new-crowned Khan of Kaloon,'" and he pointed to the gold circlet that Ayesha had set on Leo's brow, "'will lie upon the brink of the Pit of Flame'—as I foretold." An evil smile crept into his eyes and he went on—"Hadst thou not smote me dumb, I who watched could have warned thee that they would so befall; but, great mistress, it pleased thee to smite me dumb. And so it seems, O Hes, that thou hast overshot thyself and liest broken at the foot of that pinnacle which step by step thou hast climbed for more than two thousand weary years. See what thou hast bought at the price of countless lives that now before the throne of Judgment bring accusations against thy powers misused, and cry out for justice on thy head," and he looked at the dead form of Leo.

"I sorrow for them, yet, Simbri, they were well spent," Ayesha answered reflectively, "who by their forewritten doom, as it was decreed, held thy knife from falling and thus won me my husband. Aye and I am happy—happier than such blind bats as thou can see or guess. For know that now with him I have re-wed my wandering soul divorced by sin from me, and that of our marriage kiss which burned his life away there shall still be born to us children of Forgiveness and eternal Grace and all things that are pure and fair.

"Look thou, Simbri, I will honour thee. Thou shalt be my messenger, and beware! beware I say how thou dost fulfil thine office, since of every syllable thou must render an account.

"Go thou down the dark paths of Death, and, since even my thought may not reach to where he sleeps tonight, search out my lord and say to him that the feet of his spouse Ayesha are following fast. Bid him have no fear for me who by this last sorrow have atoned my crimes and am in his embrace regenerate. Tell him that thus it was appointed, and thus is best, since now he is dipped indeed in the eternal Flame of Life; now for him the mortal night is done and the everlasting day arises. Command him that he await me in the Gate of Death where it is granted that I greet him presently. Thou hearest?"

"I hear, O Queen, Mighty-from-of-Old."

"One message more. Say to Atene that I forgive her. Her heart was high and greatly did she play her part. There in the Gates we will balance our account. Thou hearest?"

"I hear, O Eternal Star that hath conquered Night."

"Then, man, begone!"

As the word left Ayesha's lips Simbri leapt from the floor, grasping at the air as though he would clutch his own departing soul, staggered back against the board where Leo and I had eaten, overthrowing it, and amid a ruin of gold and silver vessels, fell down and died.

She looked at him, then said to me—"See, though he ever hated me, this magician who has known Ayesha from the first, did homage to my ancient majesty at last, when lies and defiance would serve his end no more. No longer now do I hear the name that his dead mistress gave to me. The 'Star-that-hath-fallen' in his lips and in very truth is become the 'Star-which-hath-burst-the-bonds-of-Night,' and, re-arisen, shines for ever—shines with its twin immortal to set no more—my Holly. Well, he is gone, and ere now, those that serve me in the Under-world—dost remember?—thou sawest their captains in the Sanctuary—bend the head at great Ayesha's word and make her place ready near her spouse.

"But oh, what folly has been mine. When even here my wrath can show such power, how could I hope that my lord would outlive the fires of my love? Still it was better so, for he sought not the pomp I would have given him, nor desired the death of men. Yet such pomp must have been his portion in this poor shadow of a world, and the steps that encircle an usurper's throne are ever slippery with blood.

"Thou art weary, my Holly, go rest thee. To-morrow night we journey to the Mountain, there to celebrate these obsequies."

I crept into the room adjoining—it had been Simbri's—and laid me down upon his bed, but to sleep I was not able. Its door was open, and in the light of the burning city that shone through the casements I could see Ayesha watching by her dead. Hour after hour she watched, her head resting on her hand, silent, stirless. She wept not, no sigh escaped her; only watched as a tender woman watches a slumbering babe that she knows will awake at dawn.

Her face was unveiled and I perceived that it had greatly changed. All pride and anger were departed from it; it was grown soft, wistful, yet full of confidence and quietness. For a while I could not think of what it reminded me, till suddenly I remembered. Now it was like, indeed the counterpart almost, of the holy and majestic semblance of the statue of the Mother in the Sanctuary. Yes, with just such a look of love and power as that mother cast upon her frightened child new-risen from its dream of death, did Ayesha gaze upon her dead, while her parted lips also seemed to whisper "some tale of hope, sure and immortal."

At length she rose and came into my chamber.

"Thou thinkest me fallen and dost grieve for me, my Holly," she said in a gentle voice, "knowing my fears lest some such fate should overtake my lord."

"Ay, Ayesha, I grieve for thee as for myself."

"Spare then thy pity, Holly, since although the human part of me would have kept him on the earth, now my spirit doth rejoice that for a while he has burst his mortal bonds. For many an age, although I knew it not, in my proud defiance of the Universal Law, I have fought against his true weal and mine. Thrice have I and the angel wrestled, matching strength with strength, and thrice has he conquered me. Yet as he bore away his prize this night he whispered wisdom in my ear. This was his message: That in death is love's home, in death its strength; that from the charnel-house of life this love springs again glorified and pure, to reign a conqueror forever. Therefore I wipe away my tears and, crowned once more a queen of peace, I go to join him whom we have lost, there where he awaits us, as it is granted to me that I shall do.

"But I am selfish, and forgot. Thou needest rest. Sleep, friend, I bid thee sleep."

And I slept wondering as my eyes closed whence Ayesha drew this strange confidence and comfort. I know not but it was there, real and not assumed. I can only suppose therefore that some illumination had fallen on her soul, and that, as she stated, the love and end of Leo in a way unknown, did suffice to satisfy her court of sins.

At the least those sins and all the load of death that lay at her door never seemed to trouble her at all. She appeared to look upon them merely as events which were destined to occur, as inevitable fruits of a seed sowed long ago by the hand of Fate for whose workings she was not responsible. The fears and considerations which weigh with mortals did not affect or oppress her. In this as in other matters, Ayesha was a law unto herself.

When I awoke it was day, and through the window-place I saw the rain that the people of Kaloon had so long desired falling in one straight sheet. I saw also that Ayesha, seated by the shrouded form of Leo, was giving orders to her priests and captains and to some nobles, who had survived the slaughter of Kaloon, as to the new government of the land. Then I slept again.

It was evening, and Ayesha stood at my bedside.

"All is prepared," she said. "Awake and ride with me."

So we went, escorted by a thousand cavalry, for the rest stayed to occupy, or perchance to plunder, the land of Kaloon. In front the body of Leo was borne by relays of priests, and behind it rode the veiled Ayesha, I at her side.

Strange was the contrast between this departure, and our arrival.

Then the rushing squadrons, the elements that raved, the perpetual sheen of lightnings seen through the swinging curtains of the hail; the voices of despair from an army rolled in blood beneath the chariot wheels of thunder.

Now the white-draped corpse, the slow-pacing horses, the riders with their spears reversed, and on either side, seen in that melancholy moonlight, the women of Kaloon burying their innumerable dead.

And Ayesha herself, yesterday a Valkyrie crested with the star of flame, to-day but a bereaved woman humbly following her husband to the tomb.

Yet how they feared her! Some widow standing on the grave mould she had dug, pointed as we passed to the body of Leo, uttering bitter words which I could not catch. Thereon her companions flung themselves upon her and felling her with fist and spade, prostrated themselves upon the ground, throwing dust on their hair in token of their submission to the priestess of Death.

Ayesha saw them, and said to me with something of her ancient fire and pride—"I tread the plain of Kaloon no more, yet as a parting gift have I read this high-stomached people a lesson that they needed long. Not for many a generation, O Holly, will they dare to lift spear against the College of Hes and its subject Tribes."

Again it was night, and where once lay that of the Khan, the man whom he had killed, flanked by the burning pillars, the bier of Leo stood in the inmost Sanctuary before the statue of the Mother whose gentle, unchanging eyes seemed to search his quiet face.

On her throne sat the veiled Hesea, giving commands to her priests and priestesses.

"I am weary," she said, "and it may be that I leave you for a while to rest—beyond the mountains. A year, or a thousand years—I cannot say. If so, let Papave, with Oros as her counsellor and husband and their seed, hold my place till I return again.

"Priests and priestesses of the College of Hes, over new territories have I held my hand; take them as an heritage from me, and rule them well and gently. Henceforth let the Hesea of the Mountain be also the Khania of Kaloon.

"Priests and priestesses of our ancient faith, learn to look through its rites and tokens, outward and visible, to the in-forming Spirit. If Hes the goddess never ruled on earth, still pitying Nature rules. If the name of Isis never rang through the courts of heaven, still in heaven, with all love fulfilled, nursing her human children on her breast, dwells the mighty Motherhood where of this statue is the symbol, that Motherhood which bore us, and, unforgetting, faithful, will receive us at the end.

"For of the bread of bitterness we shall not always eat, of the water of tears we shall not always drink. Beyond the night the royal suns ride on; ever the rainbow shines around the rain. Though they slip from our clutching hands like melted snow, the lives we lose shall yet be found immortal, and from the burnt-out fires of our human hopes will spring a heavenly star."

She paused and waved her hand as though to dismiss them, then added by an after-thought, pointing to myself—"This man is my beloved friend and guest. Let him be yours also. It is my will that you tend and guard him here, and when the snows have melted and summer is at hand, that you fashion a way for him through the gulf and bring him across the mountains by which he came, till you leave him in safety. Hear and forget not, for be sure that to me you shall give account of him."

The night drew towards the dawn, and we stood upon the peak above the gulf of fire, four of us only—Ayesha and I, and Oros and Papave. For the bearers had laid down the body of Leo upon its edge and gone their way. The curtain of flame flared in front of us, its crest bent over like a billow in the gale, and to leeward, one by one, floated the torn-off clouds and pinnacles of fire. By the dead Leo knelt Ayesha, gazing at that icy, smiling face, but speaking no single word. At length she rose, and said,—

"Darkness draws near, my Holly, that deep darkness which foreruns the glory of the dawn. Now fare thee well for one little hour. When thou art about to die, but not before, call me, and I will come to thee. Stir not and speak not till all be done, lest when I am no longer here to be thy guard some Presence should pass on and slay thee.

"Think not that I am conquered, for now my name is Victory! Think not that Ayesha's strength is spent or her tale is done, for of it thou readest but a single page. Think not even that I am today that thing of sin and pride, the Ayesha thou didst adore and fear, I who in my lord's love and sacrifice have again conceived my soul. For know that now once more as at the beginning, his soul and mine are one."

She thought awhile and added,

"Friend take this sceptre in memory of me, but beware how thou usest it save at the last to summon me, for it has virtues," and she gave me the jewelled Sistrum that she bore—then said,

"So kiss his brow, stand back, and be still."

Now as once before the darkness gathered on the pit, and presently, although I heard no prayer, though now no mighty music broke upon the silence, through that darkness, beating up the gale, came the two-winged flame and hovered where Ayesha stood.

It appeared, it vanished, and one by one the long minutes crept away until the first spear of dawn lit upon the point of rock.

Lo! it was empty, utterly empty and lonesome. Gone was the corpse of Leo, and gone too was Ayesha the imperial, the divine.

Whither had she gone? I know not. But this I know, that as the light returned and the broad sheet of flame flared out to meet it, I seemed to see two glorious shapes sweeping upward on its bosom, and the faces that they wore were those of Leo and of Ayesha.

Often and often during the weary months that followed, whilst I wandered through the temple or amid the winter snows upon the Mountain side, did I seek to solve this question—Whither had She gone? I asked it of my heart; I asked it of the skies; I asked it of the spirit of Leo which often was so near to me.

But no sure answer ever came, nor will I hazard one. As mystery wrapped Ayesha's origin and lives—for the truth of these things I never learned—so did mystery wrap her deaths, or rather her departings, for I cannot think her dead. Surely she still is, if not on earth, then in some other sphere?

So I believe; and when my own hour comes, and it draws near swiftly, I shall know whether I believe in vain, or whether she will appear to be my guide as, with her last words, she swore that she would do. Then, too, I shall learn what she was about to reveal to Leo when he died, the purposes of their being and of their love.

So I can wait in patience who must not wait for long, though my heart is broken and I am desolate.

Oros and all the priests were very good to me. Indeed, even had it been their wish, they would have feared to be otherwise, who remembered and were sure that in some time to come they must render an account of this matter to their dread queen. By way of return, I helped them as I was best able to draw up a scheme for the government of the conquered country of Kaloon, and with my advice upon many other questions.

And so at length the long months wore away, till at the approach of summer the snows melted. Then I said that I must be gone. They gave me of their treasures in precious stones, lest I should need money for my faring, since the gold of which I had such plenty was too heavy to be carried by one man alone. They led me across the plains of Kaloon, where now the husbandmen, those that were left of them, ploughed the land and scattered seed, and so on to its city. But amidst those blackened ruins over which Atene's palace still frowned unharmed, I would not enter, for to me it was, and always must remain, a home of death. So I camped outside the walls by the river just where Leo and I had landed after that poor mad Khan set us free, or rather loosed us to be hunted by his death-hounds.

Next day we took boat and rowed up the river, past the place where we had seen Atene's cousin murdered, till we came to the Gate-house. Here once again I slept, or rather did not sleep.

On the following morning I went down into the ravine and found to my surprise that the rapid torrent—shallow enough now—had been roughly bridged, and that in preparation for my coming rude but sufficient ladders were built on the face of the opposing precipice. At the foot of these I bade farewell to Oros, who at our parting smiled benignantly as on the day we met.

"We have seen strange things together," I said to him, not knowing what else to say.

"Very strange," he answered.

"At least, friend Oros," I went on awkwardly enough, "events have shaped themselves to your advantage, for you inherit a royal mantle."

"I wrap myself in a mantle of borrowed royalty," he answered with precision, "of which doubtless one day I shall be stripped."

"You mean that the great Ayesha is not dead?"

"I mean that She never dies. She changes, that is all. As the wind blows now hence, now hither, so she comes and goes, and who can tell at what spot upon the earth, or beyond it, for a while that wind lies sleeping? But at sunset or at dawn, at noon or at midnight, it will begin to blow again, and then woe to those who stand across its path.

"Remember the dead heaped upon the plains of Kaloon. Remember the departing of the Shaman Simbri with his message and the words that she spoke then. Remember the passing of the Hesea from the Mountain point. Stranger from the West, surely as to-morrow's sun must rise, as she went, so she will return again, and in my borrowed garment I await her advent."

"I also await her advent," I answered, and thus we parted.

Accompanied by twenty picked men bearing provisions and arms, I climbed the ladders easily enough, and now that I had food and shelter, crossed the mountains without mishap. They even escorted me through the desert beyond, till one night we camped within sight of the gigantic Buddha that sits before the monastery, gazing eternally across the sands and snows.

When I awoke next morning the priests were gone. So I took up my pack and pursued my journey alone, and walking slowly came at sunset to the distant lamasery. At its door an ancient figure, wrapped in a tattered cloak, was sitting, engaged apparently in contemplation of the skies. It was our old friend Kou-en. Adjusting his horn spectacles on his nose he looked at me.

"I was awaiting you, brother of the Monastery called 'the World,'" he said in a voice, measured, very ineffectually, to conceal his evident delight. "Have you grown hungry there that you return to this poor place?"

"Aye, most excellent Kou-en," I answered, "hungry for rest."

"It shall be yours for all the days of this incarnation. But say, where is the other brother?"

"Dead," I answered.

"And therefore re-born elsewhere or perhaps, dreaming in Devachan for a while. Well, doubtless we shall meet him later on. Come, eat, and afterwards tell me your story."

So I ate, and that night I told him all. Kou-en listened with respectful attention, but the tale, strange as it might seem to most people, excited no particular wonder in his mind. Indeed, he explained it to me at such length by aid of some marvellous theory of re-incarnations, that at last I began to doze.

"At least," I said sleepily, "it would seem that we are all winning merit on the Everlasting Plane," for I thought that favourite catchword would please him.

"Yes, brother of the Monastery called the World," Kou-en answered in a severe voice, "doubtless you are all winning merit, but, if I may venture to say so, you are winning it very slowly, especially the woman—or the sorceress—or the mighty evil spirit—whose names I understand you to tell me are She, Hes, and Ayesha upon earth and in Avitchi, Star-that-hath-Fallen——"

(Here Mr. Holly's manuscript ends, its outer sheets having been burnt when he threw it on to the fire at his house in Cumberland.)

Printed in Great Britain
by Amazon

61456595R00160